# CREATING AUTHENTICITY

Sidestone Press

# CREATING AUTHENTICITY

Authentication Processes in Ethnographic Museums

edited by Alexander Geurds & Laura Van Broekhoven

MEDEDELINGEN VAN HET RIJKSMUSEUM VOOR VOLKENKUNDE, LEIDEN

N°. 42

Mededelingen van het Rijksmuseum voor Volkenkunde N°. 42

ISBN 978-90-8890-205-5

© 2013 National Museum of Ethnology

Published by Sidestone Press, Leiden
  www.sidestone.com

Published in Cooperation with the National Museum of Ethnology, Leiden
  www.volkenkunde.nl
  Head of Publications Committee: Fanny Wonu Veys

Lay-out & cover design: Sidestone Press

Photograph cover:
Front: Authentic productions in action. Visitors interacting with objects in the permanent Mesoamerica gallery at the National Museum of Ethnology (Rijksmuseum Volkenkunde, Leiden).
Back: top – Gold mamuli (Rijksmuseum Volkenkunde, Leiden; Liefkes 334); central – Mosaic skull (Rijksmuseum Volkenkunde, Leiden; 4007-1); bottom – Jar, Iran 13th century, metal lid 19th century addition (Victoria and Albert Museum, London; 2433-1876)

## Contents

**Preface** — vii

**Culture Sketching: The Authenticity Quest in Ethnographic Museums** — 1
An Introduction
*Dr. Alexander Geurds*

**Real, Fake or a Combination?** — 11
Examining the Authenticity of a Mesoamerican Mosaic Skull
*Martin E. Berger*

**When is Authentic?** — 39
Situating Authenticity in the Itineraries of Objects
*Prof. Rosemary Joyce*

**Authentic Forgeries?** — 59
*Prof. Oliver Watson*

**From Lukas to Liefkes?** — 73
Age and Authenticity of Gold Jewellery from Sumba, Indonesia
*Francine Brinkgreve*

**The Real Stuff: Authenticity and Photography from East Greenland in the Netherlands** — 101
*Dr. Cunera Buijs*

**Alternative Authenticities (and Inauthenticities)** — 137
*Prof. Sally Price*

**Authenticity and Curatorial Practice** — 151
*Dr. Laura N.K. Van Broekhoven*

**List of contributors and addresses** — 163

# Preface

The papers in this volume are the outcome of a one-day symposium at the National Museum of Ethnology in Leiden, The Netherlands, titled "What is Authenticity? Questions of authenticity and authentification in ethnographic museums." Originally organized by Laura Van Broekhoven, the symposium took place on November 30, 2012. Thanks are due to the staff of the National Museum of Ethnology for their organizational efforts, hospitality and interest.

Thanks are due to the symposium's participating scholars for their enthusiasm. We are grateful to Mariana Françozo for leading the panel discussion which stimulated discussions about the issue of authenticity. Two papers were ultimately not included in this volume, one by Cristiana Panella on unprovenanced objects and the opacity or transparency agendas of museum policies, and one by Wim van Zanten on living culture and authenticity in UNESCO world heritage conventions. They, together with all other participants, provided for a stimulating day of presentations and discussions, giving the inspiration to publish these papers.

Alexander Geurds and Laura N.K. Van Broekhoven

# CULTURE SKETCHING: THE AUTHENTICITY QUEST IN ETHNOGRAPHIC MUSEUMS

## An Introduction

*Dr. Alexander Geurds*

## Introduction

Objects are pliable. They can be dressed and unpacked, mimicked and feared, placed and hidden, adored and valued, commodified and singularised. Objects are thus complicated – 'bundles' of contextual meaning, to invoke Keane (2003). Though their physical form and substance allude to a seemingly limited range of interpretations and values, the object's potential force as signifier is boundless. Consider the example of artisanal and agricultural tools. A sickle and a hammer conjure up worlds of ideology (communism), colours (red and yellow), and could even be in the running for most potent twentieth-century symbol. This representational pliability adheres to all things when they are caught up in audiences that speak of them as 'objects'. There is a constant process of this kind going on in today's cultural industry, including – though not of course exclusively – ethnographic museums. While such objects and the collections they make up were once 'read' by expert custodians (museum curators), ethnographic museums in the post-colonial era invite dialogue about collections, engaging with local audiences and groups who express a form of rootedness in the things preserved in the museum, destabilising notions of fixed cultures, while simultaneously creating or reinforcing cultural identities (Clifford 1988). This paradoxical dynamic may be uncomfortable for museum professionals but it is also impossible to dismiss, given that the number of case studies narrating such dialogues is increasing at a near-exponential rate (see e.g. Van Broekhoven et al. 2010).

The symposium drew attention to the authority of UNESCO in highlighting institutionally-recognised types of cultural heritage. As the growing list of tangible and intangible world heritage testifies, these types are ranked in *orders of authenticity*, privileging some types over others. Still, these are unstable hierarchies. Certainly within the heritage industry, the notion of 'authenticity' as an objective standard for what should be preserved is now being questioned (Holtorf and Schadla-Hall 1999; Lowenthal 1995; McBryde 1997). To date, the social sciences, the humanities and the heritage sector appear to be discussing authenticity almost exclusively as historically situated – that is, *contingent and subject to change*, echoing what David Lowenthal (1995) called the 'flux of authenticity'.

This implies that the authentic is still being located and determined on a daily basis. Contemporary examples from anthropology forcefully stress this process. Anthropological studies of commodities and commoditisation, for example, suggest that even the explicitly inauthentic can be reconceptualised into something authentic. Objects and their interpretation are so pliable as to eventually overcome being branded 'inauthentic' by achieving a 'sufficient' degree of authenticity, thereby breaking the binary debate of authentic versus inauthentic, instead creating degrees of authenticity. Crăciun (2012) analyses this broadening of possible object validations as an 'approximation of the ideal', largely accomplished by stressing particular desirable material qualities of the object. As brand authenticity in commodities resides largely in their origin (a well-known commercial brand, for instance), other aspects of materiality are necessarily invoked. This is not mere strategising by sly producers and duped consumers of 'fakes'; this dynamic handling of objects by their users reveals that authenticity is a construct achieved through social experience (Brown 2010). Predictably, producers of high-end market brands would join many museum collection experts in challenging this view. As we hope that this volume will illustrate, however, authentication through provenance and/or age determination alone is as problematic as using legal arguments to prove commodity authenticity. By their very nature, objects remain pliable: they evoke ideas, realise images, and are a fundamental node in networks between people and places.

Well into the second decade of the twenty-first century, and having installed a critical museology on the shoulders of French theory, we might ask where museum practice currently stands in this debate. Where and when do museums look when framing the authentic? The festive expedition truck outside the National Museum of Ethnology in Leiden recalls the expeditions commissioned in the early twentieth century to provide authenticity for collections and museum. (Fig. 1) This kind of authentication, however, was emphasised in that particular period of early scientific collecting, in locations in Indonesia and Oceania, for instance, where the practice of collecting was in itself more important than what could be said about the collected things (see Thomas 1991). Critical theory made precisely this importance explicit, exposing the associated effects of reinforcing relations of power and knowledge. Surely we do not want to bypass all those years of deconstructivist and constructivist paradigms in favour of what are essentially colonialist arguments?

## Authenticity in the West

Traditionally, philosophy of culture tells us about the need for replication in the maintaining, indeed the solidifying, of societies. This process of replication is constant and partial and also aimed at enabling the preservation of what

*Figure 1: Expedition truck at the entrance of the National Museum of Ethnology.*

is deemed worthy of maintaining. The Renaissance took care of according precedence to innovators over imitators. Today it seems that this balance is being disrupted again, by the constant questioning of the need for original research coming from the humanities in ethnological museum-making. Instead, many appear to favour Romantic notions of collecting and exhibiting, enriched by long-standing narratives of cultural history. Copying seems to have become the *modus operandi* once again. Examples of such imitational bias are omnipresent and unsurprisingly include ad banners on the internet based on previously visited websites, library search engines replacing open stacks browsing, ceaseless debates on the importance of 'form' over 'content' in university teaching programmes, and, finally, Wikipedia as the new curatorial handyman.

A perspective such as that argued here rests on a historically deep range of philosophical debates on the definition of self, and by extension, on how to differentiate the true, authentic self from inauthentic tendencies. A discussion of the history of early and later thinking on the authentic is beyond the scope of this introduction. Still, we should note that considerable attention has been devoted to the constructed nature of the authentic and its inextricable ties to the West. Lionel Trilling's detailed history remains authoritative in this regard (1971). Linking the fragmentation of the social order in feudal Europe to the ever-increasing emphasis on the individual in Late Modernity, Trilling identifies a protracted development from preordained personal identities to the expression of a person's own sincere being, and ultimately to the fundamental belief in a sacred and universal moral self. Trilling contends that locating this self, which lies concealed beneath social frameworks, is what defines the quest for personal authenticity.

Culture depends on copying and imitating. By looking at others or other things, modern subjects realise or maintain their image of self. This self-realisation through looking at others was subsequently lamented by twentieth-century critical theorists for its perceived detriment to societal authenticity. At one point in theoretical thinking on the social, it was felt that the authentic was under siege, mostly from the onslaught of modernity, in the process *alienating* us from the authentic. At a later stage, the linguistic emphasis and postmodernism made this assumption untenable, led by thinkers such as Althusser, Foucault and Bourdieu, who argued the senselessness of tracking down an independent reality. Authenticity, it was argued, could not be the function of a norm, being highly contextual and therefore time-bound (see examples from philosophy of technology in Verbeek 2000).

Ethnographic museums actually started out as windows onto the authentic. This is partly why materialist protocols for technical and stylistic authentication have always been so important in these contexts. Such protocols ensured that subjective viewers, in studying the objects on exhibit, could contemplate a 'true' view of the distant and exotic: things produced by societies marked by Rousseau's *amour de soi*, rather than the regrettable *amour propre* dominating modern life (Lindholm 2008:8-9). In viewing these distant things, visitors were at liberty to appropriate part of the 'aura' of these objects.

Aside from reflections on the authentic self, the authentic also invokes 'naturalness'. Ethnographic objects possess a force of *empirische Einmaligkeit,* identified by Walter Benjamin (1936) – the 'aura' of an original artwork. A certain tension exists in ethnological museums as a result of the mixed composition of the objects in their holdings, being part unique works of art, part mass-produced objects. Until quite recently, ethnology museums tended to disguise the latter as the former, seeking to present themselves as guardians of 'the temple of authenticity' (Handler 1986). Authenticity tends to be a binding doctrine, finding its expression in closely contained culture histories. Visitors also come to museums as an expression of individual choice.

The networks between people, places and things, mentioned above, help to distract attention from materialist views in the context of debates on 'real' versus fakes/copies/forgeries. Fundamental as such material scrutiny continues to be for museum practice, constructivist perspectives have amply demonstrated that authenticity is a cultural product; a product that is capable of expressing desire, identity, and ultimately, a formulation of the self (*e.g.* Bruner 2007; Handler 1986; Lindholm 2008). The exhibition rooms of ethnographic museums, then, may be seen in the light of field sites – locations where people produce stories to form parts of their lives and make sense of the world around them. This may apply equally to local visitors or to cultural source communities – both objectify material things in realising their own authentic subjectivity.

It seems that ethnographic museums are increasingly listening to their visitors, who are intent on 'coming to an understanding' of the things in their exhibition areas. Ultimately, people have numerous ways in which to realise their authentic personal or group sense of reality to complement the social constructions that define their daily lives.

In view of the above considerations, we have compiled this volume to highlight the ways in which authenticities are produced, lingering less on detecting the subjective nature of communities and traditions. Such constructivist approaches are by now firmly anchored in material culture studies (Buchli 2002; Tilley et al. 2006; Oliveira Jorge and Thomas 2006/2007; Julien and Rosselin 2009; Hicks and Beaudry 2010), and ethnographic museums have been fully aware of this at least since the advent of the methodologically inclined 'new museology' (Vergo 1989) and the subsequent 'critical museology', focused more on the societal purpose and effect of museums (Shelton 2001). Since they are attached to institutions that are deeply rooted in society and are by now acutely aware of these ties, ethnographic museum professionals have opened up their research agendas to establish interdisciplinary ties within academia specifically, and more widely within local and global platforms. For this reason, the symposium that prompted the production of this book included papers by authors from professional environments other than ethnographic museums, including archaeologists, ethnographers and cultural heritage workers. Though by no means comprehensive, this breadth makes it possible to compare the ways in which different disciplinary discourses have invited their audiences to consider authenticity and inauthenticity, and to see the tenuousness of any such bipolar hierarchy. Opening the floor to 'alternative authenticities' is taking a conscious stand in the political arena of ethnographic things, where today's museums have dealings with ancestral/cultural stakeholders who at times adopt a strategic essentialism to make their voices heard. From the standpoint of social archaeology, for instance, this is a recognisable process of challenging meaning in material things. Awarding ontological primacy to the creative subject in ethnographic museums, who can subjectively experience and inscribe objects even while he or she is shaped by them, means recognising the continuous and inherently incomplete social process whereby meaning is produced – a process that we feel is the only real 'essence' about how people engage with the world surrounding them (Jones 2010).

## Structure of this book

This book addresses the practice of authentication as it has taken shape in ethnographic museums, citing examples in the Netherlands and other European countries, and indeed the West as a whole. None of the authors wishes to abolish the concept of authenticity. Instead, each reflects on ways in which it might be reconfigured and put to better use in ethnographic museums. The chapters cover a wide range of topics, from the technical determination of the authenticity of a decorated human skull from Mexico (Berger) to the loss of authenticity in the visual recycling of Aboriginal paintings through incorporation into museum architecture (Price); and from tracing the provenance of an Islamic ceramic jar and silver tray in order to argue for or against them being 'forgeries' (Watson) to the questioning of the museological use of concept of provenance (Joyce). Most authors implicitly agree that authenticity remains a central concern for ethnographic museums and that the application of the term is so wide-ranging as to defy monolithic interpretation. However, it also becomes clear that observations from the contemporary world need to be included in the stories ethnographic museums decide to tell about their collections, as Brinkgreve (this volume) argues – including giving voice to indigenous agency which is opportunely playing into the ethnographic art market.

Martin Berger opens the debate by reviewing the collection history of a particular object, a decorated human skull that stylistically invokes an origin to late Pre-Hispanic times in Mesoamerica. Deconstructing both its physical characteristics and the museological reasons for acquiring this mosaic skull, he argues, allows us to reconsider the claims that have been made identifying it as an object created before the Spanish Conquest. Berger points out that the initial assessment as to its probable age was carried out by comparing it to the general stylistic understanding of what late Pre-Hispanic ceremonial material culture was deemed to look like. In other words, he argues, such an assessment is essentially circular and therefore highly unreliable. Berger applies Dutton's distinction between expressive and nominal authenticity, which he defines as the difference between the absence and presence of convincing archaeological contextual provenience data and/or technical age determination. Both are forms of inductive reasoning, but the former is clearly more likely to produce incorrect object identifications. Separately from Berger's conclusions, the story of this mosaic skull emerges as a way of reflecting on preconfigured Romantic notions of archaeological or ethnographic cultures, with Mesoamerican culture being associated with human bone materials, turquoise mosaics, and human sacrifice. In a similar vein, classical Mediterranean culture is associated with marble, pillars and so on, and Egyptian culture is materially associated with sandstone and the inevitable Pharaonic mortuary architecture.

Rosemary Joyce questions the definitions of object provenience and provenance, and in so doing makes an unsettling ontological shift in not highlighting the 'constructed' character of people's social worlds, as is habitually done in discourses of authentication. Instead, she turns the analytical lens onto the ethnographic museum, and indeed onto 'us', by archaeologically problematising the notion of provenance to argue authenticity. Such nebulous notions are not sufficiently recognised in ethnographic museums, it seems to us, and Joyce's paper is a detailed account of the parallel yet dissimilar use of vocabularies of material culture. More reflexively, Joyce also destabilises the notion of provenance by using archaeological excavations as the starting point in an objects biography, ignoring manufacturing operational chains, subsequent uses and eventual deposition processes that may have affected the object before it was ever an 'archaeological object'.

The complexities of provenance histories, discussed by Oliver Watson, are not far removed from the point raised by Joyce. Provenance is intended as a body of knowledge that could validate an object's genuineness or unmask it as a forgery. Watson describes the curator-historian, whose expertise depends on the possibility of tracing the history of an ethnographic object's pedigree. What unfolds is an intriguing showcase of how the ascription of authenticity is achieved by authority of argument. It is emphasised that such authority has a historical tendency to shift, and at times to base itself more on power than reason. As the confidence in an authoritative voice waxes and wanes, so does the object's reception by its audience (Crew and Sims 1991).

Gold jewellery (*mamuli*) from Sumba in Indonesia is highlighted in the contribution by Francine Brinkgreve, again to question provenance, but also to reflect on the notion of viewing an object's authenticity as a function of its age. In her examination of *mamuli*, she encounters the contemporary practice of using well-known specimens of these gold ear ornaments as a source of inspiration in order to craft new ones. This highlights the capacity for object authentication, ironically, achieved through using depictions of *mamuli* in museum and auction catalogues as an inspirational source. Brinkgreve's argument comes closest of all the contributions in this volume, perhaps, to the idea that the crucial point is not so much *how* something has been produced, but *why* it is considered authentic. Sumbanese goldsmiths are apparently entirely unfazed by imperfect hierarchies of the authentic; they devise structures of meaning that merge flawlessly into the ceremonial exchange relations in which these *mamuli* play a prominent role.

Cunera Buijs's paper discusses the link between authenticity and cultural representativeness, using an example of ethnographic photography from East Greenland. While museum visitors assume that exhibition rooms show an accurate and integral cultural representation of a particular region or period of time, Buijs recognises that early collectors of ethnographic materials prioritised certain object categories over others in terms of how 'exotic' they were deemed to be. Photographs could have more to contribute in this respect, it was concluded, than some objects. They could capture a remote region in all its remoteness – and indeed its authenticity – more effectively than an isolated object displayed in the museum. Selection influences interpretation, Buijs states, and such selection criteria are seldom emphasised in museum exhibits. This hidden selection points to the construction that is inherent in portrayals of the authentic, and therefore the presence of pre-existing ideas as to what we expect to see as authentic.

The authority to decide on authenticity, and to use material culture accordingly, is the central theme in Sally Price's contribution. She takes up Buijs's point on the role of object selection in exhibits and presents a critical perspective on such curating choices. Her main observation is that in order to achieve cultural representativeness, certain discourses are mobilised in catalogues and case labelling to enable individual objects to 'fit in'. This is clearly an uncomfortable observation, one that is further stressed by Price's allusion to the 'violation' and 'cleansing' of an object's cultural authenticity, in this case its biography. Price emphatically underscores this point by using the architectural design of the Musée du Quai Branly as a second case study. For her, the planning philosophy and exterior iconography of this museum echoes the role of expressive authenticity, raised earlier by Berger. Looking specifically at the merging of Aboriginal artwork, she questions the authority of voice that determined what this museum ended up portraying as its emblem, and concludes that bargaining between aesthetics and politics significantly influences the authentic in museums.

Finally, while this introduction has outlined the materialist and constructivist backgrounds underlying thinking about the authentic, and has attempted to stress the importance of studying how museum visitors and museum professionals currently still produce realities with a *sufficient amount* of authenticity, Laura Van Broekhoven brings this volume to a close with a paper focusing on the practices of museum curatorship and the expectations of museum visitors. Drawing on ideas from tourism studies, Van Broekhoven brings attention to the reality that authority in ethnographic material culture generates certain expectations among museum visitors. Such expectations revolve around a desire to witness 'the real' and consume some of the 'aura' mentioned by Walter Benjamin. Contemporary museums are aware of such social processes going on in their exhibition rooms, and are increasingly reflective about such internal dynamics.

To conclude these introductory remarks, it must be emphasised that the authentic, in the museums of the twenty-first century, is no longer predominantly associated with the presumed 'essence' of a culture. Current thinking on authenticity is characterised by a view of human society as being engaged with ever-defective structures of meaning. Despite this essential incompleteness, people still manage to come up with apparently stable and coherent ideas about themselves and others – ideas that they invariably call 'authentic'. In an increasingly globalised world, people strategically seek out museums to satisfy their desire for an authentic experience. Subjective and staged as they may be, such visits are experiences nonetheless, and it might be argued that an analysis from the constructivist perspective alone is not fruitful. It may be more useful to study how the authentic is negotiated between objects and museum visitors, while acknowledging that people in museums and elsewhere continue to attach value to authenticity as they navigate the surrounding world.

Ethnographic museum professionals provide their audiences with a real world, an 'empirical sketch' backed up by the study of material things through their closest academic neighbours: archaeology, anthropology, and art history. Such a sketch is by definition partial and patchy, but also empirical, and thereby methodologically constrained and reliable.

## Acknowledgements

This paper has benefitted from discussions with Miguel-John Versluys, Wonu Veys, and Laura Van Broekhoven. Versluys is thanked for suggesting the idea of essential material qualities in particular culture style and transference.

## References

Brown, M. (2010), 'Changing authentic identities: evidence from Taiwan and China', *Journal of the Royal Anthropological Institute* 16: 459-479.

Bruner, E.B. (2005), *Culture on tour. Ethnographies of travel.* Chicago: University of Chicago Press.

Buchli, V. (ed.) (2004), *The material culture reader.* Oxford: Berg.

Clifford, J. (1988), *The predicament of culture: Twentieth-century ethnography, literature, and art.* Cambridge, MA: Harvard University Press.

Crăciun, M. (2012) 'Rethinking fakes, authenticating selves', *Journal of the Royal Anthropological Institute* 18: 846-863.

Crew, S.R. & J.E. Sims (1991), 'Locating authenticity: fragments of a dialogue', in I. Karp & S.D. Lavine (eds.), *Exhibiting cultures. The poetics and politics of museum display*, 159-175. Washington DC: Smithsonian Institution Press.

Handler, R. (1986), 'Authenticity', *Anthropology Today* 2(1): 2-4.

Hicks, D. & M.C. Beaudry (eds.) (2010), *The Oxford handbook of material culture studies.* Oxford: University of Oxford Press.

Holtorf, C. & T. Schadla-Hall (1999), 'Age as artefact: On archaeological authenticity', *European Journal of Archaeology* 2(2): 229-247.

Jones, S. (2010), 'Negotiating authentic objects and authentic selves. Beyond the deconstruction of authenticity', in *Journal of Material Culture* 15(2): 181-203.

Julien, M. & C. Rosselin (eds.) (2009), *Le sujet contre les objets…tout contre. Ethnographies de cultures matérielles.* Paris: CTHS.

Keane, W. (2003), 'Semiotics and the social analysis of material things', *Language & Communication* 23(3-4): 409-425.

Lindholm, C. (2008), 'Introduction' in C. Lindholm (ed.), *Culture and authenticity*, 1-10. Malden: Blackwell Publishing.

Lowenthal, D. (1995), 'Changing criteria of authenticity', in K.E. Larsen & N. Marstein (eds.), *Nara Conference on authenticity. Proceedings of the conference in Nara, Japan, 1-6 november 1994*, 121-135. Trondheim: Tapir.

McBryde, I. (1997) 'The ambiguities of authenticity – rock of faith or shifting sands?', *Conservation and management of archaeological sites* 2: 93-100.

Oliveira Jorge, V. & J. Thomas (eds.) (2006/2007), 'Overcoming the modern invention of material culture', in *Journal of Iberian Archaeology* 9/10.

Shelton, Anthony (2001), 'Unsettling the meaning: Critical museology, Art and anthropological discourse', in M. Bouquet (ed.), *Academic Anthropology and the Museum: Back to the Future*, 142-161. London: Berghahn Books.

Thomas, N. (1991), *Entangled objects. Exchange, material culture, and colonialism in the Pacific*. Cambridge: Harvard University Press.

Tilley, C., W. Keane, S. Küchler, M. Rowlands & P. Spyer (eds.) (2006), *Handbook of material culture*. London: Sage.

Trilling, L. (1972), *Sincerity and authenticity*. Oxford: Oxford University Press.

Van Broekhoven, L., C. Buijs & P. Hovens (eds.) (2011) *Sharing knowledge and cultural heritage: First Nations of the Americas. Studies in collaboration with indigenous peoples from Greenland, North and South America*. Leiden: Sidestone Press.

Verbeek, P. (2005), *What things do. Philosophical reflections on technology, agency, and design*. State College: Pennsylvania State University.

Vergo, P. (ed.) (1989), *The New Museology*. London: Reaktion Books.

# Real, Fake or a Combination?

## Examining the Authenticity of a Mesoamerican Mosaic Skull

*Martin E. Berger*

### Abstract

One of the centrepieces of the Central and South American gallery of the National Museum of Ethnology (NME) in Leiden, the Netherlands is a Mesoamerican human skull decorated with turquoise mosaic. This mosaic skull is thought to have been created by Mixtec artisans in the Late Postclassic period (AD 1300-1521). Since the skull was acquired on the art market, nothing is known about its provenance prior to 1962. As a result, some have questioned its pre-Columbian origin. Similar questions have been raised about unprovenanced mosaic skulls in other museum collections.

This article presents the findings of research carried out at the NME and at the Centre des Recherche et de Restauration des Musées de France (C2RMF), Paris in 2011 and 2012, with a view to determining whether the Leiden mosaic skull is an authentic pre-Columbian artefact, an entirely modern creation, or a modern combination of authentic elements. The article also explores the reasons for the skull's acquisition in the 1960s, in the absence of any background information, and discusses the significance of these research findings for the presentation and perception of this particular artefact.

### Introduction

In 1963, Dr P.H. Pott, who was then director of the National Museum of Ethnology (NME) in Leiden, the Netherlands, was offered for sale a human skull decorated with turquoise mosaics by the American art dealer Robert Stolper, who asserted that it had been found in a tomb at an archaeological site near Teotitlán del Camino, a town on the border of the Mexican states of Oaxaca and Puebla (see fig. 1).

Because of the style in which the mosaic was executed, the mosaic skull was said to be a product of the Mixtec culture, dating from the Late Postclassic period (AD 1300-1521). In a letter to the curators of the museum, dated 31 October 1963, Dr Pott describes it as 'an object... of such rarity and value that I would feel it wrong to reject this offer without first having made the

*Fig. 1: Map of southern Mexico, sites mentioned in the text are underlined.*

utmost effort to obtain the resources to acquire it'.[1] Standard procedure would have been for the museum's board of curators to approve the acquisition of a piece, and for the specialised curator for the region to have been involved in the acquisition process. In this case, however, Dr Pott decided independently that the skull must be acquired by the museum. According to the then curator for Central and South America, the director was 'obsessed' with the mosaic skull (R.T. Zuidema, personal communication 2011) (see fig. 2).

Notwithstanding Mr Stolper's claims about the origins of the mosaic skull, no documentation for this find was available, and the provenance of the mosaic skull before 1964,[2] when it was sold to the NME, was (and remains) unknown. The poor quality of these provenance data, combined with the fact that no such skull has ever been found in a documented archaeological context and that no depictions are known of this type of decorated skull in Postclassic Mesoamerican iconography, have led to questions being raised about the mosaic skull's authenticity. The Leiden mosaic skull is part of a group of about ten similar artefacts, preserved in private and museum collections in North America and Europe. Like the Leiden skull, all these mosaic skulls lack any verifiable provenance, and many of them have been considered spurious. For some of them, it has been suggested that, while both the turquoise on the skull and the skull itself are of pre-Columbian origin, the combination of the pre-Columbian elements is modern (Ekholm 1983; Urcid 2010).

---

1  Orig. 'een object ... dat dermate zeldzaam en waardevol is, dat ik mij niet gerechtigd acht deze aanbieding af te slaan zonder alles te hebben beproefd voor deze aankoop middelen te vinden'.

2  A discussion of the distinction in usage between the terms 'provenance' and 'provenience' is beyond the scope of this article. I use the term 'provenance' here to refer to the history of where an object has been since it was created.

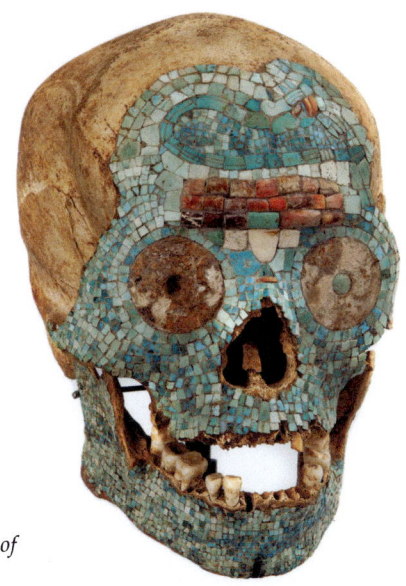

*Fig. 2: The mosaic skull in the collection of the National Museum of Ethnology, inv. no. 4007-1.*

This article reports on research carried out at the NME and at the Centre des Recherche et de Restauration des Musées de France (C2RMF), Paris, in 2011 and 2012, with a view to establishing whether the Leiden mosaic skull is an authentic pre-Columbian artefact, an entirely modern creation, or, as had been argued for other mosaic skulls of this type, a modern combination of authentic elements. The article also explores the reasons for the skull's acquisition in the 1960s, in the absence of any background information, and discusses the significance of these research findings for the presentation and perception of this particular artefact.

## Context

When the NME acquired the mosaic skull in the 1960s, few mosaic skulls of this type were known. In his letter to the board of curators in 1963, Dr Pott states that he knows of only 'two other mosaic skulls of this type in a private collection in the United States, which are in a poorer condition than the one that was offered to me',[3] as well as several turquoise mosaic pieces executed in the same style in the British Museum (see Carmichael 1970; McEwan et al. 2006; Saville 1922). It is not entirely clear to which mosaic skulls Pott was referring in this letter, but it seems probable that he was alluding to the ones in the Robert Woods Bliss collection of Pre-Columbian Art at Dumbarton Oaks in Washington, DC. Robert Stolper, the art dealer who sold the mosaic skull to the NME, was also involved in the sale of the mosaic skulls to Dumbarton Oaks.

---

3   Orig. 'Daarnaast zijn in een Amerikaanse privéverzameling nog twee schedels als de mij aangebodene, doch in een slechtere staat van conservering verkerende, aanwezig.'

This makes it likely that Pott was referring to these skulls. However, there are *three* mosaic skulls in the Dumbarton Oaks collection. Why Dr Pott mentions only two is unclear.

Since the sale of the three mosaic skulls to Dumbarton Oaks in 1959/60, seven other mosaic skulls of this type (excluding the Leiden one) have surfaced. Five of these are currently in museum collections. One is at the Los Angeles County Museum of Arts (Fields, Pohl & Lyall 2012: 200), one is at the Indiana University Art Museum (Coe 1986: 14, 31), one is at the Musée d'Arts Africaines, Océaniens et Américains in Marseille (Sourrieu 2011), one is at the DeYoung Museum of Fine Arts in San Francisco, and one is in the Museo William Spratling in Taxco (Izeki 2008:133). The other two are currently in unknown private collections, one having been sold at a Hotel Drouot auction in 1984 (Drouot 1984) and one having surfaced on the market in Paris in 2012 (Anon. 2012). Similar mosaic skulls are preserved in a few other museum collections (including the Santa Barbara Art Museum in the USA [von Winning 1968], the Museo Nacional de Antropología in Mexico City [Izeki 2008] and the Museo Arqueológico del Soconusco in Tapachula, Mexico [Michael D. Coe, personal communication 2013]) but I have decided to leave these out of consideration here, since they are markedly different in some aspects of their iconography.

Since there is no room here to discuss the history and description of all of these skulls, I shall focus on the mosaic skulls at Dumbarton Oaks, San Francisco and Marseille, in order to contextualise the research on the Leiden mosaic skull. For all these mosaic skulls it has been argued that they are not authentic pre-Columbian artefacts, but rather modern combinations of ancient elements.

Let me start by giving a brief description of the mosaic skull found in Tomb 7 of Monte Albán. This mosaic skull constitutes evidence from a controlled context of the existence of Mesoamerican human skulls decorated with turquoise mosaic. However, a brief overview will make it clear that this mosaic skull cannot serve as proof of the existence in Mesoamerica of the type of unprovenanced mosaic skulls that is under discussion here.

## *Tomb 7 of Monte Albán, Oaxaca*

The only human skull covered with turquoise mosaic ever to have been found in a controlled archaeological context in Mesoamerica is the one found by Mexican archaeologist Dr Alfonso Caso during his famous excavation of Tomb 7 of Monte Albán (Caso 1969). This mosaic skull is currently preserved in the Museo de las Culturas de Oaxaca, in the city of Oaxaca, Mexico. While the Tomb 7 mosaic skull, which is thought to be Postclassic Mixtec, looks somewhat similar to the unprovenanced mosaic skulls, it differs in two fundamental ways. First, whereas the unprovenanced skulls are decorated only at the front, the Tomb 7 skull was probably decorated all over with turquoise mosaics. This statement is made with some reservations, since it cannot be established with certainty which parts were

*Fig. 3: The mosaic skull found in Tomb 7 of Monte Albán.*

decorated and which were not on the basis of Caso's description of the find (Caso 1969: 62-9). This problem of reconstruction is compounded by the fact that parts of the skull had collapsed before Caso excavated Tomb 7. Nonetheless, the skull, which was restored and is on display in Oaxaca, today has mosaic both on the face and on the side of the skull. In addition, given the number of mosaic plaques that were found associated with the skull, it seems probable that much of the skull was covered. Also, Caso mentions that parts of the skull had rests of adhesive on them (Caso 1969: 63). I concede that all these details from Caso's description constitute only indirect evidence, not conclusive proof that the skull was originally covered entirely with mosaics. However, this is not the most important difference between the Tomb 7 skull and the unprovenanced mosaic skulls. The second, more significant, difference is that while all the unprovenanced objects are entire skulls that have not been worked, except for their decoration, the Tomb 7 skull has the top of the cranial vault cut away and all openings of the skull sealed. These alterations to the cranium have led scholars to suggest that this skull may have been used as a cup (Caso 1969:66-7), a censer (McCafferty and McCafferty 1994:144) or a resonance chamber (Urcid 2010:190). Naturally, since the unprovenanced skulls lack these alterations, they cannot have served any such function (cf. Urcid 2010). This means that while the Tomb 7 mosaic skull proves that the practice of decorating human crania with turquoise mosaics existed, it cannot be cited in proof of the existence in pre-Columbian Mesoamerica of the *type* of mosaic skull under discussion here, since different functions are involved. In other words, the basic decorative elements of the two types of mosaic skulls are the same, but from a functional point of view they cannot be grouped together, since the ways in which they may have been used simply diverge too greatly. In this respect it is important to note that the only other similar decorated skull that was found *in situ*, in the *cenote* of Chichén Itzá, was similarly cut away at the cranial vault and had all its openings sealed (Coggins 1984:155; Moholy-Nagy & Ladd 1992:132-140). Additionally, a sixteenth-century description by Diego de Landa (1959[1566]: 59-60, quoted in Urcid 2010: 190) of the creation of decorated human skulls in the Maya area describes how each skull is boiled, defleshed and has the top half sawn off, leaving intact the face and the mandible. In other words, both *in situ* finds of decorated skulls and descriptions in sixteenth century works testify to the practice of decorating human skulls that are 'cut in half', with the cranial vault removed, rather than to the use of intact skulls for decoration, as is the case with the unprovenanced mosaic skulls. Thus, while the Tomb 7 skull is definitely proof of a practice of combining turquoise mosaics and human skulls in pre-Columbian Mesoamerica, from a functional point of view this skull can hardly be seen to represent the same type of artefact. In spite of these important differences, it seems quite likely that if the unprovenanced mosaic skulls are indeed modern creations, the forgers used the Tomb 7 skull as a template.

## Dumbarton Oaks, Washington DC

The only collection to hold more than one mosaic skull is the Robert Woods Bliss collection of Pre-Columbian Art at Dumbarton Oaks. This collection contains three mosaic skulls in total, which are registered at the museum under inventory numbers PC.B.097, -098, and -099. They were acquired by Robert Woods Bliss, the founder of the collection, from the anthropologist Helmut de Terra and the art dealer Earl Stendahl in 1959 and 1960. These three mosaic skulls were also, to my knowledge, the first to appear on the art market.

Interestingly, Robert Stolper, the art dealer who sold the mosaic skull to the NME, was also involved in the sale of the mosaic skulls to Robert Woods Bliss. What is more, even though Robert Woods Bliss only purchased three of these objects, he was originally offered four (Urcid 2010: 190). He decided against acquiring the fourth mosaic skull after Robert Stolper had ordered a material examination of the skull, the mosaic and the adhesive by Norman Wiener, a restorer from New York, who also worked on the Leiden mosaic skull. During this material examination, it was determined that the adhesive used on the fourth mosaic skull was Duco cement, a type of household glue. This meant that the attachment of the mosaic to the skull was quite obviously modern. It is not known what happened to the fourth skull after Woods Bliss rejected it, but the object appears to have remained in the possession of whoever owned it at the time. Javier Urcid (2010:118) has suggested that the fourth skull offered to Robert Woods Bliss might be the one that is in Leiden today. While this may seem a logical conclusion, given that Robert Stolper was involved in both the sale of the mosaic skulls to Robert Woods Bliss and the sale of the mosaic skull to the NME, the adhesive on the NME mosaic skull is not Duco cement (see below). Although this does not exclude the possibility that the fourth skull refused by Woods Bliss is identical to the one that is currently in the NME, it does complicate the picture.

Even though the three skulls that Robert Woods Bliss acquired for his collection in 1959/60 were considered genuine at the time of purchase, research has since suggested otherwise. The skulls have not been exhibited since the 1980s, since by then they were already considered spurious, being a modern combination of ancient materials (Elizabeth H. Boone personal communication 2012). Recent detailed research on the mosaic and the skull by Javier Urcid (2010) concluded that both the skull and the materials in the mosaic are ancient, but that their combination is modern.

## DeYoung Museum, San Francisco

The DeYoung Museum of Fine Arts in San Francisco, USA holds one mosaic skull in its collection. This skull entered the museum collections through a bequest from Harald Wagner in 1978. Since the museum staff had little knowledge of the provenance of the mosaic skull and were unsure about its authenticity, Ellen Hvatum Werner of the DeYoung consulted Dr Gordon Ekholm, then curator emeritus at the American Museum of Natural History (AMNH) and the foremost expert on authenticating pre-Columbian pieces in the twentieth century, on the skull's possible authenticity. In his letter to Dr Werner, Dr Ekholm states: 'in my

*Fig. 4: The mosaic skull of the DeYoung Museum, San Francisco, without the decorated mandible.*

opinion it is without question a fake. It is, of course, a genuine ancient skull and the mosaic pieces are genuine – but their attachment to the skull is modern work.' He goes on to say: 'a number of these skulls appeared on the market in, I believe, the late 60s. I saw at least six or seven of them, – mainly at different times but in the hands of one dealer. … I was able to piece together what I believe is a fairly accurate idea of where and by whom these mosaic decorated skulls were made, but I cannot at the moment find the time to write it out' (Ekholm 1983). Sadly, Dr Ekholm passed away quite soon after writing this letter and never, as far as I know, wrote down the story he had pieced together of the appearance of the mosaic skulls. The Ekholm archives, which are preserved at the AMNH, do not contain any information on the mosaic skulls. Still, it is interesting to note that, as in the case of the Dumbarton Oaks mosaic skulls, Dr Ekholm mentions that the components of the mosaic skull are all genuinely pre-Columbian, but that the combination of the two is modern. The DeYoung Museum has not put the mosaic skull on display and the current curator considers it to be 'problematic at best' (Matthew H. Robb personal communication 2013).

## Musée d'Arts Africaines, Océaniens et Amérindiens (MAAOA), Marseille

The research conducted on the Leiden mosaic skull grew out of an earlier project at the Centre de Recherche et de Restauration des Musées de France (C2RMF) that focused on the study of a mosaic skull, similar to the one in the Leiden collections, from the Musée d'Arts Africaines, Océaniens et Amérindiens (MAAOA) in Marseille, France. This mosaic skull was acquired by the MAAOA from the French neurologist Dr Henri Gastaut in 1989. Like the one in Leiden, the Marseille skull has no known provenance prior to its acquisition by Dr Gastaut. When he was considering the purchase, the Frenchman's advisors raised serious doubts as to the skull's authentic pre-Columbian status. Dr Gastaut therefore consulted several experts on pre-Columbian material culture in France and Mexico before deciding whether or not to buy the mosaic skull, to avoid buying a forgery. During this research, two different find sites were named for the mosaic skull. While the original vendor claimed that it had been found near Mérida on the Yucatán peninsula, another contact reported that the skull was found during excavations at Yagul, a well-known Zapotec archaeological site in the central valleys of the state of Oaxaca (Sourrieu 2011). Undeterred by these contradictory statements, Dr Gastaut decided to acquire the mosaic skull for his collection in 1964.

Research on the Marseille mosaic skull by the C2RMF showed that, like the Dumbarton Oaks and DeYoung mosaic skulls, it was most probably a modern composition of ancient elements (Mogne 2011:46). This conclusion was based on several characteristics of the skull and the adhesive used to attach the mosaic to the skull. Firstly, $^{14}$C-dating of the skull suggested a date of 1180 ± 30 BP, that is to say between 772 and 900 cal AD (Calligaro et al. 2011). This date falls well within the Late Classic period (AD 600 – 900), while a Late Postclassic (AD 1300 – 1521) origin would be expected. During the Classic period, access to turquoise in the Maya area was limited, and it was only in the Postclassic period that turquoise started to replace jadeite, the greenstone material of choice during the Classic period. Additionally, the type of cranial deformation is typical of the Maya area – the skull was said to have been found near Mérida – and all other mosaic skulls are said to be Mixtec and to have been found in the Mixtec area (states of Puebla/Oaxaca/Guerrero). Lastly, and most importantly, the adhesive that was used to attach the mosaic to the skull was found to be shellac, a type of adhesive that was not used in pre-Columbian Mesoamerica (see below).

## Description of research conducted at the C2RMF and results

As mentioned, the research conducted on the Leiden skull grew out of an earlier project of the MAAOA and the C2RMF. This project entailed the detailed examination of the mosaic and the skull of the MAAOA using several techniques, including X-Ray Fluorescence (XRF), X-Ray Diffraction (XRD), Particle Induced X-Ray Emission (PIXE), radiocarbon dating ($^{14}$C-dating), and Gas Chromatography-Mass Spectrometry (GC-MS), in order to determine the mosaic skull's authenticity. Since this approach proved successful, the NME and the C2RMF cooperated, with funding from the EU CHARISMA programme, to conduct the same tests and analyses on the Leiden skull. The NME also cooperated with staff of the Faculty of Archaeology of Leiden University to study the skull itself in greater detail.

Since it has been argued for other mosaic skulls that they are modern combinations of ancient elements, I shall discuss the mosaic, the skull, and the adhesive, and their possible authenticity, separately. I shall start by describing the materials that go to make up the mosaic. I shall then describe the tests that were conducted on the skull and consider its possible provenience. The most crucial component of the mosaic skull, in terms of authenticity, is the adhesive, which I shall deal with last.

## Materials

The first step in trying to determine whether the mosaic on the skull was genuinely pre-Columbian was to characterize all the materials that formed part of the mosaic. Naturally, if these included any materials that could not be of pre-Columbian origin, such as glass in the case of the Marseille mosaic skull (Calligaro et al. 2011) or brass in the case of one of the British Museum turquoise mosaic pieces (McEwan et al. 2006:85), this would indicate that the mosaic had been, at least, modified after the conquest of Mexico.

Earlier research conducted on the Marseille skull had found that, while much of the mosaic consisted of turquoise tesserae, its overall composition was fairly heterogeneous. The materials used included amazonite, heulandite, aragonite and pyrite. The results of the research on the Marseille mosaic served as a frame of reference for the Leiden mosaic. Using X-Ray Diffraction (XRD), X-Ray Fluorescence (XRF), and Particle Induced X-Ray Emission (PIXE) the mosaic was found to be composed of the following materials: turquoise, shell, jadeite, heulandite and quartz. These tests were carried out by Dr Thomas Calligaro and Dr Yvan Coquinot (both of C2RMF).

## *Turquoise*

About 97% of the mosaic consisted of pieces of turquoise, supporting the original hypothesis that most of the tesserae would be turquoise. The turquoise was characterized using XRF analysis. The pieces analysed included all the tesserae that formed what is believed to be the feathered serpent motif on the forehead of the skull as well as some individual ones in different parts of the mosaic. Additionally, a 'map' was made of 20x20 tesserae on the right side of the mandible, in order to have a large corpus of tesserae to compare.

Turquoise is a material well known as having been used in pre-Columbian Mesoamerica. While jadeite was most used for greenstone objects in the Classic period (AD 250 – 900), Postclassic (AD 900 – 1521) greenstone objects are mostly made of turquoise, which was imported from the American Southwest and Mexican Northwest. From the Codex Mendoza, an elaborate sixteenth-century Aztec tribute list, we know that the Mixtec area supplied most of the worked turquoise that was used in the Aztec capital Tenochtitlán (Berdan & Anawalt 1997).

## *Shell*

Two important parts of the mosaic are made out of shell. First, the red and purple band that is above the eyes is composed of shell material. Second, the disks that form the skull's eyes are also made from shell material. Different types of shell, mainly of the *Spondylus* species and *Strombus* genus, were used for their colours in pre-Columbian mosaics (McEwan et al. 2006:33). In addition, in many mosaic masks the eyes are covered with white shells that have holes enabling the wearer to see through the mask. The Tomb 7 mosaic skull has similar eyes made of perforated shell (Caso 1969:30). Interestingly, the eyes of the Leiden mosaic skull are not perforated but have a piece of turquoise encrusted in the middle to form a pupil (see fig. 2).

## Concretion on shell

Examination of the shell material constituting the eyes in the mosaic revealed that both eyes were (partially) covered with some kind of brown material (see fig. 2). This material was initially believed to be glue remnants, but X-Ray Diffraction analysis revealed that it was actually a concretion of chlorphosphates, hydroxylapatite, produced by bacterial activity while the shell pieces were in the soil. This concretion forms when shell material is buried in phosphorous soil, and its thickness indicates that these pieces of shell must have been buried for some considerable time. Since the hole in the centre of the right eye is covered with the same concretion, this means that no turquoise such as now seen in the left eye was present in the right eye when it was deposited in the ground.

While the researchers initially believed this concretion to be a possible marker of the mosaic skull's authenticity, it may in fact be an indication of its spurious nature. If these skulls were authentic artefacts, they would most probably have been placed either in tombs or in dry caves, as happened, for example, with the Tomb 7 mosaic skull of Monte Albán (Caso 1969) and with several other mosaic masks and shields found in caves in Puebla and Oaxaca (Izeki 2008). However, had the mosaic skull been placed in a tomb or dry cave, it would not have been buried, and no concretion would have formed on the shell parts of the mosaic, since there would not have been any exposure to soil.[4] What is more, the unequal distribution of the concretion, which is present on both eyes but not on pieces made of the same material in between them, shows that these pieces could not have been in contact with the same soil at the same time, indicating that they did not originally form part of the same mosaic.

## Jade

One of the pieces in the middle of the mosaic, above the right eye, was clearly not turquoise to the naked eye. An initial hypothesis was that this material was amazonite, a material used on the Marseille skull – in small quantities – and on the well-known Máscara de Malinaltepec, the mosaic on which was mainly made of amazonite (Martínez del Campo 2010). PIXE analysis showed, however, that this particular stone in the Leiden mosaic was actually jadeite. It is not known at what time this stone was applied to the skull, but there are no indications that suggest a later addition of this piece. However, the stone is clearly not turquoise, even to the naked eye, and would not have been mistaken for it by the creator of the mosaic or a later restorer. It should be noted that in the Tomb 7 excavation a small plaque of jade, measuring 18 mm, was found associated with the mosaic skull. This plaque of jade still adhered to the original adhesive paste, together with some turquoise tesserae (Caso 1969:66).

---

4  I would like to thank Dr Javier Urcid for drawing my attention to this issue.

*Fig. 5: The eye of the feathered serpent motif. Copyright C2RMF.*

## Quartz

One of the main uncertainties surrounding the mosaic after the observation of the skull under ultraviolet light was the composition of the material that formed the eye of the feathered serpent design. On the basis of UV photography it was thought to be an organic material, since it glowed red in ultraviolet light. However, after examination under a digital microscope and with the use of PIXE analysis, the eye turned out to be a small piece of finely cut quartz. It was not actually the quartz itself that had glowed red in ultraviolet light, but, since the quartz was perfectly transparent, it showed the colour of the underlying adhesive (see fig. 5)

While the use of quartz has been documented for pre-Columbian Mesoamerica – for example, a cup made of cut and polished rock crystal was found during the Tomb 7 excavations by Alfonso Caso (1969) – the material is not used in any other turquoise mosaic. The most well-known use of quartz for (supposed) Mesoamerican artefacts are the famous crystal skulls that are in museum collections in Europe and the United States. These crystal skulls, which were long seen as emblematic of pre-Columbian cultures, are now believed by researchers to be sixteenth-century European objects or nineteenth-century forgeries (Maclaren Walsh 1997). While this does not necessarily mean that the quartz in the mosaic is of modern origin, its inclusion is a strong indication of modern alteration.

In conclusion, while there are no materials in the mosaic that prove that the mosaic is of modern origin, there are several incongruities that cannot be explained if we regard the mosaic as entirely pre-Columbian. First of all, the presence of the hydroxylapatite concretion on the shell pieces indicates that these pieces were buried, something that one would not expect of this type of object. Also, the distribution of the concretion shows that not all shell pieces of the mosaic could have been buried at the same time and/or in the same location. Additionally, the use of quartz is unique for mosaic work and may well be a modern addition. Nonetheless, as said, there are no modern materials in the mosaic that prove that the mosaic was constructed or restored in modern times. In view of this, and considering that microscopic research indicates that the tesserae were not manufactured with modern tools, the materials in the mosaic have been found to be authentically pre-Columbian.

## The skull

Having determined that the materials used in the mosaic are most probably of pre-Columbian origin, we turn to the skull. Two types of analysis were conducted on the skull. First, an osteobiographical assessment of the skull was carried out to determine the individual's sex and age. Second, oxygen, carbon and strontium isotope analysis was performed on the teeth of the skull, to determine where the individual had lived during his/her early life. The isotope analyses were supervised by Dr Jason Laffoon of the Faculty of Archaeology, Leiden University, while the osteobiographical study was conducted by Dr Andrea Waters-Rist and Anne van Duijvenbode of the same institution.

Ascertaining the individual's probable sex was impeded by the presence of the turquoise mosaic, since many of the facial features could not be assessed. Nonetheless, based on the observable traits of the skull, it was concluded that the individual was probably male, and approximately 35 to 49 years of age at the time of death. While some data were unobtainable because of the mosaic on the skull and the breakage or loss of parts of the skull, the available traits were suggestive of Native American (or Asian) ancestry (Waters-Rist & van Duijvenbode 2012).

The isotope analyses were supervised by Dr Jason Laffoon and carried out at the Faculty of Earth and Life Sciences, Free University of Amsterdam, and consisted of tests of carbon, strontium and oxygen isotopes. Since the mosaic skull was offered for sale in Europe and there was no documented proof that it had ever been in the Americas, a (slight) possibility existed that the skull was actually of European, African or Asian rather than Mesoamerican origin. Therefore, isotope tests were carried out to determine whether the individual had actually lived in Mesoamerica, and whether, more specifically, the individual had lived in the supposed region of origin (southern Mexico, specifically Oaxaca) during the early years of his life. The combined results of the analyses suggested

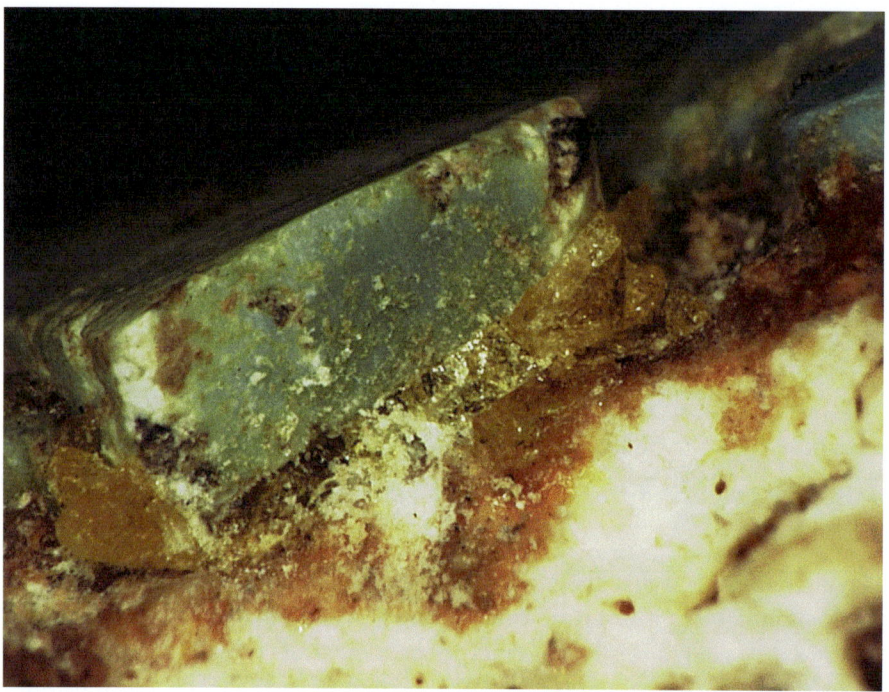

*Fig. 6: The restoration glue that was applied on top of the original glue. Copyright C2RMF.*

that the individual had lived in a drier, inland, higher altitude region of volcanic bedrock geology in the early years of life, on a diet that most probably consisted largely of maize as a staple crop. The ranges were similar to known ranges from southwest Mexico, and the Valley of Oaxaca was one of the places in Mesoamerica in which a combination of these isotope values would be expected to occur (Laffoon 2013). Naturally, this conclusion is very much in line with what would be expected for a Mixtec individual.

Taken together, the isotope analysis and the osteobiographical assessment of the skull indicate unequivocally that the skull belonged to an indigenous Mesoamerican individual. Unfortunately, it was impossible to carry out $^{14}$C-dating of the skull, since large parts of it were covered with an undefined type of varnish, which ruled out clean sampling. Even so, since nothing was found to suggest that the skull is not pre-Columbian in origin, and it is well known that pre-Columbian archaeological tombs and dry caves containing well-preserved skeletal material were often looted, there is every reason to assume that the skull is indeed of pre-Columbian origin.

*Fig. 7: The same picture as figure 6 under UV light. Copyright C2RMF.*

## The adhesive

Since no evidence emerged from the analysis of the materials used for the mosaic or the way they had been worked that the mosaic was not pre-Columbian, and the combined osteobiographical and isotope analysis of the skull indicated a Mesoamerican origin for the skull, the decisive factor in ascertaining whether the mosaic skull as we see it today is an authentic pre-Columbian artefact was the adhesive. Earlier studies on Postclassic Mesoamerican mosaics, most notably those of the British Museum (McEwan et al. 2006), have shown that the most commonly used adhesive was a type of pine resin. Pine resin is collected from several species of pines in Mexico and is still used today for different purposes, including incense and adhesives. Apart from pine resin, adhesives based on resins collected from plants of the Bursaraceae family, named copal after the Nahuatl (Aztec) word for resin, *copalli*, were also found on the British Museum mosaics, as was beeswax (McEwan et al. 2006:35-7). A similar type of copal resin was used on the mosaic skull found in Tomb 7 of Monte Albán, mixed with seeds of *Amaranthus paniculatus* (Caso 1969: 63). An experimental study of Mesoamerican adhesives, based on descriptions by Spanish friars of adhesives used in the sixteenth century, identified and tested the use of adhesives based on 'several orchid species, two copal genera, pine resin, and native beeswax' (Berdan 2007: 3).

In contrast, earlier research on the mosaic skull from Marseille had shown that the adhesive used was shellac. Shellac is an adhesive produced from the excretions of a cochineal insect named *Laccifer lacca,* or *Kerria lacca* (Butler Greenfield 2005). Since the cultivation of cochineal has been widely documented for pre-Columbian Mesoamerica, as well as colonial times, especially in the Mixteca region from which the mosaic skulls supposedly originated, it was suggested during the research on the Marseille skull that shellac might be a material of pre-Columbian origin. However, shellac cannot be a material of pre-Columbian origin since it is made from the excretions of the female lac bug, *Laccifer lacca* or *Kerria lacca* (Butler Greenfield 2005: 29), whereas the Mexican cochineal insect, *Dactylopius coccus* (ibid.: 35) is a member of a different family and does not excrete the same product. *Laccifer lacca*, which produces shellac, is an insect that lives in southeast Asia and India. The use of shellac originated here, spread to Europe in the Middle Ages, and can only have been used in Mexico after the Conquest. The confusion surrounding the possible pre-Columbian origin of shellac was probably due to the fact that both insects are referred to colloquially by the same name, cochineal, even though they belong to different families.

Examination of the Leiden mosaic skull under UV light at the C2RMF revealed that two sorts of glue had been used on the skull. One of these, by far the most prominent, glowed red under UV light, meaning that it had a certain organic composition. The other type, which was only found on certain spots on the lower jaw, the forehead and on the skull's 'upper lip', glowed yellow/green. Examination with a digital microscope showed that this yellow material had been applied on top of the reddish-brown glue. As a result, this yellow glue was thought to be an adhesive that had been used at some point for the restoration of a small number of tesserae. When the areas on which the yellow adhesive was used were compared with those that had been treated by Norman Wiener, a New York-based restorer who restored small parts of the Leiden mosaic skull in 1962, it became clear that Mr Wiener must have used this adhesive in the restoration process. This meant that the reddish-brown adhesive was the original one, which was already on the skull when it was restored in 1962 (see figs. 6 and 7).

Samples of both types of adhesive were taken by Dr Juliette Langlois of the C2RMF and analysed using Gas Chromatography-Mass Spectrometry (GC-MS). The results showed that the primary adhesive, which was used for 99% of the mosaic, was shellac, as in the case of the Marseille skull. The secondary adhesive, used for restoration purposes, was a mix of pine resin and agathis resin (Langlois 2012). This means that both types of adhesive found on the Leiden skull are of modern origin.

## Authentic, fake or combination?

In view of these findings, should we regard the mosaic skull of the National Museum of Ethnology in Leiden as an authentic pre-Columbian piece or a modern forgery? Looking at the available evidence – the authentic pre-Columbian mosaic and skull, combined with the use of a modern type of glue – a modern forgery, in this case a modern composition of authentic pre-Columbian elements, seems the most probable conclusion. This is not very surprising, considering that earlier research concluded that other, very similar, mosaic skulls were also modern combinations of ancient components.

Nonetheless, there is still a very slight possibility that we are not looking at a complete forgery, that is, an artefact invented by creative forgers, but rather a complete modern restoration of a skull that was found with the mosaic on it and was reassembled by an unknown restorer. Considering the conditions in which both skeletal and lithic materials are preserved in Mesoamerican caves and tombs, we cannot entirely rule out the possibility that the mosaic was once attached to the skull and was only reapplied in the same manner in modern times, using shellac for the restoration. In this context it would be wise to refrain from producing a wholly definitive labelling of the mosaic skull as a fake and to heed the words of David Phillips: 'Decisions are usually, in the end, matters of probability, and art-historical identifications can come anywhere on a very broad spectrum of degrees of confidence. Yet oddly little of that uncertainty is reflected in the conventions of art attribution' (1997: 2). In this case, the probability that we are dealing with a fake seems high and the degree of confidence significant, but we should always keep an open mind.

Now, having determined that the mosaic skull is most probably a modern creation, two important questions arise: 1. Why was this mosaic skull acquired in the first place, while not a single similar artefact was ever found in a controlled context? and 2. How does the finding that the mosaic skull is 'fake' affect the way it is seen, labelled and presented in a museum collection?

## Why was it acquired?

Why was the mosaic skull of the NME acquired and, we may conclude, considered authentic in the 1960s? Within the museum world, ethnographic museums appear to occupy a special place when it comes to the authentication of pieces in their collections. Whereas a painting by Rembrandt, Van Gogh or Picasso is considered authentic when it has been proven that the work was made by the artist concerned, ethnographic pieces are normally ascribed to a specified culture rather than an individual (cf. Price 1989: 56-67). As such, unprovenanced (archaeological) ethnographic pieces, most of which have been bought on the notoriously opaque art market, are, in the terminology of Dennis Dutton (2003) 'expressively authentic', rather than 'nominally authentic'. Expressive authenticity is taken to refer to 'the object's character as a true expression of an individual's or a society's values and beliefs' (Dutton 2003: 259), as opposed to nominal authenticity, which is simply 'the correct identification of the origins, authorship, or provenance of the object' (Dutton 2003: 259). In short, in ethnographic museums, unprovenanced pieces are generally authenticated on the basis of the knowledge and understanding of museum staff of the (material) culture of a given region or people. As such, I would argue that often in ethnographic museums, 'nominal authenticity' (a correct identification of an object's origin), even though not proven, is inferred or assumed from 'expressive authenticity', when a piece 'fits the style'.

This understanding of the attribution of 'nominal authenticity' on the basis of 'expressive authenticity' in ethnographic museums leads us to the perception and representation of the culture in question, since, without this understanding of the culture, pieces could not be authenticated. The (popular) perception of a culture is based on its cultural products, from artefacts and paintings to books and songs, which are presented in museums and their collections. In the words of Elizabeth Hill Boone, 'it is the collection and presentation of material culture that commands how the culture being represented is understood and received' (1993: 4). In turn, the authentication process of artefacts assumed to have been made by a certain culture depends on the knowledge and perception of the culture and its material remains. Artefacts are assumed to be authentic because they can be shown to have been found in their original context, because high-tech research methods have 'proven' the authenticity of a piece or, as is the case for most objects that are acquired on the art market, simply because they 'fit the style'. In short, knowledge of a people's (material) culture (the culture's perception) is based on supposedly authentic artefacts, which have themselves often been authenticated on the basis of the knowledge of a people's material culture. It is precisely this circle of authentication, representation and perception that has led several authors to stress the risk of the fact that students are taught what is authentic and what is not on the basis of spurious objects (e.g. Kelker & Olsen Bruhns 2010).

With this in mind, we return to the question 'why was this mosaic skull regarded as authentic and acquired, even though it lacked any documented provenance and no similar objects from controlled contexts were known?' Three main factors seem to have played a role: 1. The museum staff's knowledge of Mixtec material culture at the time of purchase; 2. The popular perception and representation of (Central Mexican) pre-Columbian cultures as 'obsessed with skulls, bones and human sacrifice', and 3. The changing view of pre-Columbian antiquities from artefacts to works of art.

*Lack of knowledge*

The most basic reason that the mosaic skull was acquired by the NME without any reservations concerning its authenticity is the fact that Dr Pott, who decided that the mosaic skull had to be acquired, was not a specialist on pre-Columbian material culture. The board of curators was hardly involved in the purchase, and the curator for the specific region, Dr R.T. Zuidema, a specialist on Andean cultures, was not consulted by Dr Pott prior to the purchase. However, even if Dr Pott had been a specialist on Mixtec culture, the fact remains that in the early 1960s, when the mosaic skull was acquired, the knowledge of the material culture of this region was not as well developed as it is today. While an image and description of the Tomb 7 skull had already been published in the early 1930s (Caso 1935), and were probably known to some museum personnel in Leiden, important publications, such as Caso's *El Tesoro de Monte Albán* (1969) and Elizabeth Carmichael's *Turquoise mosaics from Mexico* (1970), had not yet been published. Therefore, the material from the Tomb 7 excavation, especially the mosaic skull which was seen as one of the most splendid items in the tomb, was one of the few representative samples of Mixtec material culture.

Another important consideration is the fact that the Leiden mosaic skull was one of the first to appear on the art market, which means that, apart from a photo and description of the Tomb 7 skull, which may have functioned as a template for the Leiden mosaic skull, hardly any reference points were available for purposes of comparison. Still, Dr Pott's description of the mosaic skull as 'an object of [such] rarity and value' suggests that he regarded the relative uniqueness of the mosaic skull, and hence the opportunity to add an unparalleled masterpiece to his museum's collection, as an extra incentive to acquire the object, rather than a warning to thoroughly check the mosaic skull before acquiring it, especially considering his own relative lack of knowledge of the cultural region concerned. Unlike the Leiden mosaic skull, other mosaic skulls which were acquired around the same time were thoroughly checked before they were acquired.

The advances made in the knowledge of Mixtec material culture are exemplified by the description of the plumed serpent design in the upper section of the mosaic. When Dr Pott first saw the design, he described it as 'the feathered serpent clan symbol, one of the most typical cultural elements of this area'.[5] Since the feathered serpent is a well-known Mesoamerican symbol and occupies a central place in the Mixtec and Zapotec iconography and world view, the feathered serpent was seen as a mark of authenticity. Some of the mosaic tesserae that form the 'plumed serpent' design are incised with different geometrical forms, which Pott thought represented the serpent's plumes. A large number of fine illustrations of turquoise mosaics have been published since the 1960s, and it is now clear that these incised pieces must have been part

---

5   Orig. 'het clan-symbool... van de gevederde slang, één van de meest typische cultuurelementen van dit gebied.'

of the designs of mosaic shields. Some of the tesserae in the plumed serpent motif, for example, are very similar to turquoise tesserae that are incised to form headdresses, weapons and different sorts of attire of figures on the turquoise mosaic discs from the Aztec Templo Mayor (McEwan et al. 2006:fig. 94) and the Museum für Völkerkunde in Vienna (Feest 1990). Nowhere, however, do they form a plumed serpent motif similar to the one seen on the Leiden skull. The latter was probably an elaborate invention of a twentieth-century forger.

## Representation and perception

I have argued above that it is common in ethnographic museums for 'nominal authenticity' to be inferred from 'expressive authenticity'. That is to say, in the absence of any information on an artefact's provenance, the object is considered to be authentically Mixtec, for instance, if it corresponds to the criteria of what Mixtec objects are 'supposed to look like'. This 'supposed to look like' criterion is based on the representation of the given culture, and cultural region. In the case of Mesoamerica, the popular representation has generally been characterised by images of blood, skulls and, especially, human sacrifice ever since the first contacts between colonisers and indigenous peoples of Mesoamerica (see Keen 1971 for the development of this vision of Mesoamerica). An illustrative example of this popular representation is Mel Gibson's blockbuster production *Apocalypto* (2006), a historically grossly inaccurate portrayal of Ancient Maya society as obsessed with violence and human sacrifice, summarised by one critic as 'some mistakes are stupid-wrong, others are Gibson-is-kinda-racist-wrong' (Newitz 2006). Considering the wide reach of this popular representation, the question arises of the extent to which the representation and perception of a culture and the authentication process shape each other. Simply put, are artefacts, in the case of Mesoamerica, more likely to be considered authentic when they include images of skulls and bones, or actual skeletal material? In the case of the mosaic skulls, this may well have been so. These artefacts chimed with the general perception of pre-Columbian Mesoamerican (especially Central Mexican) cultures outlined above and responded to the desire of collectors for 'exotic' and 'primitive' art. In this context, the mosaic skulls, both aesthetically pleasing and, with the Tomb 7 mosaic skull in mind, seemingly culturally significant, were the perfect artefacts. They were considered 'expressively authentic', considering what was known about Mixtec culture and Mesoamerica in general. The Tomb 7 mosaic skull, which was as one of the most iconic pieces of Mixtec material culture and was probably the best-known Mixtec artefact to collectors and museum staff worldwide, played an important role in this. Not only did it probably function as a template for the creators of the modern mosaic skulls, it also heavily influenced the view and knowledge of Mixtec material culture for several decades. Quite simply, then, the newly created mosaic skulls responded to expectations of what an ideal Mesoamerican artefact should look like in the eyes of collectors (and some museum staff). In a way, 'the authentic' was replaced by what was considered appropriate (Lowenthal 1992: 186-7).

Naturally, this vision of 'what Mesoamerica should look like' to collectors and dealers was known to (and possibly shared by) restorers and forgers, which also partially explains why the concept of the mosaic skull was invented and created. In the words of Mark Jones (1992: 9), '[fakes] are also of course evidence for the history of taste; much more so than the genuine pieces ... For the fakes represent what purchasers most wanted in the class of object concerned.'

## From artefact to art

Related to questions of taste and perception (or reception) mentioned above, one final factor that possibly contributed to the acquisition of the mosaic skull was a shift in trend on the international (and especially US) art market of the way pre-Columbian pieces were appraised. Whereas until the final years of the nineteenth century pre-Columbian artefacts were valued mostly for their significance as objects of scientific study, the early decades of the twentieth century marked a shift towards the appreciation of these artefacts for their aesthetic value (Hill Boone 1993). The 1930s and 1940s were especially important periods in this regard in the United States (Barnet-Sanchez 1993). 'For an American public of art connoisseurs ... pre-Hispanic art represented an unexplored genre of human expression that was at one primal (i.e., closer to nature) and aesthetically distinct' (Brulotte 2012: 63). Combined with a sharp increase in the commercial exploitation of Maya archaeological sites and the introduction of favourable tax laws for art donations to museums, this development led to an explosion in the number of pre-Columbian pieces that were available on the market from the 1960s onwards (Coe 1993).

Robert Woods Bliss, who formed the Dumbarton Oaks collection of pre-Columbian art and who was the first to acquire a mosaic skull on the art market, was a leading figure in this movement and has been named as one of the first collectors to collect pre-Columbian artefacts *as art* (that is, for their aesthetic value) rather than as objects of study (Benson 1993). It could be argued that in this view of artefacts as art, less value is attached to an object's authenticity than to its aesthetic and expressive qualities. This may have been the case for Dr Pott when he acquired the mosaic skull for the NME. Some quotes from his letter to the board of curators in 1963 serve to illustrate this point: he describes the object as possessing 'rarity and value', notes that the technique used is one 'that is seldom encountered and is proof of a great craftsmanship' and of the black-and-white pictures he attaches to his letter, he says that 'they can hardly give an impression of the beauty of this object, which is primarily expressed in its colours'. In contrast, the letter does not say a word about the provenance of this mosaic skull, or about the way it ended up in the hands of the dealer or indeed any other information that could prove the object's authenticity. Its beauty was apparently such that its authenticity was either self-evident or not an issue to Dr Pott.

## Consequences

When presenting this research at the 2012 Authenticity conference at the NME in Leiden, I used the word 'sadly' when coming to the conclusion that the Mixtec mosaic skull of the NME was most probably not authentically pre-Columbian. After I had finished my talk, a fellow speaker asked me why I was sad that research had shown that we were probably dealing with a twentieth-century fake. Was this story about a fake not just as interesting as it would have been if the object had been authentic? And do we not learn a great deal about the past by studying spurious objects? At the time, I found myself unable to formulate a satisfactory answer to this question.

Nonetheless, in spite of the fact that I greatly enjoyed doing this research and believe that the results are worthwhile, I was being sincere when I said that I was sad that the mosaic skull was not authentically pre-Columbian (or should I say that my sadness was authentic?). But why was I sad? The answer to this question probably lies in the combination of two factors. The first, in the words of Walter Benjamin, is that the aura of an original work of art derives from 'its presence in time and space, its unique existence at the place where it happens to be' (Benjamin 1968: 220). Put simply, the older an object, the more special the simple fact of its existence. It is extremely rare for an authentic pre-Columbian artefact of this type to survive hundreds of years and, when it does, its value seems to lie more in its uniqueness and survival than in the aesthetic aspects. Drawing on the work of Sándor Radnóti (1999), Ronda Brulotte notes, 'the assumed historicity of aesthetic objects (particularly those designated as antiquities) is as important, if not more so, than their outward appearance' (Brulotte 2012:134).

However, if the artefact was made only sixty years ago, the simple fact of its existence is naturally far less spectacular. In a sense, the shift in labelling the mosaic from pre-Columbian to twentieth-century also changes the artefact's identity. Since it is no longer authentic (in the sense of authentically pre-Columbian), we might say that we are actually confronted with a different artefact altogether. In the words of David Philips (1997:5), 'authentic, used as an attribute, seems to refer to properties which are not merely discriminating, like "big" or "blue", but which identify the subject as in some way expressive of an abstract, universal truth.'

So perhaps my sadness arose from a kind of feeling of loss; the loss of an authentic pre-Columbian artefact, which had been revealed to have been mislabelled and misidentified for many years and was now revealing its true identity. By doing this, we 'lost' the old mosaic skull but, in return, 'received' a new one. But how should we label this 'new' mosaic skull?

A publication on the mosaic skulls of the Dumbarton Oaks collection, in which Javier Urcid (2010) convincingly shows that the mosaic skulls must be spurious, labels them 'Late Postclassic period, AD 1300-1520, reassembled in modern times'. This label suggests, to me at least, that, although the artefact may have been reassembled in modern times, the object itself is actually Postclassic in origin. Considering the fact that the mosaic skulls were never actually mosaic skulls, but skulls and mosaic separately, until they entered the hands of a twentieth-century 'restorer', this label seems to me somewhat off-target. At the NME, Dr Laura Van Broekhoven and I came to the conclusion that a dual label 'Late Postclassic (AD 1300-1520), Mixtec/20th-century, Mexican' would be most appropriate. This label covers all the aspects of this artefact's fascinating history. In this chapter, I hope to have shown that we can learn as much from this new mosaic skull that came to us through this research as we could have done had it been ancient, and that stories of forgeries can be just as interesting as stories of authentic objects.

## Acknowledgements

Thanks are due in the first place to Thomas Calligaro and Marianne Pourtal Sourrieu for approaching the NME about their project and its potential for examining the Leiden mosaic skull. At the C2RMF, I should like to thank Yvan Coquinot and Juliette Langlois for their assistance with the research and Claire Pacheco for coordinating the project. I am grateful to Anne van Duijvenbode, Andrea Waters-Rist, and Jason Laffoon of Leiden University for all the assistance they provided in the research for this project. I also want to thank Christina Hellmich and Lesley Bone for kindly granting me access to, and information about, the DeYoung skull. Matthew H. Robb, also of the DeYoung, provided useful comments. I should like to thank Victoria I. Lyall and Laura Leaper for their kind help at the LACMA. I am grateful to Santo Micali for allowing me to study the mosaic skull in his gallery in 2012 and for providing background information on the artefact. Juan Antonio Murro was helpful in providing documentation on the acquisition of the Dumbarton Oaks mosaic skulls. Javier Urcid supplied insightful comments and suggestions. Amy Clark at the Saint Louis Art Museum provided documentation of the turquoise mosaics at the SLAM, Rachel Menyuk provided documentation from the NMAI archives, and Kristen Mable supplied documents from the Ekholm archives. I am grateful to R. Tom Zuidema, Elizabeth H. Boone and Michael D. Coe for their help with specific enquiries. I should like to thank Laura Van Broekhoven for her assistance with this project at the NME and Alexander Geurds for his suggestions and comments on a research proposal related to this article. I wish to gratefully acknowledge the financial support provided by the Access to Research Infrastructures activity in the 7th Framework Programme of the EU (CHARISMA Grant Agreement n. 228330).

## References

Anon. (2012), 'Masterpieces of Pre-Columbian Art'. *International Herald Tribune* 15-16 September 2012.

Barnet-Sanchez, Holly (1993), 'The Necessity of Pre-Columbian Art in the United States: Appropriations and Transformations of Heritage, 1933-1945', in Elizabeth H. Boone (ed.), *Collecting the pre-Columbian Past: a symposium at Dumbarton Oaks, 6th and 7th October 1990,* 177-208. Washington D.C.: Dumbarton Oaks Research Library and Collection.

Benjamin, Walter [1968(1936)], *Illuminations,* ed. Hannah Arendt, transl. Harry Zohn. New York: Schocken Books.

Benson, Elizabeth P. (1993), 'The Robert Woods Bliss Collection of Pre-Columbian Art: A Memoir', in Elizabeth H. Boone (ed.), *Collecting the pre-Columbian Past: a symposium at Dumbarton Oaks, 6th and 7th October 1990* : 15-34. Washington D.C: Dumbarton Oaks Research Library and Collection.

Berdan, Frances F. (2007) 'The Technology of Ancient Mesoamerican Mosaics: An Experimental Investigation of Alternative Super Glues'. Report presented to FAMSI, published online at http://www.famsi.org/reports/06015/index.html.

Berdan, Frances F. & Patricia R. Anawalt (1997), *The Essential Codex Mendoza.* Berkeley: University of California Press.

Boone, Elizabeth H. (ed.) (1993), *Collecting the pre-Columbian Past: a symposium at Dumbarton Oaks, 6th and 7th October 1990.* Washington D.C.: Dumbarton Oaks Research Library and Collection.

Boone, Elizabeth H. (1993), 'Introduction', in Elizabeth H. Boone (ed.), *Collecting the pre-Columbian Past: a symposium at Dumbarton Oaks, 6th and 7th October 1990,* 1-14. Washington D.C: Dumbarton Oaks Research Library and Collection.

Brulotte, Ronda L. (2012), *Between Art and Artifact: Archaeological Replicas and Cultural Production in Oaxaca, Mexico.* Austin: University of Texas Press.

Calligaro, Thomas, Yvan Coquinot, César Dumora, Anne-Solenn Le Hô, Juliette Langlois, Pascale Richardin & Nathalie Gandolfo (2011), 'Étude Scientifique: Analyse et Datation des Matériaux', in Marianne Pourtal Sourrieu (ed.), *Xihuitl, Le Blue Éternel: Enquête autour d'un crâne,* 25-37. Marseille: Musées de Marseille.

Carmichael, Elizabeth M. (1970), *Turquoise Mosaics from Mexico.* British Museum, London.

Caso, Alfonso (1932) 'Monte Albán, richest archaeological find in the Americas', *National Geographic Magazine* 62: 487-512.

Caso, Alfonso (1969), *El Tesoro de Monte Albán*. Mexico: Instituto Nacional de Antropología e Historia.

Coe, Michael D. (1986), 'The Art of Pre-Columbian America', in Roy Sieber, Douglas Newton & Michael D. Doe (eds.), *African, Pacific and Pre-Columbian art in the Indiana University Art Museum*, 9-48. Bloomington: Indiana University Press.

Coe, Michael D. (1993), 'From *Huaquero* to Connoisseur: The Early Market in Pre-Columbian Art', in Elizabeth H. Boone (ed.), *Collecting the pre-Columbian Past : a symposium at Dumbarton Oaks, 6th and 7th October 1990*, 271-290. Washington D.C.: Dumbarton Oaks Research Library and Collection.

Coggins, Clemency C. & Orrin C. Shane (1984), *Cenote of Sacrifice: Maya Treasures from the Sacred Well at Chichén Itzá*. Austin, Texas: University of Texas.

Drouot (1984), *Antiquité, Art Nègre, Océanie: Nouveau Drouot 4 Avril 1984, salle 4*. Paris: Hotel Drouot.

Dutton, Dennis (2003), 'Authenticity in Art', in Jerrold Levinson (ed.), *The Oxford Handbook of Aesthetics*, 258-274. Oxford: Oxford University Press.

Ekholm, Gordon F. (1983), *Letter to Ellen C. Hvatum Werner, dated 13.12.1983*. On file at the DeYoung Museum.

Feest, Christian F. (1990), *Vienna's Mexican Treasures: Aztec, Mixtec and Tarascan works from 16th century Austrian collections*. Vienna: Museum für Völkerkunde.

Fields, Virginia M., John M. D. Pohl & Victoria I. Lyall; with contributions by Alejandro de Ávila Blomberg ... [et al.] (2012), *Children of the Plumed Serpent: the legacy of Quetzalcoatl in ancient Mexico*. London: Scala.

Izeki, Mutsumi (2008), 'Conceptualization of 'Xihuitl': History, Environment and Cultural Dynamics in Postclassic Mexica Cognition'. *BAR International Series* 1863. Oxford: Archaeopress.

Jones, Mark (1992), 'Do fakes matter?', in Mark Jones (ed.), *Why fakes matter: essays on problems of authenticity*, 7-14. London: British Museum Press.

Keen, Benjamin (1971), *The Aztec Image in Western Thought*. New Jersey: Rutgers University Press.

Kelker, Nancy L., & Karen O. Bruhns (2010), *Faking Ancient Mesoamerica*. Walnut Creek: Left Coast Press.

Laffoon, Jason (2013), *Report of the Results of Multiple Isotope Analyses of the Mosaic Skull of the Volkenkunde museum, Leiden*. Report on file. Leiden: National Museum of Ethnology.

Langlois, Juliette (2012), *Report on GC-MS tests conducted on adhesive of mosaic skull from the National Museum of Ethnology*, Leiden.

Lowenthal, David (1992), 'Authenticity? The Dogma of Self-Delusion', Mark Jones (ed.), *Why fakes matter: essays on problems of authenticity*, 184-192. London: British Museum Press.

Maclaren Walsh, Jane (1997), 'Crystal Skulls and Other Problems: Or, "Don't Look It in the Eye"', in Amy Henderson & Adrienne L. Kaeppler (eds.), *Exhibiting Dilemmas, Issues of Representation at the Smithsonian*, 116-139. Washington: Smithsonian Institution Press.

Martínez del Campo, Sofía (ed.) (2010), *La Máscara de Malinaltepec*. Mexico D.F: Instituto Nacional de Antropología e Historia.

McCafferty, Sharisse D., & Geoffrey G. McCafferty (1994), 'Engendering Tomb 7 at Monte Albán, Respinning an Old Yarn'. *Current Anthropology* 35 (2): 143-166.

McEwan, Colin, Andrew Middleton, Caroline Cartwright, and Rebecca Stacey (2006), *Turquoise Mosaics from Mexico*. London: British Museum Press.

Moholy-nagy, Hattula & John M. Ladd (1992), 'Objects of stone, shell and bone', in Clemency C. Coggins (ed.), *Artifacts from the Cenote of Sacrifice, Chichen Itza, Yucatan*, 132-140. Cambridge, MA: Harvard University.

Mongne, Pascal (2011), 'L'Authenticité en Art ou l'Inévitable Question', in Marianne Pourtal Sourrieu (ed.), *Xihuitl, Le Blue Éternel : Enquête autour d'un crâne*, 43-47. Marseille: Musées de Marseille.

Newitz, Annalee (2006), *Apocalypto: Myths and Facts*. Published online on 12 December 2006 at http://www.wired.com/table_of_malcontents/2006/12/apocalypto_myth/. Retrieved on 8 December 2012.

Phillips, David (1997), *Exhibiting Authenticity*. Manchester University Press: Manchester.

Price, Sally (1989*), Primitive Art in Civilized Places*. Chicago: The University of Chicago Press.

Radnóti, Sándor (1999), *The Fake: Forgery and Its Place in Art*. Rowman & Littlefield.

Saville, Marshall H. (1922), *Turquoise mosaic art in ancient Mexico*. New York: Museum of American Indian Heye Foundation.

Sourrieu, Marianne Pourtal (ed.) (2011), *Xihuitl, Le Blue Éternel: Enquête autour d'un crâne*. Marseille: Musées de Marseille.

Urcid, Javier (2010), 'Human skulls with mosaic designs', in Susan Toby Evans (ed.), *Ancient Mexican Art at Dumbarton Oaks*, 185-190. Washington D.C: Dumbarton Oaks Research Library and Collection.

Von Winning, Hasso (1968), *Pre-Columbian art of Mexico and Central America*. New York: Abrams.

Waters-Rist, Andrea & Anne van Duijvenbode (2012), *Osteobiography Report of the Mosaic Human Cranium housed at the Museum Volkenkunde, Leiden, The Netherlands. Report on file*. Leiden: National Museum of Ethnology.

# When is Authentic?

## Situating Authenticity in the Itineraries of Objects

*Prof. Rosemary Joyce*

**Abstract**

Authenticity is secured for antiquities by a variety of approaches, in part depending on the discipline of the analyst. For archaeologists today, only clear documentation of professional excavation entirely satisfies the requirement to create a provenience, which is the underlying criterion to consider things authentic. Yet historically, archaeologists have accepted, and continue to treat as authentic, objects without clearly documented excavation histories, especially if they entered museum collections during the early development of antiquarian interests. Meanwhile, art historians accept stylistic approaches to assess the authenticity of antiquities for which no clear provenience can be established. Ideally, the art historical provenance documents the transmission from someone who was the original collector (if not excavator) to the present location of the object. While today these approaches seem quite distinct, both originated in the late nineteenth century as linked practices by overlapping circles of scholars. Analytically, the provenience can be seen as one point in an ideal provenance, and the provenance of antiquities should be extended back before excavation to encompass a history of circulation beginning with the crafting of an object from original material, for which geologists use the term provenance. In practice, even today, the alternating criteria of time and place interact to determine when and for whom antiquities are considered authentic.

Authenticity is, quite obviously, a debatable term. One way to think of the conversations that take place in museums about authenticity is that what is at stake is how we secure the status of things as legitimate, meaningful, relevant to some matter at hand. For archaeologists, things have an originary moment that serves to ground authenticity. But how do we know when that moment is? As it happens, when we turn to archaeology to ask about its understandings of origins and authenticity, we find an ongoing controversy between archaeologists and art museum professionals that I believe can help us refine the question I raise in my title: '*When* is authentic?'

In this essay, I look at entwined practices and language aimed at securing the significance of past things – their true, or real, or, I would argue, 'authentic' status. To make this discussion less abstract, I will trace a single set of things both in and outside museums: carved marble vases known to have been made during the period from 600 to 1000 AD in the Ulua Valley in Honduras, where I have worked for over thirty years. These things as such are not my topic. Rather, what concerns me here is their histories of movement, what I will refer to as their itineraries, and in particular those points on their itineraries that are singled out by archaeologists on the one hand, and art historians on the other, as conferring value, especially the kind of value that rests on something being authentic.

## Authentic Things: Ulua Marble Vases

It is often easier to contest authenticity than to be sure of it: in archaeological practice, the use of tools unknown to the traditional makers, or features that are not quite the right size, in not quite the right position, are archetypal ways to deny authenticity. Implicitly or explicitly, the exercise of recognizing or denying authenticity deploys a specific temporal framework, in which there is an origin moment that secures the authenticity of the thing: because it was made in a particular way; because it was used in a particular way; because it was acquired in a particular way.

Consider an Ulua Marble Vase in the collection of the Musée du Quai Branly. The catalogue record[1] made available online describes the material as 'alabaster', and describes the class of objects as 'often recovered in funerary contexts'. Neither of these statements is accurate. The semi-translucent stone involved is, as the name 'Ulua Marble Vases' given this class of objects implies, marble. The majority of examples recovered archaeologically were buried as cached vessels, sometimes containing other objects. Only one such vase has been reported in an excavation of a burial (Wells 2007), in a site located outside the production zone in the lower Ulua Valley of Honduras' Caribbean coast. Even the characterization of these as 'luxury and exchange goods' may be misleading, since on the one hand it implies that marble vases replaced other less luxurious goods in use, or that they were produced primarily for exchange. These assumptions rest on equating the economic and social relations of the makers of this object with those of their modern owners, when what we know suggests that the patrons of the workshops that produced these objects used them for purposes distinct from other everyday actions (Luke 2002, Luke & Tycott 2007). Their arrival in locations (as the catalogue page says) 'outside their area of production, from Costa Rica to the Maya area', was more likely accomplished as a by-product of social relations (marriages, inter-family visits, attendance at ceremonies) than through concerted efforts at trade usually implied by the word 'exchange' (Luke 2010). The description of this object, at least, is inauthentic. What, then, secures the object itself as real and meaningful?

---

1   http://www.quaibranly.fr/fr/collections/explorer-les-collections/ameriques/pays/MQXAABAABAAE_Honduras/objet/70.2008.60.1.html.

The usual answer an archaeologist would give to such a question would be to cite a report of the excavation of the object, or if not that, of the history of ownership by museums and collectors known to have had access to the primary sites where these things could be collected in Honduras and neighboring countries of Central America. An art historian would find the same evidence for authenticity convincing, but in its absence, might be persuaded by a comparative analysis of inherent features of shape, design, materials and craftwork drawing on objects whose circumstances of acquisition were known. Yet it isn't actually as simple as this normative account suggests to establish that something is authentic. What counts as authentic involves questions of place, time, and person that may be worth considering in more depth.

Things with long histories in known collections often pass a test of authenticity more easily than those that emerged only recently. Stone vessels were actually the earliest objects to enter into European collections that I have documented in research on early Honduran collecting. A group of stone vessels from the Mosquitia region of the northeast coast of Honduras entered British collections in the eighteenth century, including one from the collection assembled by Hans Sloane before his death in 1753, which formed the foundation of the British Museum. The publication of a comparative study of four Mosquitia stone vessels is in fact the earliest scholarly discussion of Honduran antiquities I have identified (Pownall 1779).

None of these early acquisitions is accompanied today by an unambiguous account of its origin, beyond attribution to the wide geographic region of the Mosquito Coast. Their unchallenged status as authentic rests in part on the early date of their collection, before a market is known to have spurred creation of falsified antiquities from Honduras. I have no doubt that they are examples of objects created in Honduras, centuries before they were transmitted to British collectors. Their formal features, shape, iconography, dimensions, and raw material are all consistent with that conclusion. These stone vessels from the Mosquitia share a general shape, cylindrical with a pair of handles in the form of animal heads. These are common features of what today are called Ulua Marble Vases as well. The Mosquitia vessels are made of igneous stone, and are quite large. In the latter two characteristics they contrast strongly with Ulua Marble Vases, objects that appear in museum collections somewhat later, with equally uncertain histories of acquisition, but also are easily and universally accepted as authentic.

The earliest example of an Ulua Marble Vase that I have identified in museum collections entered the British Museum in 1931, but reportedly was collected fifty years earlier by the father of the donors (T. A. Joyce 1931). The British purchaser, James C. Madeley, traveled to Honduras around 1867, and remained until at least 1873 to work on an ultimately unsuccessful railroad project. British Museum records say it was collected 'in a native house in Spanish Honduras', suggesting it was bought directly from an unrecorded Honduran collector.

With the exhibition of an example in Genoa in 1892, and the publication in Paris of a photograph in a review of the exhibition (Hamy 1896: Plate II), Ulua Marble Vases entered the published record, more than a century after the Mosquitia stone vessels were discussed in print. The Genoa exhibition drew on a network of Honduran collectors, including government and church officials. The Ulua Marble vase included was attributed to the area around the city of Comayagua, the colonial capital, and was reportedly donated by Rita Aranda, a local resident. In 1854, a Honduran land title had been granted to Julian Aranda, for an area in the Comayagua valley around Yarumela, today identified as one of the most important archaeological sites in that area. Rita Aranda was quite likely of a landed class in the new Honduran republic that had begun assembling collections of antiquities, as likely was the unnamed collector of the vase James Madeley's family later donated to the British Museum.

These two examples of very early Ulua Marble vases, each said to have been collected by Hondurans and conveyed by them to intermediaries (one a businessman, the other a church authority) who transported the objects to Europe and ultimately to museums there, stand as authentic because we can trace not just where they came from, but when: at a moment before Ulua Marble vases were publicized, desired, collected, and thus subject to potential falsification. That situation began to change about the same time Sr. Aranda's marble vase graced an exhibition in Genoa celebrating the voyage of Christopher Columbus.

In 1896, George Byron Gordon, working on behalf of the Peabody Museum of Harvard University, visited the city of San Pedro Sula, in the lower Ulúa valley, and conducted excavations on the banks of the Ulúa river, recovering fragments of Ulua Marble vases (Gordon 1898). His field notes, and German publications (Sapper 1898; von den Steinen 1900), indicate that he learned where to excavate from a German living in San Pedro, Erich Wittkugel, who collected natural history specimens for museums in Europe and North America. Wittkugel's personal collection, now in the Berlin Museum, contains examples of Ulua Marble vessels as well as many ceramic vessels that reproduce the shape, designs, and sometimes (through application of a glossy white slip) the surface color of the marble vases. Today, the area where Wittkugel worked, and around which Gordon conducted his excavations, is recognized as Travesia, an archaeological site with evidence of patronized production of Ulua Marble vases (Luke & Tycott 2007).

These excavations in the 1890s changed the framework to consider whether Ulua Marble vases that later entered museum collections were authentic. They ensured that the international scholarly community, whether in Europe or the United States, knew that objects of this kind should come from the lower Ulua valley, even though the earliest known examples actually were collected far to the south. These scholarly publications began a history of associating carved marble vessels from Honduras with Classic Maya culture, through their co-occurrence with painted polychrome cylindrical vessels, foreclosing discussion of the relations of the marble vases to the igneous stone vessels of the Mosquitia, and deferring recognition of a much longer history of carving marble vessels in Honduras that we now understand began by 1000 BC (Luke, Joyce, Henderson & Tycott 2003).

We could consider the 1890s as the time when inauthenticity began to be a problem in the lives of Honduran marble vases, thus provisionally making 'before 1898' the answer to the question, 'when is authentic?'. Of course, things are by no means so simple. Instead of ending a period when Ulua Marble vases could be considered authentic despite sketchy histories, the publication of news about them in the 1890s started a period of intensive collecting, based on stylistically authenticating such objects. When Gordon went on to become Director of the University Museum of the University of Pennsylvania, he brought his fascination with these objects there, continuing to collect examples and publish studies of them (Gordon 1921). An active market in Honduran antiquities, including marble vases, existed in the United States by at least 1914, fueled by demand from the Smithsonian Institution, Harvard's Peabody Museum, and the University of Pennsylvania Museum, but also in part attributed to the publication of Gordon's research reports (Luke 2006: 37-38).

With the increasing number of these vessels available for scholarly study, it was only a matter of time until someone produced an authoritative study of all the then-known examples (Stone 1938). Doris Stone, a Harvard educated archaeologist, had the advantage of privileged access to sites in Honduras, due to her status as the daughter of the founder of one of the main banana companies in Central America. In the Ulua valley, excavation that was required to establish banana plantations resulted in the discovery of archaeological materials. These entered the international antiquities market through a circuit linking local people seeking sources of income, and what early archaeologist Dorothy Popenoe called banana cowboys 'on the lookout for mementos to send to the folks back home' (Luke 2006: 40).

Included in finds made by banana company affiliates were intact caches containing examples of marble vessels. Stone (1938) described the original locations of such finds more specifically than in any previous publication, identifying sites by local names. She also documented associations between the vases themselves and other objects included in the same contexts. Stone's stylistic analysis was published by the Middle American Research Institute at Tulane University in New Orleans, to which she donated complete Ulua Marble vases that she or others known to her had excavated.

Ulua Marble vases had, by the 1940s, become attractive objects of art collecting (Luke 2006:41). Yet it was not until the 1990s that renewed study of these objects was undertaken by an archaeologist, Christina Luke (2002). She combined documentation of museum collections with field survey of geological outcrops of marble, and conducted analyses of material from selected vessels.

This allowed her to define stylistic groups of marble vessels, and associate these with likely quarries for raw material in the Ulua River valley (Luke, Tycott, & Scott 2006). She argued for viewing one archaeological site located on the Ulua River, Travesia, as a likely workshop location, based on multiple lines of evidence including debris from working marble recovered in excavations there (Luke & Tycott 2007).

With Luke's work in hand, contemporary researchers can compare otherwise undocumented Ulua Marble vessels to the common profiles and characteristics of a sample of almost 200 vessels, including all the Ulua Marble vases with relatively well located find sites. It is with this background that I approached Ulua Marble vases in the museum collections I studied. As I reviewed the documentation and presentation of these objects, I began to realize that the question of their authenticity was often unstable, subject to multiple approaches. As the very name of this category of object, 'Ulua Marble vase', suggests, geographical place has become a consistent part of the grounds to construe individual vases as authentic. Yet place, like time, proves to be more complicated than it might first appear.

## Where is Authentic

Each of the propositions in the catalogue entry for the Ulua Marble vase in the collection of the Musée du Quai Branly implicitly posits an origin that is proper to a particular time and place: a place where 'alabaster' (really, marble) was worked, in places where burials were accompanied by vessels, at times of death that also marked or at least followed exchanges extending from Costa Rica to the 'Maya area': in short, in Honduras, between 600 and 900 AD. If I cast doubt on the likelihood that this vase actually was made at that time and place, because the material is wrong (or incorrectly identified), or the construction of the handles is awkward and unique, I am questioning its authenticity. Viewed this way, authenticity is embroiled in a nexus of place and time that I have previously argued underlies intertwined archaeological and art historical concepts used to secure knowledge: provenience and provenance.

The terms 'provenience' and 'provenance' seem to many people to be nothing more than variations of the same word. For contemporary archaeologists and art historians, differences between them come close to defining differences in professional disciplines. Yet the two terms are closely related, historically and, I have argued, conceptually (Joyce 2012a). In the late nineteenth century, both terms were in use, often by the same authors, who used provenance to identify stylistic assignment of objects to origins that were not known securely, and provenience to identify known find sites, which could be relatively imprecise by modern standards, such as assignment to a site or kind of feature within a site. In the century that followed, the discipline of archaeology developed an insistence on knowing the precise coordinates, in three dimensions, where things were found as a requirement to define the provenience. Provenance remained conceptually to be developed in the sister discipline of art history, where emphasis was placed on tracing the movement of artworks from their makers to their present owners.

Each of these terms involves a specific way to think about what it is that secures the reliability of an object as a focus of scholarship; in a word, what makes the object authentic. Archaeologists today define 'provenience' as the original location where an object was found through documented excavation. In contrast, the provenance of the same object can be defined as a chain of successive owners. While provenance should begin with the first owner of an object, that is, the person for whom it was made, pragmatically, for antiquities, provenance starts with the removal of the object from the location where it was buried or deposited, the same place that an archaeologist would recognize as its provenience.

Thus, the provenance of two Ulua Marble vases starts at a place in Honduras, called 'Peor es Nada' where they were first collected, and extends to the present location of these in New Orleans in the Middle American Research Institute of Tulane University.[2]

The provenience of these two vessels is the fixed point at Peor es Nada where they were encountered in excavation. Provenance intersects the location that archaeology treats as the only important point in the objects' itinerary, the provenience. The fact that there is such a point of intersection demonstrates that these concepts are inherently related, both parts of a chain of places that an object has occupied during its history.

From the perspective of modern museum practice, the provenance does not extend back before the excavation of these objects. Yet we could follow the arguments developed by archaeologists, and identify the first owner of this vessel as someone at the archaeological site of Travesia, who either crafted or patronized its crafting, prior to its movement to the house of a local dignitary at the village later called Peor es Nada by archaeologist Doris Stone (Luke & Tycott 2007:321). Not included in the conventional provenance, and over-ridden in archaeological practice by the singular importance of the provenience (the find site at Peor es Nada where they were excavated), the workshop at Travesia stands as the place that most securely provides authentication for these vessels as truly originally from the lower Ulua valley. Prior to Luke's work, the argument for local manufacture in the Ulua river valley was open to challenge. The presence of debris from marble working at Travesia; the concentration of 30 per cent of vases with known proveniences in the Travesia site and its dependencies; and stylistic ties between marble vases and pottery abundant at Travesia; form the grounds for a convincing argument that Ulua Marble vases actually originated

---

2   See figure 12 at http://www.athenapub.com/central-america2.htm.

in specific workshops at Travesia, rather than in the lower Ulua valley in general or even a wider region (Luke & Tycott 2007).

As this example demonstrates, the history of an object is unstable, subject to continuing movement in space. The recovery of an archaeological object by means of excavation begins its movement into and among the modern institutions that organize, present, and attribute value to it: universities, museums, and academic disciplines. While the concept of provenance allows more places to be noted, neither provenience nor provenance completely encompasses the history of the object in space, its journey or itinerary (Joyce 2012b).

The Society of American Archivists provides a view of these terms that reinforces the argument that, rather than being in opposition, they are intrinsically linked (Joyce 2012a, 2012b). For archivists the significance of materials 'is heavily dependent on the context of their creation', and 'the arrangement and description of these materials should be directly related to their original purpose and function' (Henson 1993:67, cited in Pearce-Moses 2005). The archivists define provenience only as 'the site of an archaeological excavation' (Pearce-Moses 2005). They equate provenance with the 'arrangement; context; creator; custodial history; entity of origin; fonds; office of origin; original order' (Pearce-Moses 2005). The references to 'original purpose and function', 'original order', 'entity of origin' and related concepts underscores the idea that authenticity is rooted in some origin. The archaeological 'origin' is recent relative to the creation of antiquities, but it is secure in place, and it is that certainty of where something originated that makes objects with provenience more authentic bases for archaeological interpretation.

Yet this privileging of one location on an itinerary, strictly because of the nature of the human agency exercised at that place, creates its own problems of authenticity. The assignment of marble vases to sites in Guatemala, Honduras, and Costa Rica, their proveniences, provide their 'secure, interpretable context', which in turn guarantees their archaeological authenticity (Luke 2010). But their cultural interpretation rests on knowledge of their provenance, which includes not only their archaeological origin, their excavated context, but also their original order, arrangement, and custodial history, something of their lives before excavation. The part of their custodial history that preceded their excavation, in the case of vases recovered in sites in Guatemala and Costa Rica, may be more significant than their archaeological provenience in these places.

Using modern analyses, the single Ulua Marble vase recovered in fragments at the Classic Maya site Uaxactun, Guatemala, is stylistically identifiable as a late product of the Travesia workshop tradition, constructing an earlier itinerary preceding its archaeological provenience that influences how we understand it (Luke 2010:48-51). In the Maya lowlands of Belize and Guatemala, vases of this late date were prized possessions in households of owners who occupied a very different level of power and authority over those around them than did the owners of these vases in Travesia and its hinterland. Reinstating the movement of the Uaxactun vase from the hands of a wealthy farmer to the house of a noble or ruler changes its significance, its value for historical understanding, and in some sense, its authenticity. The presence of Ulua Marble vases in palaces of the Maya lowlands changes their museum and market value as well, as indicated by the frequent presentation of Ulua Marble vases as 'Maya', something very few of them became by commercial consumption in the distant past, but were not by origin. The commodification of a small number of Ulua Marble vases for the ancient Maya inflects their authenticity today, both by making them ambiguous in identity, and by increasing their market value, and the subsequent motivation to create modern versions.

Consider an Ulua Marble vase in the collection of the National Museum of the American Indian, today part of the Smithsonian Institution, formerly operated by the Heye Foundation in New York City.[3] Acquired in 1917, it made this museum one of the earliest in the United States to add such a vessel to its holdings. The collection record published online describes its likely place of origin as the Ulua valley, but its 'Culture/People' as 'Probably Classic Maya (archaeological culture) (attributed)'. The string of parenthetical statements inherently expresses the uncertainty, the inauthenticity, of this identification. Who 'attributed' this vase to the Classic Maya archaeological culture? Was that original attribution qualified by 'probably', or is that qualification added by some anonymous museum worker troubled by the geographic contradiction between an origin in Honduras' Ulua valley, and a designation of the object as 'Maya'?

The ambiguity of the description is magnified in the field titled 'Collection History/Provenance'. Beginning with the assertion that the 'collection history [is] unknown', the record then provides a provenance about as good as any of the other early Ulua marble vases:

> *formerly in the collection of Marco Aurelio Soto (1846-1908, President of Honduras from 1876 to 1883); purchased by MAI from an unknown source in 1917 using funds donated by MAI trustee Harmon W. Hendricks... President Soto's son Maximiliano Soto (1881-1957) came to the U.S. in 1905 and lived in New York and may have inherited his father's collection.*

Marco Aurelio Soto himself sought refuge in the United States in 1883, first in San Francisco, and later in New York, before moving in 1903 to Paris where he died in 1908. The removal of his personal collection of antiquities from Honduras likely took place at the time of his original expatriation, which would make this marble vase, like those in the British Museum and Genoa, products of a mid-nineteenth century circle of elite Honduran collectors. The provenance actually calls into question the reported provenience of this vessel. Soto and his family were residents of Tegucigalpa, in south central Honduras, where during

---

3   http://www.nmai.si.edu/searchcollections/item.aspx?irn=65970&catids=2&place=honduras&src=1-3.

his presidency he moved the nation's capital from its colonial site of Comayagua. There is nothing to indicate he had any ties to San Pedro Sula or the lower Ulua Valley. The other objects from his collection acquired by the Museum of the American Indian reportedly came from what in the nineteenth century were the more advanced centers of commerce and society, Comayagua; the colonial city of Gracias and the neighboring town of Yuscaran; the state of Santa Barbara; and the city of Santa Rosa de Copan. Many of these are places related to the mining industry that Soto is credited with reviving, or were important places on the routes of communication between the Honduran republic and Guatemala, where Soto had studied and participated in politics.

It is likely that the reported provenience of this marble vase depends more on the conventional archaeological placement of these objects in the Ulua valley than it does on what would normally secure that location, a provenance. The vessel from Marco Aurelio Soto entered the Museum of the American Indian in 1917, not yet 20 years after the publication of Peabody Museum's work in the Ulua valley first publicized the existence of these objects to an English-speaking audience, and forged the link between place and object that is firmly embedded in their naming as 'Ulua Marble' vases (Gordon 1898). The Museum of the American Indian had already financed its own archaeological expedition to Honduras, following in the footsteps of Gordon. 'Here, too, are ceremonial vessels carved from marble, pierced ingeniously after a method so often seen in fine Chinese art, and as perfect, in spite of their rough usage in the surge of the Ulua, as though they had only recently come from the hands of the unknown sculptor' said a report on the museum's expedition by Marshall Saville (New York Times 1915). The same year, the museum added to its collections two Ulua Marble vases credited to Saville, products not of primary excavation with established proveniences, but of purchase in the authentic origin place: the Ulua valley.

## What is authentic

In practice, the provenience, the place where an object was recovered in an archaeological site, is equated with its 'original location'. As the examples discussed above show, even specifying the find site of things has historically been somewhat less straightforward than might be imagined in the logic where knowing the provenience secures the authenticity of an object, if only in part. Even when the find site is documented unambiguously, through excavation reports and contemporary museum registers, a consideration of the broader object itinerary raises the question of how we think about the life of things before they were deposited where the archaeologist finds them, and why we privilege that single point on the itinerary.

Consider another example from the collections of the Middle American Research Institute in New Orleans.[4] This assemblage, made up of two marble vases, a gold figure, and a carved jade pendant in the form of a hand, were found together at a site called Santa Ana, along the Ulua river. That is their archaeological provenience, the guarantee, for contemporary archaeologists, of their authenticity as evidence of past social life. Yet it is in no real way the origin of these things. Indeed, the four objects that make up this assemblage come from three separate places: the gold pendant from Costa Rica or Panama, the jade likely from Guatemala, and the marble vases from the Ulua Valley (Luke 2010).

The objects in this assemblage intersected at Santa Ana, near but not in the suspected workshop located at Travesia, each arriving there at a particular moment on individual chains of transmission, points on unique itineraries. The two marble vases, although both likely products of Travesia affiliated workshops, are stylistically distinct (Luke 2002), and could represent works of different producers within the Ulua valley, even within the Travesia settlement. These objects each possess individual provenances, even though there was a moment that they shared a single provenience, and even though they have continued to be associated in the museum where they are now found as they were when recovered archaeologically, maintaining a convergent provenance since their provenience was established. Their full itineraries from their origin were different, and treating only one point on their itinerary as significant undercuts their value for understanding the past. It absorbs them into a less-authentic, more homogenous whole, the category 'Ulua Marble vase', in place of treating each object as a medium for developing social relations over time, across space. Nor can we solve the problem of when objects like these become meaningful, accrue their value, and are secured as authentic by simply choosing to disarticulate them as an assemblage and trace each one back to a deferred origin in its own place and time of manufacture. Their histories actually begin before production, with the origin of raw material used in crafting, and the word used for that even-earlier moment of origin is familiar: provenance.

In a comment on a debate about provenience and provenance posted by Kris Hirst (2006) the archaeology 'guide' (essentially, editor) on About.com, the geology guide wrote that

> *geological provenance seems to differ from archaeological provenience. To the geologist, provenance is where something comes from, where it was before it arrived here. For instance, the pebbles in this conglomerate have a provenance in an ancient mountain range to the east. The provenance of these pebbles tells us something about ancient geography. What [the archaeologist] define[s] as provenience is something else: it's where those pebbles ended up. A Roman coin in the rubble would have an ancient Roman provenance, but its provenience*

---

4   See figure 11 at http://www.athenapub.com/central-america2.htm.

*is in the rubble, whether that's a Roman ruin or the remains of a coin shop* [Alden 2006].

Technical analysis of the material from which Ulua Marble vases were made shows a range of chemical composition in the marble of different vases (Luke et al/ 2006). Coupled with testing of marble from geological outcrops in the lower Ulua valley, this chemical variability creates the potential to extend provenances before the vases were crafted, let alone deposited where archaeologists later found them. Three quarries located in the southeast, southwest, and northwest edges of the valley overlap with the composition of the tested vases. One quarry, in the southeast valley, provides the best match for the majority of vases tested, suggesting that the craft workshops at Travesia used material originating near the modern town of Santa Rita. Fragments of two Ulua Marble vases, stylistically indistinguishable from other examples, have an original geologic provenance in a different quarry than all the others tested, to the northwest, hinting at Travesia-based crafters crossing the entire space of the lower Ulua valley in pursuit of their materials (Luke & Tycott 2007: 323). The stylistic uniformity argues against these two vases, both consumed at a single lowland Maya site in Belize, Altun Ha, having been produced at a different time or by a workshop unrelated to the core Travesia community of practice. Yet we may here see a trace of diversity within the crafting population, a worker or workshop pursuing different social ties both within the Ulua valley and outside it. Preceding the well-established archaeological provenience of these two fragments (Luke 2010: 50), this part of the provenance surely matters for our understanding of how these things circulated, were appraised, and the work they accomplished.

For an archaeologist, a lack of secure provenience always calls the authenticity of an object into question. Here is where it may be as useful to archaeologists as to other specialists to understand that the entire itinerary of the object matters. A geological provenance may well serve to support the perceived authenticity of a museum object that entirely lacks archaeological provenience. Yet the loss of knowledge of the remaining steps in its travels severely limits what can be said about it. Without the archaeological provenience of the two marble fragments of anomalous composition, we might have been tempted to doubt their authenticity. Without the geological provenance, we would not have seen that there was something distinctive about the exchanges that brought these vessels to that site. Geological provenance without archaeological provenience would open these objects up to appropriation, to be assigned a dubious uniform provenience (in the Ulua valley) or equally dubious cultural provenance (as of the Classic Maya archaeological culture). At issue should not be, solely, the lack of an authenticated witness at the unearthing of these things; it should be the lack of a credible narrative that follows the circulation of things throughout their long and ongoing lives.

The two categorical authenticating places in use for these things today, the provenience of the Ulua Valley, and the provenance of Classic Maya, must be questioned wherever they are found. While examples of Ulua Marble vases recovered from Maya lowland sites have bestowed on the entire class an aura of 'Maya' identity, the presence of Ulua Marble vases in other foreign places is muted. Ulua Marble vases found south and east of Honduras, in Nicaragua and especially Costa Rica, moved out of their production zone in the lower Ulua Valley earlier than those that found their way to Classic Maya sites (Luke 2010). They went from the houses of wealthy farmers to the residences of similarly situated leaders, unlike their later enlistment as luxuries for a very restricted group of people in Maya lowland sites.

Because their material carries its own trace of origin, a beginning point for the provenance of Ulua Marble vases exists even in those cases, regrettably the majority, where the object was not professionally excavated and no provenience is known. Nonetheless, this material provenance fails to secure authenticity. We can imagine a situation in which an authentic geological provenance can be demonstrated for an object made in recent times, emulating older models. This is the category we are quick to label 'fake', inauthentic not because it is the wrong material, or even (often) the wrong form and details, but because its origin is at the wrong time, historically.

## When is authentic

Let me return here to the Ulua marble vase from the Musée du Quai Branly, and add to it another: Lot 34 from the recent, and controversial, auction by Sotheby's of the Collection Barbier-Mueller of Precolumbian Art.[5] In the online listing Lot 34 is described in French as a 'vase of incised decoration of felines and saurians', attributed to the 'Maya culture', assigned a geographic origin in the Ulua valley of Honduras, with dates of 900-1200 AD. (The English text merely reads 'Maya Stone vase, Ulua Valley, Honduras'.) Unlike the Musée du Quai Branly, the Barbier-Mueller vase is more accurately described as of 'white marble'. It features a provenance that begins with a Sotheby's auction in 2004, and ends with the Barbier-Mueller collection, from which it was due to move, had it sold – which it did not.

Both the Musée du Quai Branly and Barbier-Mueller examples claim to be from the Ulua valley, which would, if true, provide them a spatial origin point to ground them as authentic. From an archaeologist's perspective, each suffers from a lack of certainty of place, signified by the absence of what an archaeologist would recognize as provenience – the three dimensional coordinates of the find spot – even if they have an attributed provenance.

---

5   http://www.sothebys.com/en/auctions/ecatalogue/2013/collection-barbier-mueller-pf1340/lot.34.lotnum.html.

In the absence of secure provenience, their identification with the Ulua valley must rest on style. The handles on the vase from the Musée du Quai Branly lurch out further from the body of the vase than on any vases of known provenience. The carving of such exaggerated forms would have added a challenge to an already difficult technical achievement. The result is a vase that is unusually bottom heavy, more awkward than any other I have seen. The Barbier Mueller vase is more balanced, yet here the handles depict bird heads in profile with details distinct from known bird head handles. The surface of the vase exhibits more relief than in any other example I have seen. I could paraphrase Gardner (1883:266) to render my opinion:

> *I am unable to state positively where the vases were found. The owners suppose them to come from Honduras: but on grounds of style this provenance would seem scarcely probable. We might search in vain among the figures from the Ulua valley for anything like it.*

I cannot say with certainty that they do not come from the Ulua valley. Yet each has physical features that are so unusual that they make the vase seem-- inauthentic.

The networks composed by circulating objects at a given time are transformed into itineraries unfolding in time. Authenticity thus becomes, like provenience and provenance, a way to characterize an object during its transit, rather than being something inherent in it as a kind of essence, lent by some particular circumstances of production or use. Consider two final examples of Ulua marble vases enrolled in museums, where their authenticity rests on the richness of their provenance, encompassing their provenience.

Both are found today in Genoa, in the Museo Castello d'Albertis. Their collections records can be found by searching the online catalogue of that museum. The first reads as follows:

> *Vaso Tripode*
> *Stile Mesoamericano (estensione meridionale)*
> *Sec. IX/XVI D.C.*
> *Honduras Nord Ovest*
> *Pietra scolpita*
> *cm. 12.5 x 16 Ø*
> *N. inv. C.A.1489*

The second is slightly different:

> *Contenitore*
> *Stilo Mayoide*
> *Sec. X D.C.*
> *Honduras, Valle di Ulúa*
> *Marmo vulcanico scolpito (tecali)*
> *cm. 15 x 17 Ø*
> *N. inv. C.A.1296*

The first provides us less apparent security of knowledge. The object is open to more scrutiny, and may be questioned as inauthentic, due to its shape, its finish, its vague provenience (north-west Honduras), and equally vague material (sculpted stone). Compared to the second, in particular, the first loses security of place, time, and circulation.

Yet that second vessel is actually, as described, completely inauthentic: 'Mayoid', a stylistic term that defers the origin of the motifs used to somewhere other than Honduras; *tecalli*, which aligns the vase with Mexican travertine; even the assignment to the Ulua Valley as a supposed locus of origin, make this vase, originally exhibited and published in the 1890s, less authentic. The museum's own records and nineteenth century publications show that this second object is an Ulua Marble vase found in the Comayagua valley, owned by Sr. Rita Aranda, and conveyed through the bishop of Honduras to become part of the 1892 Genoese Columbian exhibition. Here, as perhaps with the assignment of the NMAI's vase from Marco Aurelio Soto to the Ulua river valley, we are facing the imposition of an accepted archaeological provenience on objects that were in motion before archaeology in the Americas emerged as a profession. In the process of securing an authentic origin, these, and likely other, museums relied on a professional literature that repeatedly reconfirmed that, if Ulua Marble vases were desired, they could be obtained in the lower Ulua valley.

This is not, of course, untrue. Research on the composition and location of quarries demonstrates that the marble used to make these objects came from the lower Ulua Valley (Luke et al. 2006). Luke (2002) estimated that 60 per cent of Ulua Marble vases with known provenience were recovered in the lower Ulua Valley. Yet the distribution of the remainder is exceptionally wide, from Costa Rica to Guatemala, making it risky to assume that they all were found in the vicinity of their geological provenance. Moreover, research on collecting histories shows that the vessels that entered into circulation earliest came from those areas of Honduras where local economic and political elites by the mid-nineteenth century had begun the practice of accumulating personal collections, far to the south, primarily the Comayagua valley.

The continuing emphasis by archaeologists working in Honduras on a narrow, canonical slice of the country, projected as significant by the first professional archaeologists working between 1890 and 1930, over-emphasizes the lower Ulua valley and the zone west of it. It ensures that Ulua style marble vases will be ascribed to this significant region, rather than relegated to peripheries no longer investigated by researchers, another act of authentication, that of elevating objects as culturally and historically significant.

Yet facing us in the storage shelves of old museum collections are intransigent things, waiting to be put back into circulation, perhaps even to be engaged across the categories that archaeologists have imposed to arbitrarily divide space into units of culture. In that future discussion, Ulua Marble vases will not just be reunited with other white stone vases, from other times in Honduras (Luke et al. 2003), and other places in Central America (Luke 2010:48-49). They will be replaced in the assemblages of villages where they were made and used, confronted with the fired clay vases whose shape they borrowed, and others that in turn emulated the hard white stone. They will be compared and contrasted with igneous stone vases made in the Mosquito Coast, and the local ceramics there that seem to recall the scrolls and animal handles of the marble vases. Their authentic value and meaning will come from what they can tell us about how people crafting in new materials made more than things: they made histories, still being made today as we rediscover what lies untouched on museum shelves.

## When, Where, and What is 'Authentic': Final Thoughts

It may be objected that I have played fast and loose with authenticity here. By equating authentication as a procedure with the establishment of origin, I have allowed myself to replace direct discussion of authenticity with discussion of the practices of defining provenience and provenance, the main alternatives in museum practice for establishing the reliability in interpretation of antiquities. My larger point, I hope, goes beyond the confines of dealing with antiquities. It is that what we consider authentic is fluid, because things themselves were and continue to be in motion, both literally (as ownership changes, as physical storage location changes, and as things move about for exhibition) and metaphorically, as things are debated, published, challenged, interrogated, and even, prosaically, merely catalogued.

Authentication in archaeology rests on a peculiar nexus of knowledge of the place where something was recovered through archaeological procedures, a place that I have argued here and elsewhere also is inherently a point in time. Authentication in art historical practice engages a perhaps more expansive approach that tracks at least part of the itinerary of objects over time, yet not all the movements are included, and some are also considered more important to the project of authentication than others.

From the perspective of historical research on collecting, what is impossible for me to ignore is that the moment of authenticity is not, as archivists' definitions might lead us to expect, when something originated. It is always a moment in the contemporary world of collectors and museums, when belief in the specific agents who conveyed the object to the next collection on its route authorizes its use in cultural or aesthetic appreciation. From this perspective, it is no wonder that objects that I, as a specialist, consider extremely unlikely to have been made in antiquity continue to circulate as objects of value, prized as supposedly authentic expressions of the skills of ancient craft workers I sincerely doubt ever laid a finger on them. Their authenticity comes from now, not the past.

Nor is that simply an aspect of the emergence of the modern art world that commodifies things I think of primarily as sources of cultural history. I will close with a final addition to my inventory of Ulua Marble vases that trouble authenticity. In the 1990s, I was asked to assist in the curation of a new museum in San Pedro Sula, presenting the history of the valley from earliest times to the present. Drawing from private collections in Honduras registered with the government, the archaeological galleries are crowned by the presence of Ulua Marble vases.[6] Their original collectors knew the circumstances of their informal excavation, and thus vouched for their origin in the Travesia area. Provenance here, as in nineteenth-century European collections, provided what provenience could not: authenticity.

As work neared a close on the historic galleries, the curator of that section called for inclusion of a final object: a marble cylinder, carved in relief with fantastic designs, including handles interpreted as images of Spanish soldiers.[7] To this my reaction was, and remains, a troubled stance of doubt and uncertainty. The tradition of carving marble vases ended in the tenth century, and the last carved marble vases known archaeologically have no carved designs, and are made from a green marble undoubtedly signifying new cultural meanings were replacing the aesthetics and symbolics of white stone. Yet how can I assert categorically that no Ulua Marble vases survived to be recovered in colonial Honduras, to be reworked by colonial artists into more recognizable, hybrid forms? And if this is what happened-- when is the authentic moment of origin for such a hybrid object?

## Acknowledgments

I would like to thank the staff at the many museums where I have studied Honduran collections, including those of the British Museum, the Castello d'Albertis, the National Museum of the American Indian, Smithsonian Institution, and the Musée du Quai Branly, for their generosity in sharing their expertise with me and making my research possible. It should go without saying that nothing in this essay should be taken as criticism of the current staff of any of these institutions; this is an essay about the historical circumstances under which materials have been judged and entered into collections. If there is any critique here, it is a critique of archaeology, my own field, for its insistence that there is only one moment, and one place, that is relevant to the question of authenticity.

---

6   http://www.tiempo.hn/nacion/noticias/%C3%A9lite-ind%C3%ADgena-del-valle-del-ul%C3%BAa-utilizaba-finas-vajillas-de-m%C3%A1rmol.
7   http://archivo.laprensa.hn/content/view/full/505599.

## References

Alden, Andrew (2006), 'Comment on "Provenience or provenance? A poll"'. http://archaeology.about.com/b/a/257567.htm.

Gardner, Percy (1883), 'A statuette of Eros', *Journal of Hellenic Studies* 4: 266-274.

Gordon, George Byron (1898), *Researches in the Uloa Valley, Honduras: Report on exploration by the Museum, 1896-97.* Memoirs Volume 1, No. 4. Cambridge, Massachusetts: Peabody Museum, Harvard University.

Gordon, George Byron (1921), 'The Ulua Marble vases', *Museum Journal* 12: 53-74.

Hamy, E.-T. (1896), 'Étude sur les collections Américaines réunies a Génes a l'occasion du IVe Centenaire de la découverte de l'Amérique', *Journal de la Société des Américanistes de Paris* 1: 1-31.

Hirst, K. Kris (2006), 'Provenience, provenance, let's call the whole thing off'. http://archaeology.about.com/b/a/257574.htm.

Joyce, Rosemary A. (2012a), 'From place to place: Provenience, provenance, and archaeology', in G. Feigenbaum & I. Reist (eds.), *Provenance: An alternate history of art*, 48-60. Los Angeles: Getty Research Institute.

Joyce, Rosemary A. (2012b), 'Life with things: Archaeology and materiality, in D. Shankland (ed.), *Archaeology and anthropology: Past, present and future*, 119-132. Association of Social Anthropologists Proceedings. Oxford: Berg.

Joyce, Thomas A. (1931), 'An early Maya calcite vase from the Republic of Honduras', *The British Museum Quarterly* 6: 35-36.

Luke, Christina (2002), *Ulúa style marble vases*, Ph.D. Dissertation, Department of Anthropology, Cornell University. Ithaca, NY.

Luke, Christina (2006), 'Diplomats, banana cowboys, and archaeologists in western Honduras: A history of the trade in Pre-Columbian materials', *International Journal of Cultural Property* 13: 25-57.

Luke, Christina (2010), 'Social networks between the Maya world and lower Central America', in C. D. Dillian & C. L. White (eds.), *Trade and exchange: Archaeological studies from history and prehistory*, 37-58. New York: Springer.

Luke, Christina, Rosemary A. Joyce, John S. Henderson, & Robert H. Tykot (2003), 'Marble carving traditions in Honduras: Formative through Terminal Classic', in L. Lazzarini (ed.), *ASMOSIA 6, Interdisciplinary Studies on Ancient Stone - Proceedings of the Sixth International Conference of the Association for the Study of Marble and Other Stones in Antiquity, Venice, June 15-18, 2000*, 485-496. Padua: Bottega d'Erasmo.

Luke, Christina, & Robert H. Tykot, (2007), 'Celebrating place through luxury craft production: Travesìa and Ulua style marble vases', *Ancient Mesoamerica* 18: 315-328.

Luke, Christina, Robert H. Tykot, & Robert Scott (2006), 'Petrographic and stable isotope analyses of Late Classic Ulua Marble vases and potential sources', *Archaeometry* 48: 13-29.

New York Times (1915), 'Relics of lost city found in Honduras', *New York Times*, September 30, 1915.

Pownall, Thomas (1779), 'Observations arising from an enquiry into the nature of the vases found on the Mosquito shore in South America', *Archaeologia; Or, Miscellaneous Tracts, Relating to Antiquity* 5: 318-324.

Sapper, Karl (1898), Über Alterthümer von Rio Ulua in der Republik Honduras', *Zeitschrift für Ethnologie* 30: 133-137.

von den Steinen, Karl (1900), 'Altertümer von Rio Ulua, in der Republik von Honduras', *Zeitschrift für Ethnologie* 32: 567-569.

Stone, Doris Z. (1938), *Masters in Marble*. Publication 8, No. 1. New Orleans: Middle American Research Institute, Tulane University.

Wells, E. Christian (2007), 'Determining the Chronological Significance of an Ulúa-Style Marble Vase from Northwest Honduras'. A report submitted to the Foundation for Ancient Mesoamerican Studies, Inc. http://www.famsi.org/reports/07015/.

# Authentic Forgeries?

## *Prof. Oliver Watson*

I wonder if I am the fraud in this gathering? I will talk simply about 'forgeries', not about the more complex notion of 'authenticity". In my experience, and at the Victoria and Albert Museum where I spent many years, the word authenticity has usually been reserved for abstract and subjective questions such as 'was so-and-so an authentic country potter?', or 'is this vase in authentic rococo taste?'. Objects, on the other hand, were judged to be 'genuine' or 'real' unless they were deemed fakes or forgeries.

I want to introduce two objects which have had differing histories, and to examine the arguments and differing opinions originally advanced about them, the ongoing validity of those judgements, and the important part that 'argument from authority' seems to have played.

It is natural for museums and collectors to be concerned that their objects should be neither fakes (real things, but deceptively improved to make them more interesting to the collector) nor forgeries (things made totally new as deceptions). This concern is manifest early in the collecting of Islamic art in the Victoria and Albert Museum. In 1876, less than a quarter century after the founding of the museum, a very large collection of Persian art was accessioned and formed one of the glories of its Islamic holdings. A hundred crates had been shipped by Major-General Murdoch Smith from Iran to the UK, bringing the museum's total Persian collection to 1,889 objects. He had, as an official agent, collected these things for the museum while he directed the building of the government telegraph lines to British India.[1] Amongst this collection was a large jar with raised decoration of animals and figures in hexagons under an opaque turquoise glaze (Fig. 1) for which the museum paid the large sum of £30 12s 6d. Though no date is given in the museum register, such a sum suggests it was thought to be old, yet doubts were raised about it before the year was out. A handwritten note added to the register on 6 December 1876 reads: 'Mr Caspar Clarke lately returned from Persia says that about a dozen jars of this design were made in Persia about 30 years ago for a French gentleman, and that he knows the man who made the moulds. He believes this specimen to be 'one

---

[1] The acquisition as a whole is detailed in an accompanying publication (Murdoch Smith 1876). The figures include some earlier acquisitions of the 1870s, from the same source. For a summary of Murdoch Smith's involvement with the Museum and further bibliography see http://www.vam.ac.uk/content/articles/m/sir-robert-j-murdoch-smith/. For the British telegraph lines in Iran see http://www.iranicaonline.org/articles/indo-european-telegraph-department

*Fig. 1: Jar. Fritware ceramic, with relief decoration under a turquoise glaze.
Iran, 13th century, the metal lid a 19th century addition.
H. 78 cms
Victoria and Albert Museum, London.
2433-1876*

*Fig. 2: Jar. Ceramic, with relief decoration under a turquoise glaze.
Iran, 19th century.
H. 39.5 cms
Victoria and Albert Museum, London. 673-1884*

of the dozen'.[2] The authority of Clarke, an architect and archaeologist who in the 1870s travelled extensively in the Middle East and Europe on the museum's behalf and was later to become its Director, apparently trumped that of Murdoch Smith, and the detail he provided was sufficient to damn the piece.[3]

The museum does not hold the early location-history of objects, therefore we cannot know for how long or where it was shown in the galleries (if at all) or when it was consigned to the stores. If not out-of-sight it certainly seemed to be out-of-mind, for only eight years later the museum purchased without comment another vase (Fig. 2), smaller in size but with much the same kind of decoration under the same coloured glaze. It came as part of an extensive purchase from

---

2   Curiously, this observation passed without comment, for there is no evidence that the jar was made with the use of moulds; it rather appears to be hand-modelled in relief.
3   Caspar Purdon Clarke eventually became the museum's Director in 1896, before moving to New York as the Director of the Metropolitan Museum of Art in 1905. See http://www.vam.ac.uk/content/articles/i/indian-textiles-and-empire-caspar-purdon-clarke/

the auction sale of the highly revered Castellani collection of *objets d'art*, for the significant sum of £25 10s (Palais Castellani 1884: 205 no. 361). As before, no date was given in the records but the high price indicates that it was thought to be old. The doubts surrounding the earlier piece had apparently already been forgotten.

In 1928 yet another jar was accessioned: a gift which from its description appears to have been almost identical to the jar of 1884, but this time dated to the 13th or 14th century.[4] Annotations in the register suggest it was put on display in spite of the note drawing attention to both the earlier jars. The new piece came as part of a group of Islamic pottery given by the executors of the wife of Sir Charles M. Marling, a high-ranking diplomat and Britain's representative in Iran from 1916-1918, and a noted collector of Persian art.[5] Only a few years later, doubts were raised again. Alongside the register entry for the 1876 jar is recorded the positive opinion of Mr Philip Ziegler in February 1931 who '... has been in close touch with the Persian market since 1891 (his firm having had dealings with the country since the 60s) [and] gave it as his opinion that it was beyond the competence of the Persian potter of the 1840s to make such vases as this'. However this view is very quickly squashed for, very shortly after in a note dated 18 February 1931, Professor S. Flury and Dr H. C. Gallois 'gave it as their opinion that this vase is of 19th century date.' The opinion of these two distinguished academics – the first a palaeographer, the other a curator from the Haags Gemeentemuseum in The Hague – trumped that of the experienced man of business, Ziegler.[6]

By this time Islamic pottery, and particularly that of the mediaeval period, was much better known and these jars, if thought real, would have been heralded as masterpieces, as were similar pieces in other collections.[7] However, warnings from collectors and curators had also long been circulating about the dangers of falsifications in Islamic art.[8] The jars, subject to such early and damning opinions by a succession of authorities, are all but forgotten. The museum's singular lack of interest was demonstrated in 1951 when the Marling jar was de-accessioned.[9]

---

4   C.159-1928. The decoration alone differed slightly: '... (from top to bottom) horsemen with banners, ladies on horseback, elephants between stylised trees, & gazelles.'

5   The gift included an important celestial globe, stucco figures, and other pieces of important Islamic pottery, including two illustrated by Arthur Lane (1947; pls 56a, 89a).

6   For Flury see *http://www.iranicaonline.org/articles/flury-samuel*; for Gallois, see Kühnel (1938). For the firm of Ziegler and its activities, see the entry and bibliography on Qajar carpets: *http://www.iranicaonline.org/articles/carpets-xi*

7   Seven large jars of similar type were given whole-page illustrations (three in colour) in the monumental *Survey of Persian Art* (Pope 1939a: pls 755, 759-64).

8   The journal *Mitteilungen des Museen-Verbandes* is particularly interesting. It was produced in Hamburg from 1899 to 1939, and distributed confidentially to subscribing museums only. It enabled curators to publish notes and photographs of things they believed to be forgeries without fear of legal reprisals from their owners. The publication has now been digitised and put online by the Kunstbibliotek of the Staatliche Museen zu Berlin (http://www.ifskb.de/node/292).

9   Board of Survey, 51/1414A. The Museum disposed by sale or destruction of many forgeries, replicas and other unwanted items from every Department during the 1950s.

Successive curators, all with an interest in Islamic pottery, ignored them.[10] Even Arthur Lane, curator and then Keeper of the Ceramics Department from the 1930s to the 1960s, and the most important and perspicacious historian of Islamic pottery of his generation, never mentioned them.[11] This is rather surprising, for when we put the two surviving pieces side by side – the jar of 1876 and that of 1884 (Figs. 1 & 2) – the differences are more marked than the similarities. I was first impressed by the contrast when preparing to give a lecture in the late 1980s on forgeries. I had initially proposed, in unquestioning obedience to the earlier authorities, that both jars were modern. Sitting in a train on the way to Oxford and checking my slides, the formal differences suddenly struck me, and led me to ask why the earlier acquisition was not indeed mediaeval. And if this were so, then the other could plausibly be a modern copy of it.

The jar of 1876 is large, of good proportions, well-made, its decoration competently modelled and in its iconography of conventional mediaeval type. Its material, making, style and wear are all consistent with a mediaeval date.[12] The jar of 1884 is smaller and of completely different character: ill-formed and badly proportioned, with inept modelling and bizarre iconography, and with virtually no wear. On close inspection it fails to convince as a mediaeval object.[13] Nothing about the 1876 jar is to a modern eye suspicious, and its mediaeval date is now supported by scientific testing.[14] The pair of jars were finally recognised for what they 'really' are, and were selected for the 1990 British Museum *Fake?* exhibition where they illustrated a genuine mediaeval article as the prototype for the nineteenth century forgery. This solution had not occurred to any of the previous commentators. It seems that authority of social position (Caspar Clarke, Castellani, Marling) or academic status (Flury, Gallois) overrode what now looks the more justifiable opinion (Murdoch Smith, Ziegler). The authority wielded by such people flew in the face of the material and visual evidence, but was accepted for over a century in spite of the enormous growth of interest in

---

10   None of the vases had any publication record until my own interest in fakes and forgeries began in the 1980s; they were ignored by Rackham, Honey, Lane and Charleston in their writings on Islamic pottery. See Watson (1985) and (2004).

11   Arthur Lane's two books of 1947 and 1957 form the foundation of the modern academic study of the history Islamic pottery; though now out of date (especially the earlier volume) they transformed the field, by Lane's meticulous observation, scholarship and clarity of writing.

12   The damage – abrasion at the widest point, scattered chips and breaks, the rim missing (and fitted with a well-known type of nineteenth-century Persian metal mount and lid) – are all consistent with a mediaeval date.

13   Indeed, the flat base is unglazed, but the glaze has formed drops around the edge on which the jar stands - even these show little wear.

14   TL test carried out at the British Museum research laboratory in March 1990, sample BMT594, V&A archive paper 90/323: 'The age range is not corrected for the effects of water content or fading, both of which would increase the ages. With these assumptions, it is estimated that the jar was fired between 290 and 640 years ago.' The jar is certainly not of recent manufacture: stylistically one would put the age of the jar at the earliest of these dates, or possibly up to a century earlier.

and knowledge about Persian pottery from the 1930s onwards.[15] The mediaeval jar now plays its part in the Museum's main gallery of Islamic art; the forgery still languishes in the stores. The original story of a dozen forged jars made in the 19th century may well be true – in addition to the V&A 1884 and 1928 jars, another almost identical one is kept in storage in the British Museum, and other examples of even worse quality have been recorded in trade or private collections.

The second object I wish to address has had a different life history. It is a silver tray in the Boston Museum of Arts, known grandly as the 'Alp Arslan Salver' (Fig. 3). Silver is the rarest of Islamic historic artefacts, not because it was not used – indeed it was used in large quantities – but because it does not survive. Islamic art historians such as myself might be described as having 'treasure envy'

*Fig 3: Tray. Silver with engraved decoration*
*Inscribed 459H/1066–67AD.*
*D. 41 cms*
*Museum of Fine Arts, Boston, Martha Silsbee Fund. 34.68*
*Photograph © 2013 Museum of Fine Arts, Boston*

---

15  The 1930s was a period when Islamic mediaeval pottery was particularly fashionable to collect, and was fetching very high prices. It was accessible in great quantities in Western museums and private collections. Yet with all this new knowledge the jars were not seriously reassessed, even though the genuine piece would have been heralded as a great masterpiece had it been discovered.

when we look at the riches of the ancient Egyptian, Greek, Roman or Chinese worlds, where the furnishing of tombs with luxuries for the afterlife has preserved treasure in quantity and immaculate condition. Orthodox Islamic practice is to bury the dead wrapped in a simple shroud and without grave-goods. Silver and gold vessels have had to take their chance above ground, where the ongoing habit of reworking precious metal has eradicated all but a vanishingly small part of what was originally made. Silver was plentiful but was continually refashioned as more up-to-date vessels or, perhaps more often, as coinage in times of need. Hence the survival of a major piece of early mediaeval royal silver plate is cause for much celebration.

The Alp Arslan Salver is spectacular (Fig. 3): made from a single sheet of silver measuring 42 cms in diameter and 6.6 cms deep, it bears the title *The Sultan Aḍud al-Din* engraved in monumental script across the middle, with affronted birds against a scrolling background above, and winged-ibex similarly arranged below. The cavetto is filled with a long Arabic inscription, again in magnificent script against elaborate palmette scrolling:

> *A present to his Most Exalted Majesty, the revered Sultan, Alp Arslan, May God make his reign long: ordered to be made by the august queen, the cynosure of all women in the married state, and executed by Hasan of Kashan. In the year 459 (1066-7).*

This tray is of considerable interest. The military, economic, administrative and artistic achievements of the Saljuq rulers of Iran are legend, and they are credited with initiating the revival of culture in Iran. Here is a gift to the greatest ruler of this dynasty from another royal personage – a queen; and the inscription gives his full titles, a date and the name of the craftsman. The elaborate decoration provides a rich corpus of Saljuq motifs, for an early period from which little other than architecture remains. What could be more wonderful?

The salver was introduced for the first time in the *Burlington Magazine* of November 1933. The author was Arthur Upham Pope, by this date something of a celebrity scholar of Persian Art. He had organised the enormously successful *Persian Art* exhibition at London's Royal Academy in 1931, was a well-known advisor to museums and private collectors, and had an extensive publication record in academic and other journals.[16] He excitedly exclaims over the aesthetics of the piece:

> *The paired geese at the bottom and the winged ibexes below are of quite extraordinary force and energy. The lines may lack the sensitiveness of a brush or pencil drawing, but they have the firmness that belongs to metal, and their depth and surety, and the striking pose convey an unusual degree of vitality.*
> (Pope 1933a: 223)

---

16 For a somewhat celebratory biography, see http://www.iranicaonline.org/articles/pope-arthur-upham. More detail is given in Gluck & Siver (1996); for Pope's central role in the Exhibition of 1931 see Rizvi (2007).

For a reading of the inscription, he relies on others:

> ... *studied by a number of epigraphists. Doctors Flury and Sarasin of Basle, and Mr. Harari of London agree on the following reading... M. Gaston Wiet, who was the first to study the inscription, proposes a slight variant ...*
> (Pope 1933a: 223)

And he finishes the article with the following paragraphs:

> *The discovery of such an object, with all its historical and aesthetic implications, is so timely and has been so long sought that its genuineness must of necessity be ruthlessly tested, despite the obviously authentic character of the design itself. Although specialists in epigraphy, paleography, and ornament have all guaranteed as far as they could the genuineness of the piece, prudence required a supplementary and entirely independent investigation on technical grounds. Dr Plenderleith of the British Museum Research Laboratory submitted the piece to a variety of chemical and physical microscopic tests and reported, ' the evidence is so overwhelmingly in favour of its being genuine that it was largely a matter of form even to have doubted it. Dr. Flury is making a study of the paleography; Sir Denison Ross is further investigating the mystery of the queen who made the present; Mr. Harari is commenting on it in some detail in the forthcoming Survey of Persian Art, and its place in the history of Persian metalwork. Other students are undertaking further studies of special aspects.*
> (Pope 1933a: 224).

This insistent appeal to authority, some named and some anonymous 'specialists', seems to betray a nervousness over claims that the salver might not be genuine or that Pope's opinion alone would not be sufficiently authoritative. It is clear that difficulties had been raised with him. Some he turns to the object's credit. He recognises, for example, that the style of the ornament seems anomalous ('...it gives an earlier date than would have been expected for this particular system of arabesques, palmettes, small scrolls, and foliage.') but claims this as part of the tray's documentary importance in showing the early origins of such patterns. He raises the rather slapdash quality of the engraving – unexpected in an elaborately decorated royal object in precious metal – to a sign of aesthetic sensibility:

> ... *the presentation is dominated by a vividly felt conception which the swiftness of execution seems to have affirmed and delivered intact and which a more meticulous touch might have compromised. Such a concentration on the dominant idea is always a mark of aesthetic vitality.*
> (Pope 1933a:224).

He cites the note by eminent scholar Gaston Wiet in support of the salver, but glosses over Wiet's reservations – that the title *Adud al-Din* differs from that found in the chronicles, and that another title, though known in the period, is not recorded as used by any Saljuq ruler (Wiet 1933: 229).

In the same year Pope wrote an introduction to the detailed technical study of the salver (apparently requested by Pope) by the British Museum scientist H. L. Plenderleith, which was published in *The Museum Journal* (Pope 1933b, Plenderleith 1933). Pope displays the same nervousness, citing Wiet and other authorities, and justifying the scientific study as necessary '... despite the nigh-well conclusive evidence for its genuineness' (Pope 1933b: 281). Plenderleith's conclusion coincided with Pope's: '... that there is no reason from a scientific point of view to doubt the age or genuineness of the piece' (Plenderleith 1933: 284).

The following year the Boston Museum of Fine Art triumphantly announced the acquisition of the salver in its *Bulletin*, claiming it to be 'unique in importance and interest' and 'notable equally for its superb design and craftsmanship, and its documentary importance for the history of Persian art' (Coomaraswamy 1934). Pope had convinced the authorities of this institution at least.

However, Pope's campaign in promoting the salver did not stop here. In 1935 Plenderleith published an abbreviated version of his work in Pope's *Bulletin of the American Institute for Persian Art and Archaeology,* and Pope contributed a long article to the same issue intended to demonstrate that the foliate ornament of the salver was indeed compatible with an eleventh century date. In the same year Pope breathlessly announced the Boston Museum's acquisition to the readers of the popular *Illustrated London News*: '... which by the unanimous agreement of experts [seven of whom are named] is the most important recent discovery in the field of Islamic art in Persia. . .' (Pope 1935b). And in the *Third International Congress of Iranian Art and Archaeology* held in Leningrad in September of that year, Pope read a long paper on 'The General Problem of Falsifications' (Pope 1939b). He decries the work of the forger '... whose greed and unscrupulousness force into the market and even into public collections falsifications that mislead the public, corrupt aesthetic standards, distort history and waste money', to say nothing of 'distracting scholars from productive work' (Pope 1939: 177). However, the general thrust of the paper is to warn against excessive suspicion, which he fears will drive into the 'decorative trade' unrecognised masterpieces – and he cites the salver – where they would be lost to scholarship.

This triumphant series of announcements, the detailed arguments and the support of so many experts should surely have laid to rest any suspicions concerning the genuineness of the salver. But no. The salver makes a brief appearance in the metalwork section of the monumental *Survey of Persian Art* (Pope 1939a: 2500-1 pls 1347-8), but is questioned in a review by Maurice Dimand, Curator at the Metropolitan Museum of Art, New York: 'The style and ornament of the salver are certainly not Saljuq' (Dimand 1941: 211). This leads to an acrimonious exchange in the journal *Ars Islamica* (Pope & Dimand

1942).[17] Pope shows even greater animosity a few years later in an exchange of letters in the *Art Bulletin* with the scholar Mehmet Aga-Oglu (Pope 1947, Aga-Oglu 1947), who raised similar questions in a scathing review of Pope's book *Masterpieces of Persian Art* published in 1945. Pope cannot let the salver go – he returns to support it while defending the much-contested, quickly-condemned 'earliest illustrated Persian manuscript', the *Andarz Nama* (Pope 1960).[18]

By this date however, Pope is fighting a long-lost cause. In spite of his passion, his corralling of both named and unnamed authorities, his extensive stylistic arguments, his pleas for a rigorous approach to the condemning of objects, the Boston Salver has failed to gain a position as a recognised masterpiece of mediaeval art. It was (and is) largely ignored in both popular and specialist writing, and has been noticeably omitted from major exhibitions.[19] Silver candlesticks in similar style were acquired by the Boston Museum (in 1949) and the Freer Gallery (in 1951), but neither of these pieces have had better reception.[20] The final ignominy came in 1985 when a large silver box bearing identical decoration and '... probably made by the craftsman responsible for the Alp Arslan salver... ' was offered for auction and fetched a mere £440 – one fortieth of the price paid originally for the Salver fifty years earlier and a result which placed it definitely in the 'decorative trade'.[21]

The Boston Museum's online catalogue announces the Salver today thus: 'Salver dedicated to Alp Arslan (ruled 1063–1072, inscribed with an Islamic date equivalent to 1066– 67), *but possibly a modern-day forgery*' (my emphasis). Even more telling, lower down under the heading 'Provenance' is the sentence: 'Bought by MFA from Arthur Upham Pope in 1934' and elsewhere in the record: 'Provenance is scant: prior to 1933, when in possession of Arthur Upham Pope, the dealer from whom the MFA acquired it, it was said (by Pope) to have come from an unidentified private Russian collection.'[22] The price paid was an

---

17  Maurice Dimand was one of those who brought charges of unprofessional conduct against Pope in 1931; the other was a certain George Pratt, a Trustee of the same museum, see below and (Gluck & Siver 1996: 203-7).

18  The Andarz Nama is now completely discredited, but even in other articles by other authors in the same publication is treated warily as a forgery, and a scientific test reveals the use of a modern pigment.

19  For example, the salver is not mentioned by Basil Gray his discussion of a group of Saljuq silver (Gray 1939) nor by Marshak in his later authoritative work on Islamic silver (Marshak 1986); it is included in neither of the great London exhibitions of 1976 or 2005 (Jones & Michell 1976, Roxburgh 2005), where if thought genuine it surely would have been a key exhibit.

20  For the candlestick in Boston (48.1283) see Tomita (1949); for that in the Freer (1951.8) see Atil, Chase & Jett (1985: 267). Both are currently recognised as 20th century forgeries in their respective museum online catalogues.

21  Sale of Islamic Art, Sotheby's, Bond St, London, 16 Apr 1985, lot 410; the cataloguing gives no date, and avoids comment on the genuineness of Boston salver. The current whereabouts of the box is not known.

22  http://www.mfa.org/collections/object/salver-dedicated-to-alp-arslan-ruled-1063-1072-inscribed-with-an-islamic-date-equivalent-to-1066-67-but-possibly-a-modern-day-forgery-17905. My thanks to Laura Weinstein, Ananda Coomaraswamy Curator of South Asian and Islamic Art at the Boston Museum of Fine Arts, for additional information on the salver.

enormous $20,000 – an exceptional sum for a piece of Islamic art, or indeed any art, in the 1930s and a record for a piece of Islamic metalwork.[23] Here, sadly, finishes the story – the final explanation for Pope's ardent support for the piece – he seems to have owned it and while publicly promoting it was engaged in selling it for a record sum to the Boston Museum. His direct financial interest in the Salver is nowhere mentioned, however briefly or tangentially, in any of his writings.

Pope's prodigious activities as a dealer and agent are now publicly documented in the biography of 1996 (Gluck & Siver 1996),[24] which reveals how very deeply engaged he was in both advising and supplying art to museums and collectors, and shows the enjoyment and pride he took in it. It provided the mainstay of his income throughout his life,[25] and he was happy to boast to the Director of the Freer Gallery in 1932 that '… four-fifths of the finds in Persia are brought to my attention first' and elsewhere claiming that he had agreements with the majority of Persian dealers to be offered objects at lower prices than anyone else (Gluck & Siver 1996: 164, 207). These claims, if true, make Pope by far the major source, whether as owner or agent, for the sale of Islamic art in the West. He must have seen that such activity stood awkwardly with his strong desire to be respected as an academic. Hints or admissions of such involvement are completely absent from his writing, in which he takes the stance of a high-minded, disinterested scholar. He was very upset by a formal enquiry (in which he was however exonerated) into his relationships with dealers during the preparations for the 1931 London Persian Exhibition. Later correspondence from his own hand shows nevertheless that such concerns were real.[26] We cannot know how much he knew of 'falsifications' among the objects in which he dealt, but it is clear that his income depended on an optimistic view of the field. Then as now, these worries serve to put his claims to academic objectivity severely under strain.

---

23   Pope himself claims as much in a letter in 1943 to the dealer Rabenou when chiding him for asking too high a price for a silver candlestick (possibly that given to the Boston Museum in 1948): 'The highest price ever paid in this country for any piece of metal from the Near East was for the Alp Arslan salver, and that was paid when the museum still had large funds …' (Gluck & Siver 1996: 168). Only old-master painting regularly surpassed this sort of sum ($20,000 equalled roughly £5000 at this time) at auction sales during the 1930s, see (Reitlinger 1961-70: vols i-ii).
24   See also the review (Rogers 1977).
25   In 1940, Pope claimed to have earned an astounding $18,000 in a single month in 1917 for providing expert advice in Persian Art in New York. This was the incentive for him to give up teaching, see Gluck & Siver 1996: 72).
26   The enquiry was prompted by claims by Dimand and a Metropolitan Museum Trustee, both of whom withdrew allegations during the hearing, see Gluck & Siver (1996: 154ff). In his unfinished autobiography, begun in 1954, Pope writes that in 1931: 'Acting as agent for the Tehran dealer, I arranged the sale of the bronzes to the Boston Museum. I bought or was given some for myself. Meanwhile I retained them all in my possession, intending to show them at the London exhibition.'(Gluck & Siver 1996: 203). This runs directly contrary to his claims that he only took commissions from purchasers and had no relations with dealers, and shows how such entanglements of interest were indeed present at the 1931 exhibition.

The Boston salver today still fails to convince and on many grounds: on style and content (of the inscriptions, the animal drawing, the scrolling background, and the four arabesques which surround the central panel) and on its material and making. Plenderleith's original conclusion '... that there is no reason from a scientific point of view to doubt the age or genuineness of the piece' (Plenderleith 1933: 284) may fairly reflect the tests he had available eighty years ago and the assumptions then made about the lengths to which a forger would go, but they cannot stand today.[27] It is useful in this context to recall Florence Day's remark while discussing a major group of disputed textiles in which Pope was also involved: she rebuts the idea that we can argue what a forger would or would not do: 'We can only state, from the object itself, what the fabricator has done' (Day 1951: 251).[28]

For all his achievements in the promotion of Persian art to a wide public, in the case of the Alp Arslan Salver, Pope did help into a public collection a falsification that has over time misled the public, corrupted aesthetic standards, distorted history and wasted money, to say nothing of distracting scholars from productive work.

## References

Aga-Oglu, Mehmet (1947), 'Letter to the Editor', *The Art Bulletin* 29(2): 53-60.

Atil, Esin, W. Thomas Chase & Paul Jett (1985), *Islamic Metalwork in the Freer Gallery of Art*. Washington, D.C.: Freer Gallery of Art.

Blair, Sheila S., Jonathan M. Bloom & Anne E. Wardwell (1992), 'Reevaluating the Date of the 'Buyid' Silks by Epigraphic and Radiocarbon Analysis', *Ars Orientalis* 22: 1-41.

Coomaraswamy, Ananda (1934), 'An Eleventh Century Silver Salver From Persia', *Bulletin of the Museum of Fine Arts* 32: 56-58.

Day, Florence E., (1951), 'Review: Soieries persanes by Gaston Wiet', *Ars Islamica* 15-16: 231-251.

---

27 Re-examination by more modern examination techniques would be interesting. Plenderleith (1933 & 1935) did not seem to consider that the forgers may have undertaken a considerable degree of 'distressing' the object to suggest old wear and that they may have used old silver (perhaps medieval coins) rather than new, notwithstanding his observations. He undermines a number of his own arguments by his initial observation that '... silver ... can be made to acquire almost any characteristic of internal crystallisation or surface patina ...' (Plenderleith 1933: 281). The flimsiness of the tray and the poor quality of its planishing (Plenderleith 1933; 283), its unfinished rim, the slapdash (inept?) character of much of the engraving all add to the negative argument.

28 Many of the textiles, in whose promotion Pope played an important role, are now demonstrated by scientific testing as elaborate forgeries, see Blair, Bloom & Wardwell (1992). Florence Day had suggested already in 1951 that the same forger designed a number of the silks as well as the Boston salver (*ibid;* n. 19).

Dimand, M. S. (1941), 'A Review of Sasanian and Islamic Metalwork in 'A Survey of Persian Art'', *Ars Islamica* 8: 192-214.

Gluck, Jay & Noël Siver (eds) (1996), *Surveyors of Persian Art: A Documentary Biography of Arthur Upham Pope and Phyllis Ackerman*. Costa Mesa, C.A.: Mazda.

Gray, Basil (1939), 'A Seljuq Hoard from Persia', *The British Museum Quarterly* 13 (3): 73-79.

Jones, Dalu & George Michell (eds) (1976), *The Arts of Islam:* Hayward Gallery, 8 April – 4 July 1976. London: Arts Council of Great Britain Staff, World of Islam Festival Trust Staff, Hayward Gallery.

Kühnel, E. (1938), 'In Memoriam Henri C. Gallois 1885-1938', *Ars Islamica* 5(2): 292.

Marshak, B. I. (1986), *Silberschätze des Orients: Metallkunst des 3.-13. Jahrhunderts und ihre Kontinuität*. Leipzig: VEB E.A. Seemann Verlag.

Murdoch Smith, Major R. (1876), *Persian Art*, South Kensington Museum Art Handbooks. London: South Kensington Museum.

Palais Castellani (1884), *Collection Alessandro Castellani*. Rome: Palais Castellani.

Plenderleith, H. J. (1933), 'Scientific Examination of an 11th century Persian Silver Salver', *The Museums Journal* 33(3): 281-284.

Plenderleith, H. J. (1935), 'The Re-engraving of Old Silver', *Bulletin of the American Institute for Persian Art and Archaeology* 4(2): 72-73.

Pope, Arthur Upham & M. S. Dimand (1942), 'The Survey of Persian Art and Its Critics [with Reply]', *Ars Islamica* 9: 169-211.

Pope, Arthur Upham (1933a), 'A Seljuk Silver Salver I', *The Burlington Magazine* 368: 222-225, 229.

Pope, Arthur Upham (1933b), 'Introduction to the Scientific Examination of an 11th century Persian Silver Salver', *The Museums Journal* 33: 280-281.

Pope, Arthur Upham (1935a), 'Foliate Patterns on the Alp Arslan Salver', *Bulletin of the American Institute for Persian Art and Archaeology* 4(2): 75-78.

Pope, Arthur Upham (1935b), 'A Great Find: Alp Arslan's Silver Salver: Remarkable for Its Documentary Importance, as Well as for Its Design', The Illustrated London News, Feb. 23.

Pope, Arthur Upham (ed.) (1939a), *A Survey of Persian Art from prehistoric Times to the Present* (6 vols). London & New York: Oxford University Press.

Pope, Arthur Upham (1939b), 'The General Problem of Falsifications', *Mémoires: IIIe Congrès International d'Art et d'Archéologie Iraniens, Leningrad, Septembre 1935*, Moscow, Leningrad, 177-194.

Pope, Arthur Upham (1945), *Masterpieces of Persian Art*. New York: Dryden Press.

Pope, Arthur Upham (1947), 'Letter to the Editor', *The Art Bulletin*, v. 29(4): 284-7 (response to review by Mehmet Aga-Oglu).

Pope, Arthur Upham (1960), 'On the Discovery of Falsifications and the Recognition of Authenticity', *Survey of Persian Art* 13: 1-10.

Reitlinger, Gerald (1961-1970), *The Economics of Taste* (3 vols). London: Barrie and Rockliffe.

Rizvi, Kishwar (2007), 'Art History and the Nation: Arthur Upham Pope and the Discourse on 'Persian Art' in the Early Twentieth Century', *Muqarnas* 24: 45-65.

Rogers, M. J. (1996), 'Review: Surveyors of Persian Art: A Documentary Biography of Arthur Upham Pope and Phyllis Ackerman by Jay Gluck and Noël Siver', *Journal of the Royal Asiatic Society* 7(3): 455-458.

Roxburgh, David (ed.) (2005), *Turks: a journey of a thousand years, 600 – 1600*. London: Royal Academy of Arts.

Tomita, K. (1949), 'A Persian Silver Candlestick of the Twelfth Century', *Bulletin of the Museum of Fine Arts, Boston* 47: 56-58.

Watson, Oliver (1985), 'Fakes and Forgeries of Islamic Pottery', *Album of the Victoria and Albert Museum* 4: 38-46.

Watson, Oliver (2004), 'Fakes and Forgeries in Islamic Pottery', 2. Bamberger Symposium der Islamischer Kunst, Juli 1996, *Oriente Moderno* 2: 517-539.

Wiet, Gaston (1933), 'A Seljuk Silver Salver II', *The Burlington Magazine* 368: 229.

# FROM LUKAS TO LIEFKES?

## Age and Authenticity of Gold Jewellery from Sumba, Indonesia

*Francine Brinkgreve*

### Abstract

*The following case study focuses on questions of authenticity and age in relation to examples of gold jewellery from the island of Sumba, which were acquired on the international art market by Frits Liefkes and bequeathed to the National Museum of Ethnology. The author compares the collection with other museum collections and their histories, and presents opinions from a variety of specialists in relation to the authenticity of these particular objects, including the opinion of an indigenous Sumbanese goldsmith. Besides the questions raised about the dating of the objects themselves, the article also explores the complexity of the concept of authenticity in relation to age.*

### Introduction

Laurence A.G. Moss, in his account of developments in international art collecting in Indonesia, says that 'age appears to be the single most significant attribute of authenticity for the market' and 'fake is a constant threat, as the genuine is difficult to ascertain' (1994:101, 102). The following case study focuses on the question of authenticity and age in relation to examples of gold jewellery from the island of Sumba, in the eastern part of Indonesia. The jewellery is part of a large collection of Indonesian art and material culture, which was recently bequeathed to the National Museum of Ethnology by the private collector Frits Liefkes. The objects were acquired by him on the international tribal art market as valuable objects and he surely expected them to be genuine or authentic. When the objects were valued by two official appraisers, they were dated to the eighteenth/nineteenth or nineteenth century. Although the taxation report does not use the word 'authentic', this dating, in combination with a high monetary valuation, implies that these objects were believed to be authentic. But since their actual collection history is unknown, and because we know that there are many recently-made fakes around, the question arises as to how we can be certain of an assumed dating in such cases.

A second question to be explored is that of the relationship between age and authenticity. Would recently-made gold jewellery necessarily be non-authentic or fake, when these kinds of objects are still part of present-day Sumbanese culture? In the present article, I will discuss these questions of age and authenticity with regard to six pieces of gold Sumbanese jewellery from the Liefkes collection: four *mamuli*, omega-shaped ear ornaments or pendants; a *woridi*, a kind of ornament related to the *mamuli*; and a *kanatar*, a long chain, decorated at both ends, to be worn around the neck. I compare the collection with other published museum collections and their histories, give some information about the present situation in Sumba, and present opinions from a variety of specialists in relation to the authenticity of these particular objects, including the view of an indigenous Sumbanese goldsmith. But first a few remarks on the role the international art market plays in attributed dating and its implication of authenticity, as regards gold jewellery from Sumba.

## International art market

Although family heirloom jewellery was regarded as a sacred inheritance, passed down from generation to generation, and was essentially unmarketable, from the 1970s onwards there was an increase in the quantity and variety of gold jewellery from Sumba on the international art market (Moss 1986:6). Noble families began selling their gold objects, probably because they needed money and perhaps because the former large stock of gold jewellery was less necessary for ritual gift exchange. It is known, for example, according to Rogers (1985: 175), that when one of the former rulers in East Sumba died, his younger brother began selling off the family treasures to art dealers.

Laurence Moss (1986: 9,12) reports that by the end of the 1970s, many Indonesian (Chinese and Buginese) middlemen collected on Sumba to supply dealers in Bali and Jakarta, or on commission from museums and collectors.

Over the years, more and more collectors have set out to acquire Sumbanese jewellery and prices have risen accordingly. Dealers in the so-called tribal arts often have a *mamuli* and sometimes a *kanatar* for sale and these may cost thousands of euros. Dozens of these items are also offered for sale on the internet. As elsewhere in the world, the growing demand for objects of these kinds has resulted in an increase in the number of forgeries and fakes. New pieces were copied from exhibition catalogues, commissioned by dealers with the intention to sell them to collectors as old, authentic heirlooms (Moss 1986: 26; 1994: 102).

The preoccupation of the international tribal arts market with authenticity has influenced the dating of Sumbanese jewellery. High prices can only be demanded for 'authentic' pieces, and an authentic piece should preferably date from the nineteenth century or earlier. For probably almost all *mamuli* and other kinds of Sumbanese jewellery that have come onto the market since the 1970s,

*Fig. 1: Gold jewellery displayed in a showcase in the house of Frits Liefkes, in the upper left corner* mamuli *and* woridi *are visible. Photograph by Francine Brinkgreve, 2010.*

and that have been published, collection histories are lacking. Year of acquisition or source are rarely mentioned. Although some publications refrain from providing dating, many pieces, despite any supporting evidence, are dated '19th century', '19th century or earlier', '18th-19th century' and '18th century or earlier'. Such dates are accompanied by captions such as: 'It appears that sometime in the 18th century, new wealth and changing tastes resulted in larger *mamuli* with increasingly exuberant finials' (Richter & Carpenter 2011: 133), an interesting hypothesis but without supporting evidence. Elsewhere, however, Carpenter writes 'Since the 1960s *mamuli* have become larger and more complex' (2011: 204); here of course first-hand information may well have been available.

Questioning such instances of early dating is not to imply that, among all these pieces of jewellery, there are not some that do indeed date from the nineteenth century or earlier. It is just that in the present state of knowledge such dating is speculative. Such problems arise not only in relation to Sumbanese jewellery, of even Indonesian jewellery as a whole, but a wide range of Indonesian ethnographical objects. Bearing this in mind, let us now turn to the items of Sumbanese jewellery in the Liefkes collection.

## The Liefkes collection

In 2010, the National Museum of Ethnology received a large bequest from the late Frits Liefkes, a collector and lover of Indonesian art and material culture. The collection consists of about 900 objects, half of them being precious textiles from all over the archipelago, which generally do not give rise to questions of authenticity, since in Indonesia, copies or replicas of textiles are usually not made as fakes, or are readily identified as such. However, the other half, more than 400 statues, pieces of jewellery, furniture, ritual objects, and so on, are more problematic, since their provenance is unknown. Liefkes bought all his objects from art dealers and at auctions in the Netherlands, between the late 1970s and the day of his death in March 2010. He literally lived with his collections and kept his precious gold objects in showcases in his bedroom.

For him as a private collector, the unknown provenance of most of his objects was not a problem. He bought objects that he found aesthetically pleasing. The aspect of authenticity only became relevant after the collection was bequeathed to the museum. In preparation for the exhibition from May to July 2013, devoted to the Liefkes collection, that was a condition of the bequest, and in the preparation of the accompanying catalogue (Brinkgreve & Stuart-Fox 2013), objects were examined from a variety of viewpoints such as origin, materials, cultural significance, and dating. Only then did the estimated date provided by the seller of the object (usually an auction house or art dealer) or by the appraisers start to play the role of a stamp of authenticity. Our research concentrated on a selection of 150 objects of high quality. It became clear that for most of Liefkes' gold objects, from Java, Bali, Sulawesi and Sumatra, there is no question about their authenticity. Among them is a beautiful gold container with filigree decorations and although we do not know exactly when and even where it was made, nobody would call this wonderful object a fake. The object is unique, not a replica of something else and an inscription in Buginese, inscribed at the bottom, gives an indication of its cultural function in South Sulawesi. However, the gold jewellery from the people of the island of Sumba was a more complex case.

## Identification of the gold jewellery in the Liefkes collection

In the East-Sumbanese[1] language (Kambera) – Dutch dictionary, compiled by Louis Onvlee, who from 1925 worked for decades in Sumba as a language specialist, a *mamuli* is defined as an ear pendant made of precious metal, worn

---

1   There are differences in terminology, form and function of this jewellery between East and West Sumba, and also between the various regions or principalities of the island. In this article, I present only a brief general overview.

*Figs. 2 and 3: Two gold* mamuli pawihi *with cockatoo decorations,* mamuli kaka. *Collection of the National Museum of Ethnology, Liefkes-334 and -335. Photograph by Ben Grishaaver.*

*Fig. 4: Gold* mamuli pawihi *with buffalo decorations,* mamuli karambua. *Collection of the National Museum of Ethnology, Liefkes-337. Photograph by Ben Grishaaver.*

*Fig. 5: Gold* mamuli pawihi *with monkey decorations,* mamuli buti. *Collection of the National Museum of Ethnology, 6181-1. Photograph by Ben Grishaaver.*

in ceremonial circumstances. The most precious ones are part of the family heirlooms, the *tanggu marapu*, 'what belongs to the ancestors'. *Mamuli* are also part of the bride wealth. Traditionally, there are different categories of *mamuli*.

Old *mamuli*, *mamuli ndai* are *patuku* Ropa, made by Ropa and new *mamuli* of pure gold are *patuku* Lombu, made by Lombu.[2] *Mamuli bara* are silver *mamuli*, *mamuli rara* contain gold and are called *mamuli Humba* (from Sumba) and *mamuli Jawa* are imported *mamuli*, of copper or brass. An important distinction

---

2  I am not sure about the meaning of Ropa and Lombu, whether they are ancestors or mythical heroes, and what they have to do with *mamuli* making. But in the context of this article it is interesting that apparently *mamuli* can be classified in Sumba as being either old or new.

*Fig. 6: Gold chain,* **kanatar**. *Collection of the National Museum of Ethnology, Liefkes-363. Photograph by Ben Grishaaver.*

is between *mamuli pawihi,* mamuli with feet, two horn-shaped decorations of its lower half, used as base for little figures, and *mamuli kamuluku,* bare, undecorated *mamuli.* The *mamuli* with feet are classified as male, the ones without as female. A *mamuli pawihi* can take the name of the figure represented on the feet (Onvlee 1984: 260).

The four *mamuli* in the Liefkes collection are all *mamuli rara, mamuli Humba* and *mamuli pawihi,* and the feet are decorated with three different pairs of animal figures: two with cockatoos[3], one with buffaloes, and one with monkeys. In Sumba they would be called respectively *mamuli kaka, mamuli karambua* and *mamuli buti.* This last one is different from the others in its having movable parts; the monkeys seem to be drumming.

The animals depicted on the extensions of the *mamuli* have symbolic meaning in Sumbanese culture. Native to Sumba, the cockatoo is a white bird with orange-yellow crest and curved beak (Adams 1969:140). According to Adams, 'as an initial gift given by the prospective groom to the bride's family the *mamuli* is called "the bird's crest which stirs within"' (1969:142). The buffalo is an important animal, a sign of wealth and prestige. At major rituals dozens are slaughtered and serve as offerings to the ancestors and festival food for the guests (Adams 1969:136). The monkey, according to Onvlee (1984:27), is associated with thieves and stealing. This attribution appears in a story published by D.K. Wielenga, in which a monkey with the name I Dari plays a prominent role; the

---

3   These *mamuli* were both exhibited in Museum Nusantara in 1984 (Wassing-Visser1984:60, 118, pl on cover, pl.95, cat.nr 462).

*Figure 7: Gold ear ornament,* woridi. *Collection of the National Museum of Ethnology, Liefkes-336. Photograph by Ben Grishaaver.*

monkey, who referred to himself as a 'hairy man', helped (indeed by stealing and lying) a mythical ancestor to grow up and find a wife (Wielinga 1913: 16-25).

A *kanatar*, in the dictionary called *kanataru*, is defined as a chain, plaited from gold thread, and like some *mamuli*, classified as precious heirloom (Onvlee 1984:164).

The last gold object from Sumba in the Liefkes collection to be discussed here is called *woridi* in Kambera, the language of East Sumba, according to Susan Rogers (1985: 347), who did fieldwork in Sumba in 1983 to collect material for her book *Power and Gold*, but the word has no entry in the Kambera-Dutch dictionary of Onvlee. The object has the basic shape of a *mamuli* and of other ear ornaments from East Indonesian cultures. Rogers included a number of *woridi* in her publication, but she admits that the *woridi* were largely unrecognized in Sumba, when she conducted field interviews (1985:183, 292, 330).

## Expert opinions

When we started working on the Liefkes collection in preparation for the exhibition and the catalogue, first the whole collection was evaluated by two official appraisers. In their valuation report they evaluated the six pieces of Sumbanese jewellery as dating from the nineteenth century or even earlier. But when I sent photographs of the objects to two collectors I knew and who lived in Indonesia in the 1970s, they both expressed their doubts. We also organised an expert meeting at which various specialists examined closely all the gold objects in the Liefkes collection (not only the Sumbanese jewellery) whose authenticity we were not certain of. Among those present were a specialist who used to be an art dealer, an expert who is also a goldsmith, and an art historian who had seen many objects of these kinds while working for an auction house. They all questioned the early dating of nineteenth century, and thought the objects were of more recent make.

The *mamuli* with monkeys was said to have some wear and tear, the figures are lively and not too modern. But one of the specialists told us that he had seen many of this type being made in Sumba in the 1970s, to be sold on the art market. Also, the newly-made copies were apparently often given to Sumbanese families, to be used for a while in order to give them traces of age, such as patina and small surface scratches, and thus to make them look more authentic and also again collectable in a village setting. Cases like these involved the creation of a false provenance.

When photographs of this particular *mamuli* were sent to a Chinese dealer who lives in Sumba, his answer was: 'probably made in the 80s.' All specialists agreed that the *mamuli* with the buffaloes was made in a traditional way, but dates from the twentieth century.[4] Both *mamuli* with cockatoos have an unusual round shape, and, according to our experts, may have been made for the European market, perhaps as early as in the 1930s or 1940s, or may be more modern creations. In any case, they would seem to have been made by the same hand.

The *woridi*, according to one of our specialists, is a very modern piece of work. A collector who had seen a lot of gold jewellery in Sumba did not trust it, since he had never seen one in Sumba. The expert who is a goldsmith noticed some modern technical aspects in the making of the object, like the flat granulation. The ornament shows striking similarity with a *woridi* in the Musée du quai Branly,[5] published by Rogers (1985:183, 292). About the *kanatar* all the experts agreed that it was a modern piece, and as such not very valuable.[6]

## Ritual use of gold jewellery in Sumba[7]

In the old days *mamuli* were worn by people in artificially elongated earlobes, but also as pendants, suspended around the neck, hanging from a necklace, or fastened to a head cloth. To make *mamuli* and *kanatar* the Sumbanese used silver and gold coins, originally received as payment for the selling of slaves. But from the mid-nineteenth century, the income from the export of the famous

---

4  The *mamuli* with the buffaloes was sold at auction at Christie's, Amsterdam, 24 April 1996, lot no. 285 (Christie's 1996:112).
5  Inv. no. 70.2001.27.741.
6  The *kanatar* was sold at auction at Christie's, Amsterdam, 14 March 2005, lot no. 91 (Christie's 2005:19).
7  Since *mamuli* are an important aspect of traditional Sumbanese culture and society, over the years, but especially in the 1980s, many anthropologists have written about their meaning and ritual use, for example Susan Rogers (1985), Janet Hoskins (1988), Gregory Forth (1981), Webb Keane (1988) and Danielle Geirnaert (1989).

*Fig. 8: Detail of man's cloth from West Sumba, with* mamuli *motifs. Collection the National Museum of Ethnology, Liefkes-1004. Photograph by Ben Grishaaver.*

Sumbanese horses became more important than that derived from the slave trade. The import of gold and silver coins rose accordingly, increasing the availability of material for precious jewellery.

In Sumba *mamuli* and *kanatar* are much more than just beautiful pieces of jewellery. They are 'packed with many layers of kinship, political and mythic meaning' (Rogers 1985:27). They play an essential role in the elaborate ceremonial gift exchanges that take place on important occasions like weddings. *Mamuli*, as 'male' goods, are given as part of the bride wealth by the family of the groom, the wife-takers, in return for the fertility of the bride, who marries into the groom's house. In return, the family of the bride, the wife-givers, present 'female' goods, like textiles. Items of gold jewellery like *mamuli* are sometimes woven as motifs into these textiles, especially in West Sumba.

The status and wealth of the families or clans (*kabihu*) involved in the marriage ritual determine the total amount and different categories of the *mamuli* presented. For weddings of important *maramba*, the highest nobility, *kanatar* are also part of the bride wealth.

This gender classification is also applied to the different gold ornaments. If the *mamuli* are given in pairs, one of each pair should be a *mamuli kamuluku*, bare *mamuli* which represents the female aspect, and the other one, considered masculine, a *mamuli pawihi*. If they are fastened to a *kanatar*, the chain represents the male principle as opposed to the female principle embodied in the *mamuli* (Onvlee 1977:157). *Mamuli* and *kanatar* are also part of symbolic kinds of exchange between entities classified as male and female. For example, in his article about the construction of a dam in Mangili (East Sumba), Onvlee (1977:159) presents the following analysis:

> *What happens now follows the example of the past and obeys the ancestors' exhortation that the sawah (ricefields) must be seen as ancient ear pendants, and the channels as their woven chains. And so I Umbu and I Rambu, the Lord and his Lady, are united. [...]* Muni-kawini, *male and female, have been brought together.*

The most precious *mamuli* and *kanatar* are part of the ancestral heirlooms, the *tanggu marapu*, 'what belongs to the ancestors'. The most sacred ones are the *tanggu marapu, la hindi*, the *marapu* objects which are kept in the attics high in the roofs of the houses of important Sumbanese clans. These *mamuli* served to maintain contact with powerful ancestors and divine beings. They are seldom allowed to be seen, and then only at certain rituals, when they are handled by *ratu*, priests. They are called *banda mbana*, hot, dangerous goods. Other items of the *tanggu marapu* which are called *banda la kaheli* or *banda la uma*, are *marapu* possessions which are kept in the lower parts of the house (Onvlee 1984:12, 13; 478). These are heirlooms of the *kabihu*, the clan, and handed down to the next generations. *Tanggu marapu* were never worn as jewellery (except at royal funerals, as we will see later), nor were they exchanged at weddings and other ceremonies, and, ideally, never sold. A variety of metaphors stress the importance of these inalienable pieces of jewellery. For example, *mamuli* are called 'the eyes of the deceased' or the 'shape' of the spirits of the dead (Geirnaert 1989: 454; 460), or a 'mat' upon which the ancestors may sit (Keane 1988:5).

At funerals, the dead receive many objects of gold jewellery, especially *mamuli* and *kanatar*, to serve as wealth in the afterlife. As evidence of the high status of the deceased, *mamuli* and *kanatar* are often carved as decoration on a monumental stone, erected after the funeral of a *maramba*. Just as was the custom a hundred years ago, as reported for example by D.K. Wielenga ([1926]: 72-74), the giving of gold jewellery is still an important aspect of large-scale funerals in present-day Sumba. In October 2012, Wahyu Ernawati, Head of the Ethnography Department of Museum Nasional in Jakarta, went to Sumba to witness an important funeral of four members of high nobility in the principality of Pau in East Sumba.[8]

> *At the present time,* mamuli *still play an important role in Sumbanese society, especially among the aristocracy (*maramba*) and especially in death rites. When someone dies, the body is washed and placed in foetal position.* Mamuli *and gold coins are placed in the mouth, hands, and folds of the shroud. Then the body is wrapped in layers of textiles, as many as a hundred. For the burial itself, when the bereaved family sends notice to other families, the envoy brings a* mamuli *for male relatives and a textile called* lau *for female relatives. In return the families of male*

---

8   I am grateful that Erna shared her research results with me and that I may use the photographs which were taken by her and by a friend who went with her, Claude Lavalle.

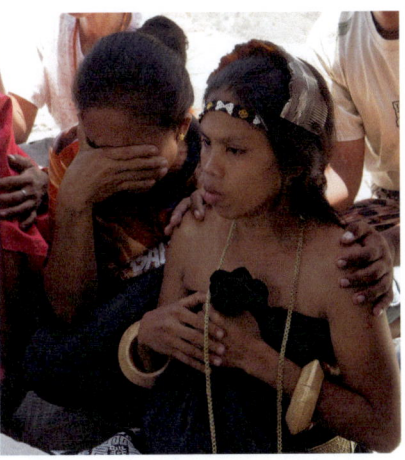

*Figs. 9 and 10: During a royal funeral ceremony the papanggang wears two gold mamuli attached to a gold head ornament, lamba. Among a group of women mourning at the grave, a young lady wears a kanatar chain.*
*Photographs by Claude Lavalle, 2012.*

> *relatives bring a horse, buffalo or pig, while the families of female relatives bring an unsewn cloth if the deceased is male or a tabular skirt if female. During the burial ritual, a slave or servant, known as* papanggang, *dresses up in ceremonial attire with full jewellery accessories such as* mamuli, lamba, kanatar and mutisala. *The* papanggang *is not allowed to touch the ground, so he must be carried when put on a horse which is believed to be the mount of the aristocrat (*marimba*) on his or her journey to the abode of the ancestors (*paraingu marapu*). … The final ceremony is a 'cooling' ritual in which all the objects worn by the* papanggang *are 'cooled' by means of washing in water. Only then can the heirloom objects such as the* mamuli *and* lamba *be safely stored again in the sacred part of the house* (Ernawati 2013:275).

The *woridi* is apparently not unknown in present-day Sumba.

> *According to Umbu Agung from Prailiu, East Sumba, a* woridi *is actually a* mamuli *with globular motifs around the edge.* Woridi *are made for the rajas and families, and like* mamuli *are used ritually in betrothal ceremonies, as bride price, and for death rites. According to Rambu Margarita, wife of Umbu Agung,* woridi *is derived from* wuaridi, rua, *meaning fruit, and* ridi, *referring to a mythical "tree of life"* (Ernawati 2013:279).

*Fig. 11: Silver* mamuli, *collected by H.F.C. ten Kate in 1891. Collection of the National Museum of Ethnology, inv. no. 858-89. Photograph by Ben Grishaaver.*

## Historical sources and museum collections

During research on the possible age and authenticity of the gold jewellery in the Liefkes collection, I compared his *mamuli, woridi* and *kanatar* with similar jewellery, in various sources. I first looked at old ethnographic museum collections known to date from the nineteenth or very early twentieth century, since their collection history is well documented.[9] I also looked at field reports, searched for older visual materials, and finally I compared the six items with other Sumbanese jewellery in collections which have been published since the 1980s. The oldest published *mamuli* that entered museums prior to the Second World War were collected in the field in the second half of the nineteenth century and the first half of the twentieth century, for the colonial museums at that time, whose collectors also reported about their journeys, work and research in Sumba.

### Roos 1871

The first *mamuli* known so far to have entered a museum collection was a gold *mamuli* given in 1871 to the 'Ethnological Cabinet' of the Museum of the Batavian Society of Arts and Sciences (Voorwerpen 1871; Van der Chijs 1885:200). The collector was S. Roos, who was one of the first two civil servants of the Dutch Colonial Government on Sumba, stationed there in 1866. He described the *mamuli* (inv. no. 3439) as a 'gold ear pendant. Made on Sumba with as general purpose to present as gift, but in the mountain areas one sometimes see the *raja*s wear them, that is why they have enormous holes in their ear lobes.' He does not give any further information as where and how he obtained the *mamuli* (or any of the other objects in his collection), or who made the object. We might wonder what the *mamuli* Roos collected looked like, since in a report on Sumba,

---

9   There are a few other *mamuli* in Dutch collections and in Jakarta, but nothing is known about their collection histories. Further research in European collections may turn up other early collected examples.

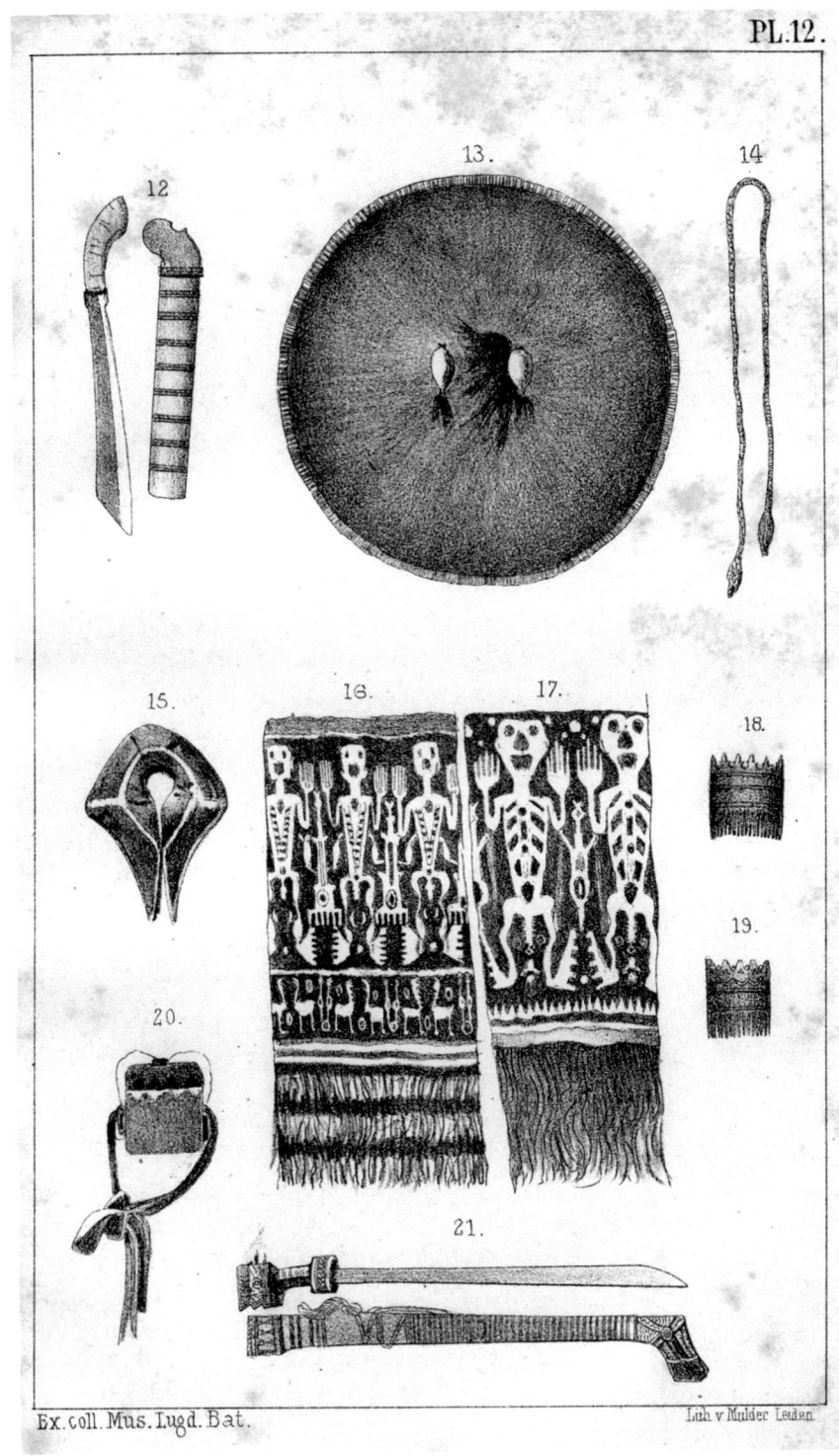

*Fig. 12: Illustration of this* mamuli, *in 'Verslag eener reis in de Timorgroep en Polynesië: III. Soemba' (Ten Kate 1894), plate XII, fig.15.*

published in 1872, he expresses a fairly negative view of *mamuli*, which he calls 'ear pendants of a type that to us appears unimaginably coarse'.[10] He reports that 'some men make plaited copper chains and they have a certain capability in the making of gold *mamuli*' (Roos 1872:21) and he mentions that 60 to 100 gold coins are needed to make one *kanatar* for the bride wealth of a *maramba* (Roos 1872:48).

According to Roos (1872:79), the brother of a man of Arab descent, Sjarif Abdoel Rachman, who had considerable influence in a coastal village with market and harbour, Waingapu (the present capital of the island), made *mamuli* and *kanatar* on order for the nobility. Could the *mamuli* he collected for the museum in Batavia have been made, perhaps, by this Arabian man? Another interesting point in Roos' report relates to his figures for the island's imports and exports, in which he includes 41 gold *mamuli* exported in 1870 (Roos 1872:39). Where did this jewellery go to? Who would use them outside Sumba?

## Ten Kate 1891

The oldest *mamuli* in the National Museum of Ethnology, inv. no. 858-89, was collected by Herman F.C. ten Kate (Fischer & Rassers 1924:126).

In 1891 he made a field trip to Sumba, sent by the Royal Dutch Geographical Society (Koninklijk Nederlands Aardrijkskundig Genootschap), with a grant from the Dutch Government, to collect objects for the Rijks Ethnographisch Museum, as the National Museum of Ethnology was called at that time. He visited the *maramba* (ruler) of Rendeh (Rindi), one of the most powerful little states in East Sumba, who was apparently rather suspicious and distrustful, and only opened up a little after Ten Kate presented him with some gifts. However, Ten Kate did not succeed in collecting any ethnographic objects. 'Neither the *raja* nor anybody else was inclined to hand anything over,' noted Ten Kate regretfully (1894:579). However, in Memboro (West Sumba) he was helped by the local colonial civil servant, R.G.F. Baumgarte, who had for some time lived alongside the local people in the same impoverished conditions, spoke the language, and had managed to collect a number of objects before Ten Kate's arrival (Ten Kate 1894:623). Among them was a plain, undecorated silver *mamuli* (*mamuli bela*)[11], which was illustrated in his report (plate XII, figure 15) and is now in the National Museum of Ethnology. In one sense there is no doubt about the provenance of this object, since we know the collector and the date of collection, but we do not know anything about the cultural context of this particular *mamuli*. Was the *mamuli* newly made, or had it been used in the gift exchange system as a wedding prestation? Was it given or sold to Baumgarte, by whom, and what was the counter prestation?

---

10   Unfortunately, this *mamuli* is not in the museum anymore.
11   *Bela* means both white and silver in Memboro language (Ten Kate 1894:623).

*Fig. 13: Brass* mamuli, *collected by H. Witkamp in 1910. Collection of the Tropenmuseum, inv. no. H 1998b*

During his travels, Ten Kate did not see many *mamuli* in use, since he did not come across or was not invited to any ritual, such as a wedding or funeral. But he did notice many robbed graves, and he was told that a lot of gold jewellery, especially *mamuli* and *kanatar*, which were meant to serve as wealth of the deceased in the afterlife, were stolen by members of a neighbouring clan or by people from Endeh (Flores), during slave raids (Ten Kate 1894:573). What has happened to all those pieces of stolen gold jewellery?

## Witkamp 1910

The Tropenmuseum in Amsterdam has a number of *mamuli* from the colonial period. Almost twenty years after Ten Kate, H. Witkamp travelled to Sumba and, like Ten Kate, he published a report in the journal of the Royal Dutch Geographical Society (1912-1913). In 1910, besides a betel quid (a sign of hospitality everywhere in Indonesia), he 'was given a *mamuli*, according to an old Sumbanese custom'. He immediately added a disparaging comment on this gift: 'of course it was not a real gold one, but one made of yellow copper (brass), as there are plenty for sale in the Chinese shops in Waingapu. The real ones only appear at important ceremonies' (Witkamp 1913:504). In 1911 he presented this *mamuli* with minor decorations (a photo was published in his report) to the Colonial Museum in Haarlem, whose collections became part of the Tropenmuseum, together with another, similar *mamuli* (present inventory numbers: H1998a,b).[12]

Might this other one have come from the Chinese shop? Who were the craftsmen of these shop-sold *mamuli*? It is curious that what we might think of as being authentic (received as present in Sumba, in an 'authentic way'), in the eyes of the collector himself is 'not real'. Witkamp's *mamuli* are registered

---

12  Thanks to Pim Westerkamp, Ingeborg Eggink and Jacqueline Weg for providing information and photographs.

CREATING AUTHENTICITY

*Fig. 14: Gilded silver* mamuli, *collected by D.K. Wielenga.*
*Collection of the Tropenmuseum, inv. no. 386-2*

*Fig. 15: Gold* mamuli buti wilak, *collected by G.P. Rouffaer in 1910.*
*Collection Museum Nasional Indonesia, inv. no. E1348 or E 1199*

as '*mamuli Jawa*'. This does not mean that the *mamuli* actually came from the island of Java, for 'Jawa' was also a general expression to indicate that something came from outside, not from Sumba itself (Onvlee 1984:260).

## Wielenga 1921

A more in-depth knowledge of Sumbanese culture, laid down in extensive reports and many articles (Wielenga n.d.), was obtained by one of the first missionaries of the Dutch Protestant Church, D.K. Wielenga, who started his work on Sumba in 1904 and lived there for many years. Although he often describes the ritual use of gold *mamuli* and *kanatar*, he does not mention in detail what they look like, nor does he mention who the craftsmen are or how they have been made, or the fact that he collected them himself. But he did donate some handsome examples of *mamuli* to several museums and institutions in the Netherlands. In 1921 he donated to the Tropenmuseum a *mamuli pawihi* with a little skull tree on either foot (inv. no. 386-2) (Brakel 1987:188).

Another one, with two little roosters on the feet, came into the collection of the museum in Rotterdam, the present Wereldmuseum (inv. no. 21300) (Leven en dood [Adams] 1965: cover; 32).[13]

---

13  This *mamuli* was lost after an exhibition in the 1980s.

*Fig. 16: Portrait of a Sumbanese women wearing two gold* mamuli buti, *painted by Mas Pirngadie in the 1930s. Collection Museum Nasional Indonesia, Jakarta.*
*Photograph by Claude Lavalle, 2013*

## Rouffaer 1910

Towards the end of 1910, the museum in Batavia, the present Museum Nasional Indonesia in Jakarta, was offered the first known gold *mamuli* of the type with little movable figures along the base. This can be dated with certainty as being over a hundred years old, since it was collected in Sumba in 1910.

This lovely *mamuli* (inv. no. E1348 or E1199) is on show in the museum's treasure room and has a well-documented collection history (Rouffaer 1911: bijlage II). In the late nineteenth century, Savunese soldiers, on behalf of one of the small Sumbanese states, not mentioned by name in the report, went to war with the neighbouring small island of Salura (or Halura), off the south coast of Sumba.[14] They slaughtered all the inhabitants of the island, and they took two precious *mamuli* back home. These very special heirlooms, according to legend the very reason for going to war, were called *buti wilak* (meaning 'monkeys which look back') and *kaka mbelu* (cockatoos from Belu, in Timor).

The last one was handed over to the ruler of Rindi (in East Sumba), while the *mamuli* with the monkeys was first held by a noble family from Savu, who lived in Melolo on Sumba. They finally sold the *mamuli* to the representative of the Dutch colonial government, lieutenant A.A. Streiff, for 125 guilders. Meanwhile, the *raja* of Rindi had a replica made of the *mamuli* with monkeys, so that he had the important pair of *mamuli* complete. In 1910 G.P. Rouffaer, a well-known scholar attached to the Batavian Society of Arts and Sciences in Batavia, travelled to Sumba, met the lieutenant and bought the original *mamuli buti wilak* from him for 150 guilders, to be placed in the museum of the Batavian Society, the present Museum Nasional. But even with this excellent provenance,

---

14  As for the historical evidence of this story, I have not found any information about an actual raid on the island of Salura towards the end of the nineteenth century.

how can we be certain that this is the original *mamuli* and not the replica, or another copy of this apparently extremely valuable object?[15]

## Mas Pirngadie 1930s

In old collections of photographs there are no illustrations of gold jewellery in Sumba, and especially not of the elaborate heirlooms. But the *mamuli* with monkeys in the Museum Nasional is depicted on a portrait of a Sumbanese woman, who wears two of them in her elongated earlobes.

This portrait is one of a series painted by Mas Pirngadie in the 1930s, used as a frame around a large map of the various ethnic groups in Indonesia in the Museum of the Batavian Society (Brinkgreve 2005:112). A detail of this portrait[16] shows that Mas Pirngadie, who worked at the Batavia Museum at that time, must have used the *mamuli* which Rouffaer had collected in 1910 as his example. This is obviously not an 'authentic' representation of the use of this particular *mamuli*, which would never have been worn by a common Sumbanese woman, let alone two of them.

## De Roo van Alderwerelt 1890

Although J. de Roo van Alderwereldt did not contribute to museum collections, his extensive study of the island of Sumba from 1890, based on his travels in Sumba in 1885, contains interesting information on Sumbanese gold jewellery in the nineteenth century. He mentions that the island of Salura (where the *mamuli* collected by Rouffaer came from) was deserted, and that many graves had been robbed. Sumbanese informants confirmed that a great deal of gold jewellery could be found on the island. According to myth, two men from the island of Solor (an island between Flores and Timor) made the first *mamuli*. They had been shipwrecked on Salura. Eventually these men were buried there, together with many of their *mamuli*. The *mamuli* made by the two Solorese men were called *pateku* Lumbu (made by Lumbu), or *mamuli ndai*, old *mamuli*.[17] They were very expensive and cost up to 250 guilders, which was ten times as much as their actual gold value. Often such old *mamuli* were the cause of war. De Roo van Alderwerelt reports further that *mamuli* with birds, human beings

---

15  Although this *mamuli* has been published many times in catalogues (for example Girard-Geslan 1999:70; Sulitianingsih 2006:270-271; Maxwell 2010:80), this original collection history is seldom referred to. Hoskins (ca.2010:239), obviously unaware of the name of the legendary *mamuli*, calls the two monkeys 'Two human figures in front of a bowl. The figures with apparently covered faces are squatting with upraised hands and seem to be supplicating the spirits. Because of the importance of mamuli as exchange valuables at funerals, they probably represent slave attendants mourning beside the body of a nobleman'. Although the only evidence for the age of this mamuli is that it was collected in 1910, in one catalogue this mamuli was even dated '17$^{th}$-18$^{th}$ century' (Sulistianingsih 2006:270).

16  This portrait is shown on a postcard in the collection of the KITLV (no.1405603).

17  This contradicts the view expressed by Onvlee (1984:260), who calls the *patuku* Lombu new *mamuli*, and not *mamuli ndai*, old *mamuli*.

and monkeys, respectively called *mamuli mahawurung, mamuli tau* and *mamuli buti*, and the *pateku* Lumbu could only be in the possession of the *maramba*, the nobility (1890:592).

He also writes about the two other types of jewellery in the Liefkes collection. He notes that for the wedding ceremony of one of the *maramba*, two *kanatar* (with a value of 1,200 guilders) were given by the groom's family, in exchange for 40 women's skirts, *lau*, from the bride's side. He had even heard of a *kanatar* being worth 7,500 guilders (De Roo van Alderwerelt 1890:574)!

According to him, 'one also finds *mamuli* on Savu, where they are called *woridi*' (De Roo van Alderwerelt 1890:592). This would explain why the word *woridi* is not found in Onvlee's dictionary of the Kambera (East Sumbanese) language, and why they were not recognised by Rogers's informants.

## *Published collections after 1970*

Since World War II, and especially in the 1970s and 1980s, many pieces of jewellery, especially gold *mamuli* with figures along the base, entered collections of art museums and galleries in Europe, the United States and Australia. But these museums began collecting Indonesian art only quite recently, and usually via the international art market, such as Frits Liefkes himself used to do. Some of these pieces have a provenance in relation to place of collection, but none of them can be dated conclusively to the nineteenth century.

Robert Holmgren and Anita Spertus collected *mamuli* in Sumba in the 1970s and 1980s; Baing and Kanatang are mentioned specifically. Some of their gold jewellery is now part of the collections of the Metropolitan Museum of Art (Holmgren & Spertus 1989:32,33; Taylor & Aragon 1991:216,217) and the Australian National Gallery (Maxwell 2010:81).

The Musée du quai Branly in Paris has a large and famous collection of ethnic jewellery from Indonesia and the Philippines. This whole collection, published by Susan Rogers in her book *Power and Gold* (1885), formerly belonged to the Barbier-Mueller Museum in Geneva, but was donated to the museum in Paris by Jean Paul and Monique Barbier-Mueller in 2001, without any further documentation.[18] Out of twenty or more *mamuli*, three gold *mamuli* are said to have been acquired directly from the younger brother of the raja of Pau (Melolo), after his elder brother had died (Rogers 1985:330-331). In 1976, when J. Gabriel Barbier-Mueller travelled in Sumba he acquired two brass *mamuli* 'from lower-class people', published by Webb Keane (1988:3).

Recently, other large ethnic jewellery collections containing gold objects from Sumba have been published (Vanderstraete 2012; Richter & Carpenter 2011; Carpenter 2011), but they do not provide any provenance for the objects.

---

18  Personal communication from Constance de Monbrison, April 2013.

## Comparison with the Liefkes jewellery

Returning to the six pieces in the Liefkes collection, the *mamuli* with buffaloes displays certain similarities to one of the *mamuli* from the treasure of Pau[19] (Rogers 1985:293). Recently published collections also include *mamuli* with buffaloes (Richter & Carpenter 2011:144; Vanderstraete 2012:350). Both *mamuli* with cockatoos have a rather unusual round shape, which is not found in any published museum collection. But cockatoos on the feet of a *mamuli* are not uncommon (see for example Rogers 1985:294). Although they are not found in the old museum collections, a very fine *mamuli* with cockatoos, from the collection of Robert J. Holmgren and Anita E. Spertus, collected in Baing (South Sumba), is said to date from the nineteenth century (Holmgren & Spertus 1989:32).

The *mamuli* with movable monkeys is the only *mamuli* of the four in the Liefkes collection[20] which looks similar to a *mamuli* in an old museum collection, proven to date from the nineteenth century, the one in the Museum Nasional. Originally I had hoped that this could have been the *mamuli* the *raja* of Rindi had ordered in 1910 as a duplicate of the one that was sold to the Dutch. However, during the research I came across a *mamuli* with monkeys in the Musée du quai Branly[21] and in at least three other collections.[22] These were assembled much more recently and do not have published provenances. Holmgren and Spertus (1989:32,33) collected in Kanatang a *mamuli* with warriors, accompanied by little figures who look like the monkeys of the *mamuli* in the Museum Nasional. This *mamuli* is now in the Metropolitan Museum of Art (Taylor and Aragon 1991:216, 217).

Of the two other gold objects from Sumba in the Liefkes collection, the *woridi* (ear ornament) and the *kanatar* (chain), no examples exist in the old museum collections, but they are present in the more recent collections, for example the collection of Musée du quai Branly. The *kanatar* is said to have come from the treasure of Pau but the *woridi* is of unknown provenance (Rogers 1985:183, 296, 332).

So we may conclude that most of the Liefkes jewellery has parallels in pieces in recently published collections. Pieces may have been copied from the catalogues, like *Power and Gold*. It is also possible that they were copied directly from old treasures, or that they really came from old treasures that have been sold after the 1970s, as happened with the royal treasury of Pau.

---

19  Musée du quai Branly, inv. no. 70.2001.27.747.
20  Actually, Liefkes did not buy this *mamuli* himself, but after his death I bought it for the National Museum of Ethnology with money from the so-called Weegenaar-Liefkes Fund, inv. no. RMV 6181-1.
21  Inv. no. 70.2001.27.751.
22  Dallas Museum of Art, the Mandala Foundation (Richter & Carpenter 2011) and the Manfred Giehman collection (Carpenter 2011).

And indeed, the historical sources and museum collections show that the kind of jewellery Frits Liefkes had in his collection did indeed exist in Sumba in the nineteenth century; but they were not collected at that time. Gold *mamuli* with animals on their feet and *kanatar* were exclusively in the possession of the *maramba*, the nobility, who had no interest in negotiating with outside collectors a hundred years ago. The one exception is the *mamuli buti*, the gold *mamuli* with movable monkeys in the Museum Nasional (collected by Rouffaer in 1910), probably because it was in the possession of a Savunese family and not of a Sumbanese ruler. The Sumbanese ruler involved is said to have had a copy made of this important *mamuli*, so copying was already taking place in the nineteenth century!

The collection histories also show that already around 1900 *mamuli* were for sale in the Chinese shops in Waingapu and a man of Arab descent had taken up the craft of gold smithing.

## The craftsmen

Compared to discussions of their use and function and role in culture and society, remarkably little has been written about the technical aspects of the process of *mamuli* making or about the makers themselves. In the *Encyclopaedie van Nederlandsch Indië* (1921:2) it is stated that a few men practise smithing, and that the manufacture is largely confined to metal ornaments. Still, considering the enormous quantities of jewellery needed for bride wealth of the nobility (50 to 100 gold *mamuli* in 1920 in Kambera, as reported by A.C. Kruyt (1922:501)), one would expect more attention from researchers for this aspect. Gregory Forth, who did fieldwork in Rindi in 1975-1976, merely reports that a few men made gold, silver and tin [?] *mamuli* (pendants) and plaited chains made mostly of copper wire (Forth 1981:16).

Robert Holmgren and Anita Spertus write:

> *It is not known whether fancy gold* mamuli *were actually made on Sumba. Although Sumba men smith, the technical and stylistic uniformity of many older* mamuli *suggests routine workshop production, while the finest examples were probably the work of specialized artisans. Such* mamuli *may have been imported from nearby islands, or made by resident Chinese.* (Holmgren and Spertus 1989:32)

According to Sumbanese oral tradition, the arts of metalworking came from the neighbouring island of Savu, and many Savunese living on Sumba continued to practise the traditional art of goldsmithing (Hoskins 1988:129; Keane 1988:5). Craftsmen from the tiny island of Ndao (like Sumba and Savu part of the archipelago of Nusa Tenggara Timur), were also known to visit Sumba to ply their craft, as observed by anthropologist James J. Fox (1978:24). But according to Susan Rogers, 'a Waingapu smith interviewed in 1983 said that

*Figs. 17 and 18: Bapak Lukas Kaborang, goldsmith from Lairuru, East Sumba. Photographs by Claude Lavalle (17) and Wahyu Ernawati (18), 2012*

many Sumbanese have now gone into the same business'. Besides Sumbanese craftsmen, 'some wealthy East Sumbanese families patronize Balinese or Chinese-Indonesian goldsmiths in Bali when they want a new piece made or an old one repaired' (Rogers 1985:167). Janet Hoskins also noticed during her fieldwork on Sumba that expertise from outside the island was required: 'Noble families have also brought in goldsmiths from places like Java and Makassar, but have always asked that they produce objects which conform to local aesthetic traditions' (1988:129).

More recently, Richter and Carpenter (2011:144) talk about the continuing creative powers of the East Sumbanese craftsmen, especially in Melolo and the 'royal seat of Pau', but they do not give further information about the artisans themselves. However, thanks to Wahyu Ernawati, we can refer to very recent field data about an indigenous Sumbanese goldsmith: Lukas Kaborang.

## Lukas Kaborang

During a field trip to Sumba in October 2012, Wahyu Ernawati visited Bapak Lukas Kaborang, who is a goldsmith from the village of Lairuru in Melolo, East Sumba.

She interviewed him at length:

> *According to him, Sumbanese living in Bali and in Java also make* mamuli, *though quality varies. They are still being made because demand remains high, particularly for marriage rituals (as bride price) and death rites. But besides fulfilling the demand for their role in ritual, many* mamuli *are now made just as decorations, and as collector's items, not only among Indonesian collectors but also throughout the world. Many go to Sumba to search for heirloom pieces, and this has pushed dealers to have them made in quantity to satisfy demand since genuine heirloom pieces are rare ...*
>
> *Originally made of gold or silver, with the rising price of gold and difficulty in procuring the raw material,* mamuli *are now often made of other materials such as*

*Fig. 19: Wahyu Ernawati wears a new creation made by Bapak Lukas Kaborang, a combination of traditional* mamuli *and* kanatar.
*Photograph by Francine Brinkgreve, 2012*

bronze or brass. Apparently bronze and brass are also difficult to obtain in Sumba, a concern expressed by the mamuli *master of Lairuru, Lukas Kaborang. According to him, the demand for* mamuli *has risen in recent years, especially to satisfy the demand from Jakarta, to participate in exhibition activities, and fulfil requests from private collectors.*

*To satisfy this demand, the raw material for* mamuli *such as metal sheeting or brass plaques is brought in from Jakarta or other areas of Java or even Bali; they are ordered and transported directly by Sumbanese who travel back and forth between Sumba and Jakarta exhibiting their products. This has strict limits, for each person can only afford to carry about five kilograms of brass plaques, because of the price. According to Lukas Kaborang, gold* mamuli *have not been made since 2008; they are only made of gold or silver plating.*

*Lukas Kaborang is one of four brothers, all of whom are capable of making* mamuli, *skills which have been handed down the generations from his grandfather. But of the four brothers, only Lukas'* mamuli *are finely and carefully crafted. For a time he lived in Bali making* mamuli, *but he could stand Bali for only one year before moving back to Lairuru. Lukas was born in 1966 and started making* mamuli *in 1981 when he was only 15 years old. At that time he was taught by his father first just to draw the design. He has done the same with his own son Yudias Umbu Yiwa who is still at primary school in sixth grade. Yudias also makes hanging ornaments for* kanatar *necklaces, fashioning out of stainless steel animals in the shape of monkeys, birds, ducks, horses and so on. Lukas's wife, Ndunga Ata Djuwa, also helps her husband in the cleaning processes in which completed kanatar necklaces and* mamuli *have to be submerged in distilled battery water to remove blackened remnants from the smithing before being gold or silver plated, according to order. Since 1998 Lukas, as a craftsman of experience and regarded the best in Lairuru, has often been approached to make* mamuli *for people who then sell them on to those interested. Mostly such orders come from antique dealers who do business in Sumbanese art objects, including ikat textiles and jewellery. They travel back and forth between Sumba and Jakarta, where they exhibit their wares.* (Ernawati 2013: 276-277).

When I met Wahyu Ernawati in Jakarta in October 2012, she had just come home from her trip to Sumba with pieces of jewellery, given to her by Pak Lukas: examples of modern creations he makes as well, based on the traditional *mamuli* and *kanatar*.

As a pendant, the *mamuli* has become very popular and well-known as a Sumba icon to such an extent that it is now worn in Indonesia by anybody irrespective of origin, not only by the Sumbanese. So the *mamuli* has entered the flourishing world of modern Indonesian fashion. Can they be called authentic pieces? In their own way, of course they are. It is known exactly who made them, when, where and for what purpose. For the National Museum of Ethnology I ordered a modern *woridi* of this kind, made by Pak Lukas from silver-plated metal.

Erna also took photographs of the six pieces of gold jewellery from the Liefkes collection with her to Sumba, and she asked the opinion of Pak Lukas.

> *When recently we came to meet Pak Lukas, bringing photographs of* mamuli *in the Liefkes collection, spontaneously he indicated that he thought that two of the three items [as published in the catalogue], a* mamuli *and a* woridi *were his own work. He said that he made these items at the request of an acquaintance who planned to sell them again in Jakarta. He did not know who had ordered them or who bought them in Jakarta, but he remembers clearly and memorizes* mamuli *of his own making. Of every* mamuli *that he makes, he takes a photograph as documentation. He showed us these photographs, as he does also to people who order from him. According to him, his work possesses certain characteristics that only he can recognize. However, since Lukas Kaborang only saw the photographs of the Liefkes collection, and not the actual objects, we cannot be absolutely certain that the* mamuli *and the* woridi *in the Liefkes collection were indeed made by him. But in any case, he has made similar pieces, and in the view of those who often order jewellery from him, the work of Lukas Kaborang is among the best in East Sumba.* (Ernawati 2013:278-279).

With regard to the *kanatar*, Pak Lukas said that he himself did not make this one, although in principle he could do this kind of work. The *mamuli* he recognised as his own work were the *mamuli* with the buffaloes and also the one with the monkeys, which, like the *kanatar*, was not included in the Liefkes collection catalogue.[23] Lukas could have copied both *mamuli* from collection catalogues, like *Power and Gold* (Rogers 1985). Interestingly, in relation to the two *mamuli* with the cockatoos, Pak Lukas commented that they were really old, antique pieces, probably precious heirlooms from an important family

---

23  Personal communication from Wahyu Ernawati, October 2012.

(Ernawati 2013:279). Obviously he had never seen the unusual, round shape of these *mamuli*. Pak Lukas also claimed to have made the *woridi* himself, like the two *mamuli*. Since it shows such similarity with the *woridi* published in *Power and Gold*, the photograph of this *woridi* may have been used as an example. However, when I received the new *woridi* I ordered for the museum from Pak Lukas, I started to wonder whether he had really made the gold *woridi* in the Liefkes collection. The quality of the smithing and granulation is less refined.

## Conclusion

So did three of the six objects indeed travel from Lukas via Liefkes to Leiden? We will never know for certain. Of course we have to bear in mind that Pak Lukas only looked at photographs; he has not seen the actual objects. But if he made the Liefkes objects, he probably did not regard them as fakes. It is only on the journey to the collector, in the long chain of dealers and middlemen, Indonesians and foreigners, who order them and sell them as authentic pieces, in the sense of being old and having been used as precious heirlooms, that they become misrepresentations or fakes.

Pak Lukas as a Sumbanese craftsman is well known in East Sumba and he is proud of his work. The objects made by him are all authentic pieces in a certain sense, whether they are made in a modern fashion, traditional pieces ordered for paying a bride price, or in response to an order to copy an old heirloom from a photograph. So even if we still do not know the answer whether the jewellery in the Liefkes collection date from the nineteenth century or were recently made by Pak Lukas or another goldsmith, Pak Lukas has certainly added his indigenous voice to the complexity of authenticity.

In the course of this article, three categories have become clear with regard to the possible relationship between age and authenticity of the six pieces of gold Sumbanese jewellery in the Liefkes collection. It is possible that some of them are authentic and recently made. As the fieldwork of Wahyu Ernawati has shown, the jewellery is still part of present-day Sumbanese culture, so they could have been made recently for ritual purposes and presented to the art market after having been used as such. In theory, it is also possible that one or two of the pieces are older (nineteenth-century) objects, belonging to the old, sacred treasures of Sumbanese noble families, who sold them on the international art market in the 1970s or 1980s, as Rogers has described sometimes took place. So these would be authentic and of old age. The third possibility is that some of the objects are recent copies made from catalogues or from examples provided, to deceive buyers, since that is also part of reality in present-day Sumba. In that case they are recently made but not authentic. Because provenance is lacking, there is no firm evidence to determine which of these possibilities might apply. The actual age of the jewellery cannot be proven one way or another. But one conclusion is clear: the concept of authenticity in relation to age is flexible and complex.

## References

Adams, Marie Jeanne (1969), *System and meaning in East Sumba textile design: A study in traditional Indonesian art*. New Haven: Yale University.

Brakel, J.H. van [et al.] (1987), *Budaya Indonesia: Kunst en cultuur in Indonesia / Arts and crafts in Indonesia*. Amsterdam: Royal Tropical Institute.

Brinkgreve, Francine & Itie van Hout (2005), 'Java: Gifts, scholarship and colonial rule', in Endang Sri Hardiati & Pieter ter Keurs (eds.), *Indonesia: The discovery of the past*, 100-121. Amsterdam: KIT Publishers.

Brinkgreve, Francine & David J. Stuart-Fox (eds.) (2013), *Living with Indonesian art: The Frits Liefkes collection*. Leiden: Rijksmuseum Volkenkunde/National Museum of Ethnology; Amsterdam: KIT Publishers. (Collection series).

Carpenter, Bruce W. (2011), *Ethnic jewellery from Indonesia: Continuity and evolution: The Manfred Giehmann Collection*. Singapore: Editions Didier Millet.

Chijs, J.A. van der (1885), *Catalogus der ethnologische verzameling van het Bataviaasch Genootschap van Kunsten en Wetenschappen*. 4th edition. Batavia: Albrecht; 's Hage: Nijhoff.

Christie's (1996), *Indonesian pictures, watercolours, drawings and works of art*. Auction catalogue, 24 April 1996. Amsterdam: Christie's.

Christie's (2005), *Indonesian art*. Auction catalogue, 14 March 2005. Amsterdam: Christie's.

Encyclopaedie (1921), *Encyclopaedie van Nederlandsch-Indië: Vierde deel*. 2nd edition. 's-Gravenhage: Nijhoff; Leiden: Brill.

Ernawati, Wahyu (2013), 'Gold jewellery from Sumba', in Brinkgreve, Francine & David J. Stuart-Fox (eds.), *Living with Indonesian art: The Frits Liefkes collection*, 274-279. Leiden: Rijksmuseum Volkenkunde/ National Museum of Ethnology; Amsterdam: KIT Publishers.

Fischer, H.W. & W.H. Rassers (1924), *Catalogus van 's Rijks Ethnographisch Museum: Deel XVII, De oostelijke Kleine Soenda-Eilanden*. Leiden: Brill.

Forth, Gregory L. (1981), *Rindi: An ethnographic study of a traditional domain in eastern Sumba*. The Hague: Nijhoff. (Verhandelingen van het Koninklijk Instituut voor Taal-, land- en volkenkunde, 93).

Fox, James J. (1978), 'Island of gold- and silversmiths,' *Hemisphere*, 22 (12): 24-27.

Geirnaert, Danielle C. (1989), 'The Pogo Nauta ritual in Laboya (West Sumba)', *Bijdragen tot de taal-, land- en volkenkunde*, 145 (4): 445-463.

Girard-Geslan, Maud [et al.] (1999), *Indonesian gold: Treasures from the National Museum, Jakarta*. Brisbane: Queensland Art Gallery.

Holmgren, Jeff & Anita Spertus (1989), *Early Indonesian textiles from three island cultures: Sumba, Toraja, Lampung*. New York: Metropolitan Museum of Art.'

Hoskins, Janet (1988), 'Arts and cultures of Sumba', in Barbier, Jean Paul & Douglas Newton (eds.), *Islands and Ancestors: Indigenous styles of Southeast Asia*, 120-137. New York: Metropolitan Museum of Art; Munich: Prestel-Verlag.

Hoskins, Janet [2010], '*Mamuli*, ear ornament', in Benitez-Johannot, Purissima (ed.), *Paths of origins: The Austronesian heritage in the collections of The National Museum of the Philippines, The Museum Nasional Indonesia and The Netherlands Rijksmuseum voor Volkenkunde*, 238-239. Philippines: ArtPostAsie.

Kate, Herman F.C. ten (1894), 'Verslag eener reis in de Timorgroep en Polynesië: III. Soemba', *Tijdschrift van het Koninklijk Nederlandsch Aardrijkskundig Genootschap,* tweede series 1: 541-638.

Keane, Webb (1988), 'Ombres des hommes et des esprits: Les mamuli de Sumba / Shadows of men and spirits: Mamuli of Sumba', *Art tribal*, 1988, II: 3-15.

Kruyt, A.C. (1922), 'De Soembaneezen,' *Bijdragen tot de taal-, land- en volkenkunde*, 78: 466-608.

*Leven en dood op Sumba / Life and death on Sumba* [1965]. Rotterdam: Museum voor Land- en Volkenkunde. [Text: Monni Adams].

Maxwell, Robyn (2010), *Life, death and magic: 2000 years of Southeast Asian ancestral art*. Canberra: National Gallery of Australia.

Moss, Laurence A.G. (1986), *Art of the Lesser Sunda Islands: A cultural resource at risk*. San Francisco: San Francisco Craft and Folk Art Museum.

Moss, Laurence A.G. (1994), 'International art collecting, tourism, and a tribal region in Indonesia,' in Paul Michael Taylor (ed.), *Fragile traditions: Indonesian art in jeopardy*, 91-121. Honolulu: University of Hawaii Press.

Onvlee, L. (1977), 'The construction of the Mangili dam: Notes on the social organization of eastern Sumba,' in P.E. Josselin de Jong (ed.), *Structural anthropology in the Netherlands*, 151-163. The Hague: Nijhoff. (Translation series / Koninklijk Instituut voor Taal-, land- en volkenkunde, 17).

Onvlee, L. (in samenwerking met OE. H. Kapita en met medewerking van P.J. Luijendijk) (1984), *Kamberaas (Oost-Soembaas)-Nederlands woordenboek, met Nederlands-Kamberaas register*. Dordrecht: Foris Publications. (Koninklijk Instituut voor Taal-, land- en volkenkunde).

Richter, Anne & Bruce W. Carpenter (2011), *Gold jewellery of the Indonesian archipelago*. Singapore: Editions Didier Millet.

Rodgers, Susan (1985), *Power and gold: Jewelry from Indonesia, Malaysia, and the Philippines from the Collection of the Barbier-Mueller Museum Geneva*. Geneva: Barbier-Mueller Museum. (2nd ed. Munich: Prestel, 1990).

Roo van Alderwerelt, J. de (1890), 'Eenige mededeelingen over Soemba', *Tijdschrift voor Indische taal-, land- en volkenkunde* 33: 565-595.

Roos, S. (1872), *Bijdrage tot de kennis van taal, land en volk op het eiland Soemba*. Batavia: Bruining & Wijt. (Verhandelingen van het Bataviaasch Genootschap van Kunsten en Wetenschappen 36, 1).

Rouffaer, G.P. (1911), 'Zeldzame gouden memoeli van Soemba', *Notulen van het Bataviaasch Genootschap van Kunsten en Wetenschappen* 49 (bijlage II): xxix-xxxi.

Sulistianingsih Sitowati, Retno & John N. Miksic (2006), *Icons of art: National Museum Jakarta*. Jakarta: BAB Publishing Indonesia.

Taylor, Paul Michael & Lorraine Aragon (1991), *Beyond the Java Sea: Art of Indonesia's outer islands*. Washington: The National Museum of Natural History.

Vanderstraete, Anne (2012), *Magie van de vrouw: Weefsels en sieraden uit de Gordel van Smaragd*. Rotterdam: Wereldmuseum.

Voorwerpen (1871), 'Voorwerpen afkomstig van Soemba aan het Ethnol. Museum aangeboden doos S. Roos, kontroleur 1e klasse (Notulen 3 Oct. 71, VIII a)', *Notulen van het Bataviaasch Genootschap van Kunsten en Wetenschappen* 9 (1871) (bijlage F): 71, [xxxi]-xxxvi.

Wassing-Visser, Rita (1984), *Sieraden en lichaamsversiering uit Indonesie*. Delft: Volkenkundig Museum Nusantara.

Wielinga, D.K. (1913), 'Soembaneesche verhalen,' *Bijdragen tot de taal-, land- en volkenkunde*, 68: 1-290.

Wielenga, D.K. [1926]. *Soemba*. 's-Gravenhage: Zendings-Studieraad; Algemeene boekhandel voor inwendige- en uitwendige zending. (Onze zendingsvelden 5).

Witkamp, H. (1912-13), 'Een verkenningstocht over het eiland Soemba,' *Tijdschrift van het Koninklijk Nederlandsch Aardrijkskundig Genootschap*, tweede serie, 29: 744-775; 30: 8-27, 484-505, 619-637.

# The Real Stuff: Authenticity and Photography from East Greenland in the Netherlands

## Dr. Cunera Buijs

### Introduction

In the context of anthropological museums, the concept of authenticity is often discussed in relation to the state of artefacts. In seeking to determine whether an object is real or falsified in some way, museum curators and other professionals often use photographs as evidence (Banta & Hinsley 1986; Collier Jr & Collier 1986:13; Edwards 2001:9). It is perfectly admissible to use photographs to prove that objects were already in the museum at a certain date, or that a specific object was in use in a specified village. However, Richter and Carpenter (2011) stress the complex nature of photography:

> *While reference to museum collections and historical photos is an important tool for determining authenticity, it is not foolproof. For example, the Wutulai mask crowns of South East Moluku only appear in a few photos and are absent in collections... The reason they were not seen before is simple: they were so sacred they were concealed from strangers.*
> (Richter & Carpenter 2011: 3)

The general public qualifies museum objects and historical photographs pre-eminently as 'authentic', as the 'real thing'. Yet in the course of my PhD research it became clear that clothing collections from the East Greenland of the 1930s were completely unrepresentative of 'real life' situations. In the early period of colonisation, between 1894 and 1930, most East Greenlanders switched in part to European clothing, such as skirts, textile trousers and jackets. Even so, these garments were absent from museum collections, not because they were sacred, as appears from Richter and Carpenter's example, but because they were simply not collected. European researchers and museum collectors thought them of too little interest at the time, considering them modern and insufficiently exotic. Photographs were deemed more convincing and 'authentic' than the objects in the museums. The same holds good for anthropological photographs taken during fieldwork:

> *Anthropological truth value has been grounded in a cultural representation, extracted from real time, authenticated through real-time observation, captured and stilled through the action of the camera.*
> (Edwards 2001: 157)

But how 'real' are photographs, given that they are artificial images or 'quotation[s] from appearances' (Berger & Mohr 1982: 128). What constitutes reality in, and in respect of, photographs, as references to real objects and situations, or as portraits of (living) human beings? Nearly all the people who appear in the photographs taken in Greenland in the 1930s have since died. We still see them in the photographs as human beings, and yet they no longer occupy the world of reality. Elizabeth Edwards argues that 'photographs are no different than other historical sources in that they must be integrated with other ways of articulating the past' (Edwards 2001: 9).

During Greenland's colonial period, for instance, photographs depicting Greenlandic life were mainly taken by outsiders, in specific circumstances. In many cases, we do not know the conditions in which they were produced. In present-day museum practice, photographs are often 'returned' to the source communities,[1] to the people depicted or their descendants. Experience with this practice, which has been dubbed 'visual repatriation', reveals that photographs of deceased relatives are frequently more important to their descendants than to the museums in which they are stored. Furthermore, for most native peoples it appears that both the image as image and its availability – having access to the picture of a beloved relative or unknown ancestor – is more important than the precise way in which the person is depicted (frontal or in profile as was the custom in physical anthropology, or posed in a photographic studio) or the original material that was used (see Banta & Hinsley 1986; Edwards 2001; Peers & Brown 2006).[2]

> *Photographs taken by professional photographers or government officials have proved to be extremely valuable to aboriginal people as historical documents, even though they are often heavily influenced by the artistic or political inclinations of the photographer and by misguided and racist beliefs resulting in the portrayal of Aboriginal people as savages, beggars, or as the last of a dying race. I have, however, often seen Aboriginal people look past the stereotypical way in which their relatives and ancestors have been portrayed, because they are just happy to be able to see photographs of people who play a part in their family's history. I have watched as a woman viewed photographs taken in the 1890s of her grandmother posing bare-breasted in a photographic studio. This image was in*

---

1 The 'source community' is where the material originated (see Peers and Brown 2003).
2 Biometrical science, biological or physical anthropology traces back to seventeenth century discoveries of new worlds. In the nineteenth century, archaeologists brought back home their fieldwork results, such as artefacts, tools, and human remains, among which skulls were the most collected. It was obvious to use photographs in physical anthropology from the middle of the nineteenth century onwards. The main goal of research was to establish evolutionary models and classifications of body types and races. Photographs were believed to provide 'purely visual evidence' and could 'reveal important truths about the laws of human physical variation' (Banta & Hinsley 1986: 64). After the Second World War the practice of portraying and measuring indigenous peoples became suspect and those concerned were accused of having racist motives. Strong reactions of indigenous organizations from the 1960s onwards resulted in the abandonment of the method of anthropometric photography (Banta & Hinsley 1986: 57ff, 73ff; see also Edwards 2001: 131ff).

*contrast to the way the woman remembered her grandmother, a woman who was always fully clothed. Yet she seemed undisturbed by the uncharacteristic way in which the photographer portrayed her grandmother and was simply grateful for the opportunity to view a photograph of her taken so long ago.* (Aird 2003: 23-25)

The above quotation confirms that certain values and ideas, whether or not articulated, are at stake here. How do people want to be represented in photographs and who has the right to determine the manner of representation? (See also Peterson 2003: 119ff).

Edwards and Hart (2004) state that photographs are more than just images, and stress their object character. Images printed on paper can be touched, turned over to reveal the back, sometimes inscribed with the names of those depicted.[3] A photograph printed from a negative on paper can be retouched manually, put in a frame and hung on the wall of a private home, or exhibited in a museum gallery. This transforms it from two to three dimensions. The material properties of printed photographs make them into social objects *par excellence*. They can be shared, looked at together, exchanged as gifts (see Edwards 2004: 13), consequently becoming part of the broader social sphere. As Edwards and Hart point out: 'Photographs are both images *and* physical objects that exist in time and space and thus in social and cultural experience' (Edwards & Hart 2004: 2).

Outsiders, such as tourists, may visit people in their homes and find photographs made by other visitors, by the local inhabitants, or possibly even by themselves on an earlier visit. Photographs can then be taken on the same spot, this time including the ones taken before. To some extent, the presence of earlier photographs disturbs what the outsider hoped would be an 'authentic' experience (of ethno-tourism), in the ideal sense of discovering peoples not yet discovered by others. This leads to the complex relationship between photography and authenticity, which will be the focus of this article.

## Authenticity and photography

Authenticity has been widely discussed in the field of tourism studies (Cohen 1988, Graburn 1984; Laxon 1991; Littrell, Anderson & Brown 1993). Tourists travel to remote places in search of new experiences, undiscovered areas, unmissable cultural highlights, and unspoiled nature and authentic ways of life, which they feel have been lost from the overpopulated areas of Europe and North

---

3   During fieldwork in East Greenland, while using photo-elicitation as a research method (Collier Jr. and Collier 1986) on material culture studies, one of the viewers looked at the back of a photograph and asked what the sticker 'copyright *Rijksmuseum voor Volkenkunde*, Leiden' meant. He was astonished to learn that the museum 'owns' this photograph, since it is *his* grandfather who is depicted. Printed photographs can trigger unexpected emotional reactions that digitised images may not. It turns out that virtual images have their own specific characteristics and provoke different but equally interesting reactions.

America. 'Tourists may seek opportunities to move from the front stage or more superficial aspects of travel to the back stage authentic life' of a community or region (Littrell, Anderson & Brown 1993: 197-198). Tourists are eager to find 'real life' as they expect it to be, and they yearn to find it still intact in places they want to visit. Yet tourism itself often destroys the unique character of a region, transforming the so-called 'real life' into something more artificial and modern. Tourists hoping to encounter wild native dances performed in authentic costumes often witness 'native-like' expressions of folklore instead. These they duly capture in photographs to take back home as souvenirs, as shadows of culture. Of one Steinberg, who travels the world in search of authentic costumes, we read:

> *Acknowledging her drive for the authentic, [she] labels her tourism behavior 'ethnic costume dementia'. Souvenirs acquired during the special conditions of travel often become among the most valued possessions of individuals.* (Wallendorf & Arnould 1988 in Littrell, Anderson & Brown 1993: 198)

This is reminiscent of fieldwork carried out by anthropologists, who often select remote, rural, homogeneous 'authentic' areas – those 'backward' local places where life appears less disturbed, unchanged as yet by modern Western cultures or their political and economic systems. But anthropologists, like tourists, change the supposedly undisturbed nature of communities that are remote from the Western centres of power.

Authenticity is apparently seen as almost synonymous with the 'real', the pure and undisturbed.[4] It is defined as 'of undisturbed origin, reliable, trustworthy. It derives from the Greek word *autentikos*. [To] authenticate means to establish as true, genuine, or valid' (Thompson 1993: 49).[5] Photography and photographs are often valued as truthful images of life, being evidence of, or genuine recordings of, situation, people, or a specific place in time. This assessment is apparently based on the medium-specific characteristics of photography: the photographer, a camera, and the people depicted were really there. Photographic techniques guarantee an undisturbed and unaltered presentation (and representation) of reality. Nothing else – barring possibly films or artefacts – is seen as containing

---

4   Littrell, Anderson and Brown did research among tourists in North America focusing on and arts and crafts. Tourists' definitions of authenticity encompassed aspects such as 'uniqueness and originality, workmanship, cultural and historical integrity, aesthetics, and function and use. 'Furthermore, they narrate that 'craft authenticity was also associated with characteristics of the craftsperson or artisan, their materials and with the shopping experience. ' (Littrell, Anderson & Brown 1993: 204)

5   Definition of 'authentic' according to etymological source: mid-14c. 'authoritative,' from Old French *autentique* (13c., Modern French *authentique*) 'authentic; canonical,' and directly from Medieval Latin *authenticus*, from Greek *authentikos* 'original, genuine, principal,' from *authentes* 'one acting on one's own authority,' from *autos* 'self' (see auto-) + *hentes* 'doer, being,' from PIE *\*sene-* 'to accomplish, achieve.' The sense of 'entitled to acceptance as factual' is first recorded mid-14c. http://www.etymonline.com/index.php?term=authentic. See also the article on philosopher Nelson Goodman's views on authenticity: 'Goodman's Aesthetics' at http://plato.stanford.edu/entries/goodman-aesthetics/#Aut

more truth than photographs. From its invention, photography became a welcome addition to scientific methods of recording data in the field:

> ... *from early on many pioneer ethnographers were motivated by the desire to document what they observed. Nineteenth-century anthropologists can be accused of having a naïvely realist perspective on film and photography, and of failing to see the constructed nature of the imaginary and cultural biases of their own ways of seeing. ... Photography was viewed as an enhanced presentational method and not merely as a medium of transcription.*
> (Morphy & Banks 1997: 7)

During the twentieth century, however, especially after the 1950s, technological advances improving the scope for photographing processes and social situations during fieldwork were embraced by many anthropologists, especially those working with material culture and the performing arts, including the Dutch scientists Adriaan Gerbrands and Gerti Nooter (see Buijs 2010: Banta & Hinsley 1986). They, like other scientists, such as Baldwin Spencer and F.J. Gillen,

> *were motivated to take photographs not by their evolutionary paradigm but by the documentary ethos of participant observation. Spencer and Gillen's excitement was over the potential of the camera to record what they had seen and felt otherwise inadequate to convey. They focused on recording ritual events and, to a lesser extent, daily life; they used the camera because they could see no other way of recording what occurred* (Morphy & Banks 1997: 8).

In the Netherlands, Gerbrands became the founding father of the ethno-cinematography at the department of Social and Cultural Anthropology of Leiden University. And while working for the Dutch Museum of Education (Museon), Nooter recorded stages of kayak-building in photograph sequences, showing the movements and specific actions of the builder, as well as half-finished parts of the kayak-to-be. Through its narrative sequencing, the series produces effects similar to those of film.

> *Behavior as an object of study cannot be served by single still photographs alone; the sequence of actions through time can increase analytic significance. ... Using photography to record behavior has an additional advantage: it enables the anthropologist to 'bring the field back home' to the laboratory or classroom [or to the museum visitor].*
> (Banta & Hinsley 1986: 66)

In Nooter's opinion, material items were to some extent 'scientific evidence', the very basis for his anthropological research. He photographically recorded processes of making objects, like the construction of a kayak and the making of a woman's knife (*ulu*). Photography provided the means for documenting separate stages in processes of material production, which is difficult to record unambiguously in written language. He collected and photographed objects

*Fig. 1. Building a kayak depicted in a series of photographs taken by Gerti Nooter, 1968, Diilerilaaq,*
*East Greenland (Museon, a. no. 67-4-33-7 ( 10224-58) ; b. no. 68-1-31-2 (10226-32); c. no. 68-1-31-7 (10226-33); d. no. 68-1-31-10 (10226-35) ; e. no. 68-1-31-11 (10226-36); f. no. 68-1-31-14 (10226-39)*

during the 1960s and compared them with older items of material culture, from 1884, 1932 and 1934, housed respectively in the National Museum in Copenhagen, the Museum of Education (Museon) in The Hague, and the Musée de l'Homme in Paris. He interpreted these collections as 'evidence' of material culture, as benchmarks in time. He stated that these collections were the very basis for re-examination and reinterpretation in the future (Nooter, personal communication 1982, see also Morphy & Banks 1997: 17).[6]

Thus photographs – like objects – can be seen as important documents that are unique and real – that is, as authentic documents. Yet East Greenlanders do not view their material culture or daily life as unique phenomena, since they all build their kayaks and almost all East Greenlandic women still use women's knives every day. This raises the question: to whom are foreign cultures and photographs authentic, as testimony to this life? To outsiders, or to local people and their relatives? And what is the level of authenticity of photographs from East Greenland preserved in Dutch museums?

## An overview of East Greenland Collections in the Netherlands

The Arctic region is under-represented in Dutch museums. There are only three major collections from the circumpolar areas. These small but important collections are at the National Museum of Ethnology in Leiden (4,000 objects, including 2,000 from East Greenland), the Museon in The Hague (1,800 objects, mainly from East Greenland), and the Wereldmuseum in Rotterdam (approximately 600 Canadian Inuit objects). There are also roughly 11,000 Tunumiit photographs in the Netherlands: 1,500 at the Museon (copies in Leiden); 4,000 negatives (including prints thereof) and 7,000 colour slides at the National Museum of Ethnology in Leiden.

Between about 1880 and 1930, copies of the same photographs were distributed among several European museums of ethnography. It is often difficult to locate originals, since provenance is not always (well) recorded.[7] During the first half of the twentieth century, museum directors in the Netherlands often

---

6  'Interestingly Ucko justifies the study of material culture objects in exactly the same terms that Mead justifies the use of visual recording methods : 'the essential quality of material culture objects is that reanalysis is possible at all times'.' (Morphy & Banks 1997: 17). Probably these ideas were introduced during the 1950s and 1960s. In that period anthropology was highly influenced by theories of functionalism of Bronislav Malinowski and cultural relativism of Margaret Mead. Both were also active photographers. Nooter was familiar with their work and he was acquainted with the work of Jeness, Van der Steenhoven and Pater van der Velde, who were photographers too.

7  A collection of c. 60 photographs from historical Vladivostok and the native peoples of the Amur region, in the Russian Far East, dating from the end of the nineteenth century, is kept in the National Museum of Ethnology in Leiden. During research in the 1990s, identical photographs were discovered in *Kunst Kamera*, the Russian State Museum of Ethnology and Anthropology in St. Petersburg. Further research may lead to the discovery of copies in the museums of Vladivostok, Khabarovsk, and Yuzhno Sakhalinsk as well.

exchanged collections. The early Arctic collections of objects acquired by the National Museum of Ethnology in Leiden exemplify this practice, having been exchanged with the National Museum of Copenhagen in 1926. The objects were collected, and the photographs taken, in the nineteenth century, mainly by civil servants and merchants in the Danish colonies. Contextual documentation is limited, usually consisting of static descriptions of the culture in question. Evolutionary theories inspired by the German *Kulturkreise* ('cultural field') still dominated museum studies in Europe at the time. Cultures were believed to be evolving from 'primitive' to complex industrial societies. Such theories ignored the unique ways in which indigenous peoples perceive their own cultures. The paradigm of development was a very Western concept that was projected onto cultural 'others'.

## The 1930s: Collections built up by Tinbergen and Van Zuylen

The Tunumiit artefacts at the Museon in The Hague were collected by Niko Tinbergen, a Dutch biologist and Nobel Prize laureate, and by De Bruïne and Van Lohuizen. They originated in the Tasiilaq (Ammassalik) area of East Greenland and were collected during the International Polar Year (IPY) of 1932-33. Tinbergen wrote a PhD dissertation on his ornithological research, besides which he amassed biological and ethnographic collections for the Museon in The Hague. Jacob van Zuylen, leader of the 1932-33 IPY expedition, stayed one year longer than the other members to continue his meteorological research. During this extra year he took about 250 black-and-white photographs in Tasiilaq, Kuummiit, and Diilerilaaq.[8]

After World War II, Dutch museums were enriched by several Arctic collections purchased from art dealers or donated by private individuals. A few university professors donated small collections to the National Museum of Ethnology in Leiden. One of these gifts was a minor but interesting collection of Canadian Inuit objects donated by the Dutch anthropologist Van den Steenhoven in 1957, after a year-long stay among Inuit in Canada while studying Inuit law (Marcus 1998: 192ff; Steenhoven 1959, 1962). After 1960, Dutch anthropologists became more actively involved in fieldwork, combining research with collecting. They grew increasingly interested in Inuit artists as individuals with personal styles at times when the dominant paradigm was still the general category of primitive art, preferably perceiving the makers as 'anonymous' (e.g. Gerbrands 1990; Nooter 1972; Price 1989).

---

8   First displayed in Leiden in 2001 and first published in Buijs & Van Zuylen 2003.

## 1960-1990: Photographs taken by Gerti and Noortje Nooter

From 1960 to 1970 Gerti Nooter was a curator at the Museon in The Hague, and from 1970 to 1990 he was curator of the Native American and Arctic collections in the National Museum of Ethnology in Leiden. He was inspired by Tinbergen's work, and by earlier collections from Greenland in Europe.[9] He conducted fieldwork in East Greenland between 1965 and 1990. Nooter combined anthropological research with collecting, resulting in the wealthy Inuit collections of objects and photographs in The Hague and Leiden.

Nooter focused on the hunting village of Diilerilaaq in East Greenland, where he conducted eight field trips,[10] including a one-year stay in 1967-1968 with his wife Noortje and their three children. At the time, the Diilerilaamiit had a subsistence economy of hunting for seals and fishing. Life was in many ways still traditional, mainly based on kinship interactions between men and women, and among families.

The Nooter family lived and shared their lives with the Diilerilaamiit. The two eldest children went to elementary school in Diilerilaaq and learned Danish and East Greenlandic. Gerti and Noortje paid visits to the people in the village and shared their lives as much as possible. Gerti studied kayak-building and Inuit hunting techniques while accompanying the hunters. He also collected items for the Museon and the Museum of Ethnology in Leiden. Most colour slides were taken by Noortje, who almost always accompanied her husband. The couple photographed a culture in rapid transition, including its hunting and fishing activities, equipment manufacture, travel, and village life. They photographed women and children, school activities, the church, Christian holidays such as Christmas and Easter, *Mitaarneq* or *Uaajeerneq*,[11] sailing on the Sermilik fjord, dog sledding, sewing clothes, and the preparation of sealskins. Their images are surprisingly free of stereotypes of the 'noble savage' or salvage ethnography, the documentation of vanishing cultures (figs. 1 to 5). During their first few visits, they extensively photo-documented the construction and uses of material culture. There are few staged poses. The Nooters indeed recorded life 'as-it-was', depicting 'real people' and their lives as they were lived at the time.

---

9   Nooter was not acquainted with the photographs of Jacob van Zuylen.
10  When Nooter returned in Diilerilaaq after his first stay in 1965, he expected to find a more important fisheries branch of the economy. In the meantime, however, the cod had disappeared due to fluctuations in the sea temperature and the village was mainly focussing on seal hunting as subsistence. Gerti and Noortje Nooter visited Greenland in 1965 (without Noortje), 1967-1968, 1970, 1973, 1975 (in Upernavik, West Greenland), 1977, 1979 (without Noortje, with his eldest son Aartjan), 1982, 1986, 1987 (on the west coast), and 1990 (in Nuuk, West Greenland).
11  The last two events are midwinter activities with disguised performers, vestiges of a former spiritual culture (see Buijs 2004: 74-78, 210).

Nooter conducted research on continuity and changes in material culture (especially kayaks and hunting equipment), subsistence economy, authority patterns and changing sociopolitical structures.[12] East Greenlandic Inuit society was changing rapidly in response to Danish colonisation, modernisation, centralisation, the introduction of currency, and industrialisation. Western influence and modernisation made an imprint on material culture. Nooter was not motivated by 'salvage anthropology', nor did he describe East Greenland as a vanishing culture. He viewed culture as a phenomenon that undergoes constant change, adaptation and transformation. He therefore collected plastic household utensils, sealskin and textile clothing and modern rifles alongside wooden meat containers, blubber lamps, harpoons, fishing equipment, and sealskin kayaks.

Gerti Nooter recorded his experiences in a diary, using these notes for articles, books, and exhibitions about the Tunumiit (Buijs 2006; Buijs and Rosing Jakobsen 2011; Veerman and Buijs 2011). His documentation and the many photographs he took still constitute a valuable source of information today.[13]

## Context and content of Nooter's photographs from East Greenland

The context in which a photograph (or a series of photographs) was taken determines its meaning. Let us have a closer look at the conditions in which the Nooter couple lived, worked, and photographed in East Greenland. The advantage of a prolonged stay, as the Nooter family experienced in 1967-68, is that it enables you to forge close relationships with the local people. This method of 'participant observation' often conflicts with the outsider's role that a researcher will need to some extent, to do 'objective' scientific research. Participant observation is sometimes an obstacle to taking photographs (see e.g. Collier Jr and Collier 1986). In one of the photographs, Gerti Nooter can be seen helping two Greenlanders to transport a heavy bearded seal. The participant

---

12   Some of Nooter's major publications are *Old Kayaks in the Netherlands, Mededelingen van het Rijksmuseum voor Volkenkunde*, Leiden, volume 7, Leiden: E.J. Brill, 1971; *Leadership and Headship: Changing Authority Patterns in an East Greenland Hunting Community*, Mededelingen van het Rijksmuseum voor Volkenkunde, Leiden, volume 7, Leiden: E.J. Brill, 1976; *Life and Survival in the Arctic. Cultural Change in the Polar Regions* (G.W. Nooter ed.), The Hague: Government Publishing Office, 1984. 'The East Greenland Kayaks', in *Contributions to Kayak Studies, Canadian Ethnology Service, Mercury Series* 122, E.Y. Arima et al., eds., Hull: Canadian Museum of Civilization: 319-348. (See Nooter Bibliography in Cunera Buijs, *Continuity and Discontinuity in Arctic Cultures*, CNWS Publications volume 15, Leiden: Centre for Non-Western Studies, 1993: 1137-39.)

13   It is along these same lines that National Museum of Ethnology curators have carried out fieldwork to document social and material change. Their work also focuses on intangible aspects of heritage (e.g., oral history, social practices, and identity symbols) that relate to material culture. The Leiden photographical and artefacts collections from the 1970s to 2010 combined with the 1930s and 1960s objects from the Museon constitute a unique East Greenland collection in Europe. The museum's older East and West Greenland collections have intrinsic value, yet these later historical collections hold even greater interest because 20th century 'modern' objects have been incorporated, thus providing a diachronic and comparative perspective.

*Fig. 2: Massenti Akipe and Gerti Nooter with a bearded seal, 1967 (Museon no. 67-3-58-14 / 10222-31).*

situation prevents him from photographing the action. The situation looks very real; the viewer gets the impression that a spontaneous moment of everyday life has been captured, in spite of the presence of an outsider in the photograph. Yet the description in the museum's archives proves that the scene in the picture was posed. Nooter typed these descriptions at the museum's typewriter back home at the office, while documenting the collection.

In that case, who took this photograph? Over half of the photographs in the Leiden collections were taken by Noortje Nooter, most of them on colour slides. Yet the description of this black-and-white image states: 'The Greenlanders were keen to have me in the photo with the bearded seal they had caught. To the right of the seal is Massanti Akipe, to its left Gert Nooter. On the far right of the picture are two hungry dogs' (www.roots2share.gl).

The explanation omits any mention of who took the photograph. It was not their eldest son Aartjan, whose legs can be seen on the left. Noortje may have taken it herself. Alternatively, one of their local friends may have done so, although no such person is named in the description.

Does it matter who took the photograph? Analysing the Nooters' collection of images, we get the impression that Gerti Nooter made most – if not all – of the series of photographs on material culture. This includes a series on kayak-building and a black-and-white series documenting Billiam Jonathansen's

# Creating Authenticity

*Fig. 3: a-h. Billiam Jonathansen making a woman's knife, 1967 (Museon, a: 67-3-42-30A; b. 673-42-12A; c. 673-42-16A; d. 673-42-19A; e. 673-42-20A_; f. 673-42-26A; g. 67-3-58-1).*

*Fig. 4: Classroom with the Greenlandic pupils on the left and the Nooter boys separated from them on the right, probably for the photograph. Nooter's description: 'Two of my children also attended the school in Diilerilaaq (Tiniteqilaaq): Arthur in front and Aartjan behind in this photo. Unfortunately, in this picture they are sitting separately from the other children, which was normally not the case' (1968; Source: www.roots2share.gl nr 139; Photo: Museum no. 68-3-46-11 /10232-32).*

construction of a woman's knife. Nooter's original description in the archives explains: 'Billiam Jonathansen is making a woman's knife. In his right hand he is holding a small file'. In his exhibition *Life and Survival in the Arctic* (1985), he states that making a woman's knife is man's work. There are only a few colour slides of Billiam Jonathansen engaged in making a woman's knife, probably taken by Noortje Nooter. [14]

Images from the Nooter collections were shown at the community centre in Diilerilaaq during community meetings in 2011. After seeing some of these photos of Billiam making a woman's knife, one of the Tunumiit joked: 'suli Billiam aggestita sakeq, suli, sukangaju, sukangkajugei' ('Billiam is still making a woman's knife – how slowly, very slowly'; Field recordings 2011).

Nooter took most of the photographs purposefully to support his research. They depict his research themes, such as kayak-building, the making and uses of material culture, dog sledding, hunting and fishing, and community meetings at election time (part of the changing political situation and Danish influence in the village). These photographs were made with a specific focus in mind. Gerti

---

14   In 1965 Gerti Nooter used two cameras, one with black and white photographs and the other with colour slides. In 1967/68 he took ca. 30 photographs of the making of a women's knife and Noortje about 5 images.

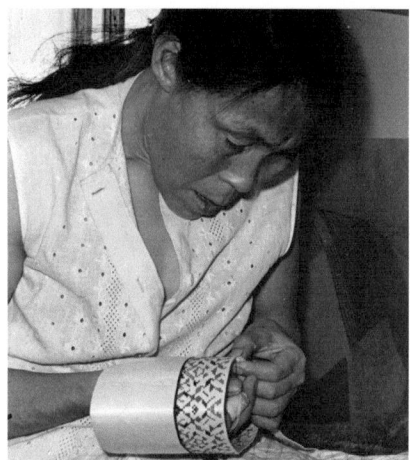
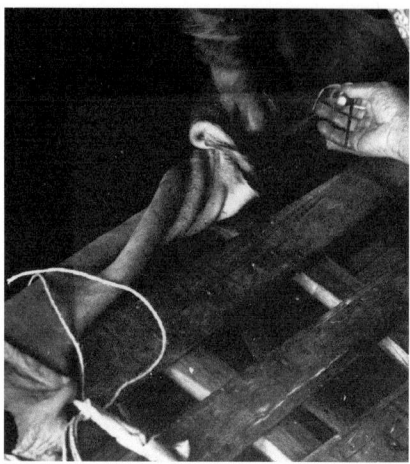

*Fig. 5: Melina Larsen sewing sealskin boots, 1968 (Photo: Museon no. 68-2-15-16 /10228-6).*

*Fig. 6: Sewing the cover on a kayak frame, 1967 (Photo: Museon no. 67-4-33-11 / 10224-62).*

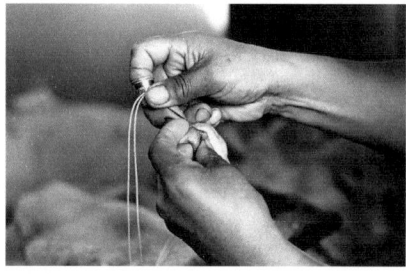
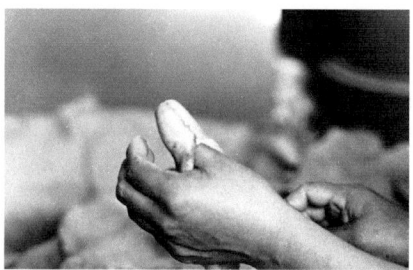

*Fig. 7: Details of sewing a kayak cover; the tip of the kayak is being covered with sealskin, 1967 (Photo: Museon a. no. 67-4-33-9 / 10224-60; b. no. 67-4-33-10 / 10224-61).*

Nooter also photographed local schoolchildren in their classroom (changes brought by Danish institutions constituted another of his research topics). At the same time, these pictures would not look out of place in a family album). Interestingly, the Greenlandic teacher moved Nooter's children to the other side of the room. One of the sons explains this in a manner that differs from Nooter's own account (see fig. 4): 'partly because all the other tables were already occupied' (A. Nooter, personal communication 2013). Again, Nooter's description focuses on his own children, while Greenlanders revisiting the pictures now react to the Tunumiit children in the glass room. It is simply a matter of perspective.

There are also some black-and-white photographs of clothes being sewn, though not as many as might have been expected from a one-year stay, when one recalls that clothing is an essential part of material culture, and that over 10,000 photographs and slides were produced in total. The Nooter family ordered sealskin trousers for their three children and sealskin boots for the entire family. The Nooters had to make a considerable effort and visit seamstresses on multiple occasions to obtain these garments.[15] There are scarcely any photograph series documenting the stages of making a garment. Only Melina Larsen, one of the best seamstresses in Diilerilaaq, can be seen making several parts of a festive costume that had been ordered for Noortje.

One of the photographs focusing in detail on the sewing process is actually a fragment depicting the tip of a kayak being covered by sealskins. As we noted earlier, kayak building was one of Gerti Nooter's main research interests.

There are also photographs of family life, including both black-and-white and colour slides. Nooter's youngest son, *nukatsepartai* Jeroen '*appalotoq*' (the red-haired one) can be seen playing with Moses Jonathansen, both about five years old when the photo was taken. The images look as though they belong to a family album. In a sense they are in fact part of a Nooter family album, but since they were taken a long way away in an unfamiliar country, they strike continental European viewers as exotic. However, photographs taken during the first few months of the Nooters' stay in 1967, while they were staying with the Jonathansens before acquiring their own house in Diilerilaaq, are not posed and are part of daily life as it occurred in the village.

> *Anthropologists thus function in an uncertain relationship with the peoples they study and the wider public. In the field they are in an ambivalent power relationship, seeking access to information over which their subjects have control yet sometimes capitalizing on unequal social or political status in order to gain that access. At home anthropologists are in the sole control of the interpretive process and the product presented to the public. Finally, when the material enters the public domain, anthropologist and subject have very little control over the wider uses and interpretations of the original information.*
> (Banta & Hinsley 1986:23)

Besides the context in which photographs are taken, the context in which they are viewed does at least as much, if not more, to shape interpretation and understanding, depending on the available information about the production (see Berger and Mohr 1982). Greenlanders looking at the two boys playing, one *Kalaaleq* (Greenlander) and the other *Qalluna* (white), pointed out that the Greenlandic boy was Mosesi, but they had no idea of the other boy's name. It did not matter to them (field observations 2011). These issues are a matter of perspective. The fifty-year distance sets the people depicted and the situation back in time, turning them and the images of them into history (see Edwards 2006).

---

15 Noortje Nooter, personal communication 2001, 2009, 2013 and Nooter Diaries 14-9-1967; 23-10-1967; 28-10-1967; 8-11-1967; 9-11-1967; 14-11-1967; 20-11-1967; 22-11-1967; 8-12-1967; 9-12-1967; 11-12-1967; 4-1-1968; 13-1-1968; 23-2-1968 about ordering a Sundays costume of Noortje, this theme is documented with several photographs; 7-3-1968; 11-4-1968. Ca. 20% of the photographs depicting material culture contain clothing related themes.

The photographer clearly plays an important role not only in determining the content or theme of the photographs he or she takes, but also in selecting the scenes or objects to photograph, and in changing the context. In the case of the Nooter photograph collection, two photographers were involved. Noortje Nooter shot some 6,000 of the total of 10,000 images in the collection. Women photographers – even trained photographers, professional journalists or scientists – have frequently been described by male authors as 'unprofessional' or 'amateurs'. The Danish photographer Jette Bang, who worked extensively in Greenland, was a notable exception (see Bernardin *et al*, n.d.: 1-3; Johnson 2010).[16]

> *Yet these photographs, like those made by women teachers [Noortje was a trained and experienced nursery-school teacher], government employees and missionaries, remain largely absent from official public photographic archives, often characterized as amateur, they do not follow the conventions of content, framing, and pose used by the men engaged in 'the grand endeavours' of scientific, anthropological, or aesthetic photography. . . . These photographs constitute a counter-archive, inviting comparisons with other images of indigenous peoples from the nineteenth and early twentieth century.* (Bernardin et al, n.d.:3)

Noortje's photographs have received less public exposure than those taken by her husband. Her work was less accessible in the past, partly because of the specific conditions in which colour slides are preserved in the archives in order to prevent the film and its colours from decaying. Furthermore, the printing and publishing of colour photographs was still expensive in the 1970s and 1980s.

This raises the question of whether significant differences are discernible between the photographs taken by Gerti and Noortje, besides those in the photographic material used. According to a study carried out by Diederik Veerman,[17] Gerti Nooter published 198 photographs (some of them several times), 11 of which were made by himself, 69 by other photographers and 18 by Noortje. Leaving aside the question of limited financial resources, why were so few of Noortje's photographs used in Gerti Nooter's publications? Colour slides might perfectly well have been printed in monochrome instead of full colour.

Noortje Nooter owned her own camera, a semi-automatic Canonette with a 50mm lens. 'I always had the camera set to automatic' (Noortje Nooter, personal communication 2013). In the 1960s, Gerti used a Canon FX with a 85mm lens (as well as 50mm, 28mm, and zoom lenses). A rough analysis of the photographs'

---

16 In 1973, Gerti Nooter met Anna Bang, the daughter of Jette Bang, in East Greenland. Both women were professional photographers. He used several of their photographs as illustrations for his publications and included a few of them in exhibitions. He was impressed by Anna Bang and admired her work (Veerman, *Overzicht* - unpublished).

17 Appendix 1. Veerman n.d. 'Gert Nooter – afbeeldingsanalyse in publicaties', part of the master thesis 'Veranderingen vastgelegd – plaats, perceptie en potentieel van fotografie in het antropologische discours', unpublished (2013).

*Fig. 8 a: Colour slide made by Noortje Nooter, children at play, the family of Erinatek Jonathansen and on the left Jeroen Nooter, 1967 (Photo: Museon no. 67-19-20 / 13162-67-019-020).*

*Fig. 8 b: A boy with a bow and arrow, photo taken by Gerti Nooter, material culture in the context of play, 1968 (Photo: Museon no. 68-3-51-15 / 10234-38).*

*Fig. 9: Black-and-white photograph of three women and children in their festive Sunday best taken by Gerti, Diilerilaaq, 1967 (Photo: Museon 67-3-58-26 / 10222-37). Nooter's description reads: 'Official "Sunday photograph" made on request. From left to right the adults Elisa Sivartsen, Thomassine Tarkissimat and Melina Larsen in costume, on the right (in costume) one of Melina's daughters, Bathsheba, and between them two of Melina's young daughters.' (Media archives of the National Museum of Ethnology, photo no. 10222-37).*

subject-matter reveals that Noortje tended to focus less on people and more on landscapes and outside activities like camping, sailing and sledging. One would expect that she concentrated more on children with or without their mothers, the education or instruction of children by their elders, and children at play. Being a mother herself, Noortje connected with, or related to, the Greenlanders through, or in the presence of, her own offspring. As a professional teacher at a nursery school, one would expect that she was attracted to themes surrounding children and education. Taking the number of photographs into account this turns out not to be the case. What we see is that the slides, taken by Noortje, depicting people show remarkably many images of her own family. On half of the small amount of photographs depicting children, her own children can be seen. Her private interests as a mother influenced the kind of pictures she took. In addition, she also focussed on the themes of interest to her husband, like kayak related themes.

Gerti and Noortje made very few close-up portrait photos. There are fewer than twenty, most of them black-and-white photos dating from 1967/67 taken by Gerti.[18] However, there is one excellent portrait photograph taken by Noortje,

---

18   In later years the amount of portrait photographs increases.

*Fig. 10: Colour slide portrait of Elisa Sivartsen taken by Noortje Nooter, Diilerilaaq, 1968. (Photo: Museon no. 67-019-025 / 13162-67-019-025). Taken on the same occasion and at the same time as fig. 9.*

an appealing colour slide of Elisa Sivartsen, taken with a 50 mm lens from a distance of about two metres. Noortje told me that she took this photograph in the slipstream of Gerti, who was taking a group portrait at the same time. A group of women (Elisa Sivartsen and her adult daughters Thomasine and Melina with some of their daughters, see figs. 9 and 10) asked him to take their picture wearing their Sunday best. Noortje followed, moving closer to the women than usual:

> *Normally I did not dare to take photographs at such close range. But I was following Gerti, who was taking photographs at Thomasine's request. Since it seemed natural to be taking photos at the time, I followed Gerti as I sometimes did, and in this way I was able to take this photograph. It always feels a little awkward to be taking pictures at such close range.* (Noortje Nooter, personal communication 2011)

When people ask a photographer to take their picture, the request transforms him or her into a kind of instrument. There is a brief change in their relationship, at least while the photograph is being taken. As Edwards states: 'The photographer becomes, through re-enactment, facilitator, envisioner or director of continuity, active in the performance of culture.' (Edwards 2001:169)

Both Gerti and Noortje photographed scenes of everyday life in East Greenland, seldom staging them. Their individual interests, professional and otherwise, are reflected in the subject matter of the images. This example suggests that photographers influence the context of a photograph's production (see Banta & Hinsley 1986:23ff.). It may have been more difficult for Noortje to take photographs than it was for Gerti. When Tunumiit came to visit, she

*Fig. 11: Nooter children in their teenage years in East Greenland,1977. From left to right Thomasine Tarkissimat, unknown boy, Jeroen Nooter, Paula Larsen, Arthur Nooter (Photo: National Museum of Ethnology no. 10253-3).*

was expected to be the hostess serving coffee and tea, or baking bread for family and friends. She was also responsible for cooking and cleaning, which left her with less time and energy to take photographs. This helps to explain why most of the photographs taken of Greenlanders visiting their home were made by her husband. It would have been easier for Gerti; the Tunumiit thought him a 'clumsy Westerner' and therefore did not expect him to do what they called 'Greenlandic work' (even though both, in fact, did so). 'It is sad to notice that the Greenlanders are significantly more skilful at handling objects from the European culture than I am at handling theirs.' (Nooter Diaries 2-9-1967.) This comment reflects Nooter's own position and function in Greenlandic society, while at the same time revealing great admiration for the practical skills of the Tunumiit in many aspects of daily life, the subsistence economy, and material culture. How the Greenlanders regarded the Nooter family, however, is less clear. Evans Pritchard (1989: 90) states that the reason why 'so little has been written about how "they" see "us" is that the attention of social scientists has been elsewhere, focused on cultural relativism, ethnic identity, and symbolic systems.' In other words the focus was on 'them' and not on the overall field situation of which the anthropologist is an inextricable part.

Gerti was highly aware of his position as an anthropologist and that his mere presence influenced the local situation. Having his family with him brought certain advantages, in that it made contact with other families easier and more natural, not least because they took their children with them. But it also posed a challenge, especially on their later visits to Diilerilaaq, when their sons became

*Fig. 12: Noortje on a dog sled driven by a Greenlander, West Greenland, 1975 (Photo: taken by Gerti Nooter, National Museum of Ethnology no. 75-3-3 / 10249-2).*

teenagers. If a member of his family acted in way that was 'too European' or at odds with the way of life in Greenland, Gerti would shout to them by way of humorous impulse: 'Mind my research!' His sons would affectionately poke fun at him, calling his winter jersey outfit 'Malinowski trousers'.[19]

The Nooter family did their utmost to adapt to the way of life in East Greenland. 'When I leave for East Greenland I "switch over in my mind" and do things the Greenland way' (Gerti Nooter, personal communication 1982). One very non-Greenland situation involved Nooter's long journeys by dog sledge, on which he took his wife with him. In 1967, during the Nooters' first few days in Diilerilaaq, Lars Jonathansen invited Gerti and his three sons for a short fishing journey in his boat. They left their respective wives Noortje and Asta at home, as Tunumiit men usually do. Noortje was not yet able to speak East Greenlandic, so she was unable to talk to Asta and her children.

> *It was then, as I sat in Asta's house, ill at ease, unable to talk to her and only understanding a few words, that I found myself thinking: is this it? Can I cope with this for months on end?* (Noortje Nooter, personal communication 1998 and 2012)

---

19  Personal communication with Gerti Nooter and his sons, and participant observations in 1982.

After that, Noortje always accompanied her husband on journeys outside the village.[20] They sometimes left their youngest son with one of their Greenlandic friends, while taking the eldest sons with them. Women rarely travelled with their husbands in the winter months, although one would occasionally join a group to take care of the catches made along the way.[21] Gerti himself relied on Noortje as his primary companion. She had a far better grasp and memory of complex kinship relations than he did. At an advanced age, she could still recall the names and family relations of many of the villagers of Diilerilaaq. In December 1967 and March 1968 she kept a diary, and indeed on one occasion added an entry in Gerti's diary, 'when he was too busy to record his observations himself' (Noortje Nooter, personal communication 1994; see also Nooter Diaries).

## Shaping the context

Studying the work of Gerti and Noortje Nooter leads us to conclude that they observed and recorded the everyday lives of the Tunumiit as closely and in as much detail as is possible for outsiders. They did their best to avoid influencing situations, and exerted only a limited impact on context. Their photographs provide a unique 'participant-observer' view of village life in Diilerilaaq from the late 1960s onward.

Even so, situations may arise in which the presence of a researcher/photographer encroaches deeply on the local situation, or creates a new one. I experienced this myself in East Greenland on 6 January 2013. I was doing fieldwork in the city of Tasiilaq as part of the Dutch museum project *Roots 2 Share,* while also researching winter festivals in East Greenland.[22] On 6 January, during the festival of Epiphany, I was told the city would be full of wandering *Mitaartiit* (actors in disguise), who enter people's houses and put on a comical or frightening act while asking for sweets and gifts. I was planning to make some photographs and videos of these events. However, due to a delayed flight I spent all day waiting at the local airport, while *Kongipingasiit* ('Three Kings' Day') slowly passed by; in that season, the sun is already setting at 2 p.m. By the time I returned to Thomasine Umerineeq's house, where I was staying, it was already too dark to take pictures. I lamented the fact that I had missed Three Kings' Day without even seeing a single *Mitaartut*. Suddenly a fully-dressed female *Mitaartut* entered the house. She made an immense amount of noise and threatened the family members with a wooden stick. She wore a stuffed indigenous coat (*amaat*), her clothes arranged

---

20  My interpretation of a causal relationship of the event mentioned before. The character of Noortje herself, who was always eager to participate in holidays and travels abroad, greatly facilitated Gerti's work in Greenland and was a great advantage.

21  In that case there would be a lot of gossip in the village. The activities of a woman accompanying a man during the hunt would not be limited to processing the cash alone. (Field data 1985, 1998, 2001).

22  See www.roots2share.gl and www.roots2share.nl.; and see for Greenlandic winter feast the blog at the website of Rijksmuseum Volkenkunde www.volkenkunde.nl.

to make her look pregnant, she had a doll on her back as if she was carrying a baby, and a mock penis dangling from her loins. She wore a big red cowboy hat and high heels to complete the outfit. The *Mitaartut* danced frantically as she moved from room to room, causing raucous laughter among the family by the sexual gestures she made with her mock penis. I filmed and photographed all these antics. At some point it was revealed that our *Mitaartut* was none other than Thomasine Umerineeq. She had felt sorry for me having missed the *Mitaartut* at the festival of *Kongipingasit*, and had therefore decided to dress up as a *Mitaartut* herself. Her disguise was not typical – 'not authentic' – but her family explained that she is such a good performer that had she performed at the town's sports hall earlier that day, she would have won the *Mitaartut* contest. She adopted the role of Nalikatseq, an authentic character in Tunumiit mythology, one that had been included in earlier *Mitaartut* performances. It was only the context – the fact that she performed for me alone, and did not enter other houses – that was non-original. This brings us back to questions of authenticity in relation to cultural performances and their documentation by outsiders. How authentic is authentic? In other words, are some situations more authentic than others? How authentic are the photographs that I took during this event, which was both a 'real' and an 'artificial' performance at the same time?

In 2011, I accompanied the Museon curator Diederik Veerman to East Greenland. He was looking for the exact location in the mountains where Nooter had photographed the Dutch filmmaker Jan Veenman in 1965. Local schoolchildren helped him to identify the location, and he asked one of them to take a photograph of himself at the same spot and from the same angle as the 1965 photograph, a practice known as 'rephotography' or 'repeat photography'.[23] Another example is the moment in 2010 when Veerman showed Paulus Larsen the published book, which Veerman had edited, and photographed Larsen looking at it. Probably he drew inspiration from one of Nooter's photographs, which he had been studying closely. On a visit to Greenland's west coast in 1990, Gerti Nooter had visited a local library, where he spotted a young West Greenlander reading Nooter's book on old Greenlandic kayaks preserved in the Netherlands, co-published with Rosing in West Greenlandic. Nooter took a photograph of this scene. Is there a difference in the level of authenticity between the two photographs? Should the staged photograph be considered less authentic or 'fake'?[24] On the surface, the images address identical topics, yet they

---

23 See for example http://en.wikipedia.org/wiki/Rephotography (retrieved June 19, 2013).
24 Photographs can easily be manipulated technically. Dramatically altering the situation witnesses the famous photograph of Lenin and Trotsky at a political meeting. Trotsky was removed from the photograph and the manipulated image was published widely, which had the intended effect of changing history. (David King, *The Commissar Vanishes: The Falsification of Photographs and Art in Stalinist Russia*, New York 1997. http://www.amazon.co.uk/The-Commissar-Vanishes-Falsification-Photographs/dp/0862417244/ref=wl_it_dp_o_pC_nS_nC?ie=UTF8&colid=39XG1FKSGD1LR&coliid=I2R2TOEF4KNOIH See also John Tagg, *The Disciplinary Frame: Photographic Truths and Capture of Meaning*, Minneapolis, MN 2009.

were made in completely different contexts. The more recent, to some extent 'shaped' or manipulated context has its own premises and its own background, recording a different social process, situated in the twenty-first century.

## Authenticity as a process of selection

Selection influences interpretation. This applies both to the selection of certain scenes from everything that is visible in reality and to the selection of certain photographs from a large number of them. This severely limits the scope of our understanding of documented actions or situations. If the viewer cannot see all the photographs that have been taken, – getting a 'fuller picture', so to speak – he or she is offered only a fragmentary and isolated image. In the Nooter collection, for instance, we find a photograph depicting women wearing beautiful bead-collar costumes. The viewer gets the impression of an exotic people, and might conclude that these people always dress in this way. Other photographs in the series show local people walking down the street to the central square in the village in order to pose for East Greenland photographers, who are taking pictures on the occasion of the youngsters' Confirmation in church. That explains why they are wearing festive costumes, which would often be ordered especially for this event.

Another example of selection is a photograph showing Gerti Nooter in Diilerilaaq's main square, looking through the lens of a camera on a tripod. A recent caption wrongly explains: 'Gerti Nooter taking photographs'. This is what an experienced museum employee was expecting to see. However, other photographs from this series, which were not selected for publication, prove otherwise. On one of these we see Gerti and Noortje Nooter walking through the village, passing a film camera that someone has placed on a tripod. In the following photographs we see Gerti taking a quick look through the camera, which wasn't his. However, in the first photograph in the sequence we see a Greenlander standing at some film equipment, recording the Confirmation ceremony. This example demonstrates the difficulty of avoiding stereotypes and Western bias when interpreting what we see. A viewer's implicit cultural frame of reference is often a decisive factor when it comes to interpreting the photographs he or she is looking at.

Some photographs are selected time and again, while others are never used at all. The same small few images keep reappearing in publications and exhibitions, in a sense becoming stereotyped representations of the peoples or cultures depicted. These isolated photographs indeed take on a life of their own, divorced from the original context or flow of multiple images from which they originated. Stereotypes often reveal more about selection processes than about the people who are represented. Selections made by exhibition makers, journalists, anthropologists, or museum PR staff, for instance, may be made with specific aims in mind. Almost never are those depicted in photographs

*Fig. 13: Dina Jonathansen, Diilerlaaq, 1968. (Photo: Museum no. 68-1-31-36a/ 10226-52). Nooter's caption, published in Headship and Leadership, explains: 'Dina, one of Billiam Jonathansen's daughters, grinding coffee. The dishes and oil lamps standing by the sink were bought at the store. The large hooded seal lying on the floor was killed by Billiam's son Erinatek' (Nooter 1976: 54).*

responsible for selecting photographs for publication. National and international museums are powerful institutions, and their collections, which exist at such a great physical distance from native communities, are hard to access, even in the digital age. In addition, skewed power relations are involved. Yet Aird has stated that the production and selection of photographs is sometimes less important to native peoples: 'I have, however, often seen Aboriginal people look past the stereotypical way in which their relatives and ancestors have been portrayed, because they are just happy to be able to see photographs of people who play a part in their family's history (Aird 2003: 25).

For some of his articles, Nooter made selections from the photographs and slides he and his wife had taken in Greenland.[25] Nooter selected these for their photographic or aesthetic qualities (he included Anna Bang's photographs, for example), depending on the subject matter of publications (e.g. kayaks, changing material culture and leadership patterns, and fishing activities), and readily available photographs printed before. Many of the photographs selected by Nooter show a combination of traditional cultural traits with Western technologies and imported products. These images represent the village of Diilerilaaq and its inhabitants as not only a traditional society of seal hunters still employing kayaks, but also linked to the wider world of globalization.

As I have already noted, taking photographs during fieldwork is itself a selection process (see also Banta & Hinsley 1986; and Edwards 1997). Additional choices are made during the technical processing of photographs, which is beyond the scope of this article.[26] Afterwards, while incorporating the results of research and photographic material into exhibitions and publications, another selection process takes place. Anthropologists scarcely have any influence nowadays in the media (including the social media) on the use of their visual materials, and 'their' people are represented by policy-makers at museums and elsewhere for PR purposes. Native peoples often express their frustration about this, and claim the right to have a say in the way they are represented.[27]

## Source communities and 'the authentic experience'

In 2010 the 'visual repatriation' project *Roots 2 Share* was launched officially, after a preparatory period in which the photographs taken in Greenland by the Nooters proved to be of great emotional value and significance to the Diilerilaamiit. They considered the images to be part of their personal, family

---

25   Following research on the collection done by Veerman, Nooter published a 1965 black-and-white photograph of a kayak placed on an oil container along the coast of Sermilik Fjord, in five of his publications. A photograph from 1970, also appearing in five publications, shows Paulus Jonathansen with his family in their kitchen, while Paulus' wife Ebba – in a glittering short dress from Denmark – is scraping a sealskin on a scraping board (*qapiapik*). Other popular photographs featured the Danish princess Margarethe visiting Diilerilaaq in 1973; Harald Boassen in his kayak (1967); Harald Boassen pointing the way (1973, photograph by Anna Bang), Paulus Jonathansen fishing cod (1967); the young Pili Tarkissimat getting lessons in a kayak (1968); and three hunters returning to the village in their kayaks (1973). (D. Veerman – Appendix 1. 'Gert Nooter : analysis' in master's thesis 'Veranderingen vastgelegd, Plaats, perceptie en potentieel van fotografie in het antropologische discours', 2013 (unpublished).

26   For example, sepia images tend to evoke romantic notions. Nooter's negatives were developed by the photography department of Museon (1965 and 1967-68) and by Ben Bekooy, photographer at the National Museum of Ethnology (1970-1986). Bekooy worked with Nooter for many years. He recalls: 'Gerti had a strong preference for printing his photographs in high contrast, as can be seen on the photograph of the kayak on a drum container. The processing of photographs was connected to the technical constraints of photographing in cold and snowy areas. Too much exposure to light in processing the negatives into positives would turn white snow into grey, and Gerti definitely did not want that!" (Ben Bekooy, personal communication 2011.

27   See also Pia Arke's critical essays.

*Fig. 14: Screenshot with the recently-added story of Mikilina Larsen, a twenty-three-year-old East Greenlander, written by herself in East Greenlandic, on the website www.roots2share.gl.*

and regional histories, and important documents of their culture and identity. The website www.roots2share.gl was developed, hosted by the Museon in The Hague. Many of the Nooter photographs were scanned and returned in digital form to the communities from which they originated and where they can now be accessed. As a product of cross-cultural interaction, the photographs depict the ancestors of present-day Tunumiit and carry multiple meanings: ethnological and/or exotic meanings for most viewers outside East Greenland (including the Dutch), and historical or ancestral meanings for the people of Diilerilaaq. Many stories have been told about these photos and we expect many more stories to be told through them.

In May 2011, we introduced the website to the source communities in East Greenland.[28] Carl-Erik Holm, director of the Ammassalik Museum, arranged for an introduction in the museum including coffee and tea with plenty of biscuits and sweets (in accordance with the national tradition of *kaffemik*). Community consultation meetings were held at the *kaatersortapik* (community centre) in the village of Diilerilaaq. Using a laptop and a beamer we introduced a stand-alone version of the website and showed about 900 photographs. For research purposes we filmed the feedback from the audience. Afterwards we visited some of the

---

28  A 'source community' is where the collected materials originated, including audio and video recordings (see Peers and Brown 2003). In January 2012, nine schoolchildren and two teachers visited the Netherlands and donated their handmade art objects to the museum in Leiden. In the winter of 2012/2013, the curator of the Leiden museum revisited the area for an update of the project and visited the school (Anne Mette Holm being the teacher in charge for Roots 2 Share) in Kulusuk to extend the project to that village as well.

families at their homes to gather additional information on the photographs, and stories about them, with the aid of Kaaleeraq Larsen, a local hunter aged twenty-two (with a Facebook account). The stories have been posted (in East Greenlandic) on the website. Nooter's photo captions have been translated into Danish and English as well as West and East Greenlandic for the website.

Responses from the community have been largely positive. One of the meetings was chaired by Paulus Larsen, a local coordinator and previously our guest in the Netherlands. As a result, many of the older visitors stepped forward to tell their stories to their own people, thereby gradually taking their fair share of 'ownership' in the project. We left a laptop in the village and another one with the museum in Tasiilaq. The unreliable and expensive internet service in the village remains a challenge.

A school programme was added to the project. In 2011 we were inspired by our visits to the senior classes (students aged fifteen to sixteen) at the high school in the district capital of Tasiilaq. In 2012 I visited the school in Kulusuk and launched a similar project with the help of the teacher Anne Mette Holm. Some of the pupils were amazed by what the pictures showed them ('Did they really butcher seals right there in the kitchen?'); for others, the sight of the photos produced unexpected emotional experiences. The pupils were asked to interview the community elders and to record the interviews on user-friendly audio recorders. They were also asked to transcribe the spoken words to paper, translate the texts into English and upload them to the website. Anna Kuitse Kuko, teacher and deputy director of Tasiilaq's regional school, visited the homes where the elders were living, together with her pupils. Some of those interviewed were the students' grandparents, which created a new connection between the generations. The way the photos are dealt with now on the internet not only produces a connection with the past, but also fits into the present day; we may even make a link to Facebook, on which the students are very active.

Repatriating images in digital format or as paper copies is not the same as returning the original photographs.[29] Nevertheless, the Tunumiit people responded emotionally and with evident pleasure to this initiative (Buijs and Rosing Jakobsen 2011; Veerman and Buijs 2012). During the visit of consultants in the Netherlands, Thomasine Tarkissimat found herself confronted with the image of her deceased twin sister. Thomasine was deeply moved and she approached the image on the wall and touched it. The act of touching this image became in a sense a new 'authentic experience'. Having access to the images and being able to make prints from them on paper seems to be more important than owning the originals or being involved in their conservation, although claims in that direction may develop in the future. Since the start of our project, East Greenlanders have been able to add information to the collections of photographs

---

29 The question to what extent are original, fysical photographs authentic, compared to virtual images is beyond the scope of this article. See for images as objects the work of Elisabeth Edwards and Janice Hart 2004 and Edwards 2006.

taken in East Greenland that are preserved in Dutch museums. The launch of the Roots2Share-website has made them less dependent than in the past on museum anthropologists for selections and contextual information related to the images. Greenlanders reflect on life in the past, retrieving photographs of people from earlier generations, or perhaps of their younger selves. Information they might add is different from stories told by spokesmen from these earlier generations in the past. Stories told by Greenlanders display different levels of connectedness compared to those told by Europeans. It is this connectedness that makes the newly-added texts authentic on the basis of their own premises.

## Conclusion: Creating authenticity

> *The camera is a kind of passport that annihilates moral boundaries and social inhibitions, freeing the photographer from any responsibilities towards the people photographed... The photographer is supertourist, an extension of the anthropologist, visiting natives and bringing back news of their exotic doings and strange gear... Meaningful interaction is replaced by the passive observance of spectacles and attractions... Travel may become a strategy for collecting pictures, and tourists turn into image junkies, experiencing the world vicariously through the associated images they consume.*
> (Laxon 1991: 372)

Most museum collections in Europe, including those in the Netherlands, were originally built up within colonial contexts. There is no colonial relationship between East Greenland and the Netherlands, but there is nonetheless a skewed balance of power regarding the control of, and access to, the Tunumiit collections. The East Greenland photographs from the Nooter collection, together with related knowledge, constitute the nucleus of a so-called visual repatriation project, which was initiated by two Dutch museums in collaboration with two museums in Greenland, and is being carried out in cooperation with representatives of the local communities. Photographs and objects embody information, revealed through the interactions with people who are willing to share their knowledge about them. Their responses can teach us many things. During nearly two decades of regularly showing 'old' photographs to the people in East Greenland, I noticed that Tunumiit reacted strongly and often very emotionally to the sight of members of early generations, their deceased relatives. Looking at the images together often gave the people immense joy. In some regard we may call this an 'authentic experience'. For the Tunumiit, their kinship relations and daily lives are neither accentuated nor valorised as 'special'. Even so, looking at photographs taken over forty years ago, taken in their village, is a unique experience. Some people became so emotional that they started crying at the sight of the images. This leaves us with the question to what extent these emotional reactions are indicative of 'authenticity'.

The photographs are evidence of cross-cultural encounters, depicting members of the Nooter family in contact with Diilerilaaq villagers. They therefore belong just as much to the cultural heritage of the Nooter family as to the inhabitants of Diilerilaaq. The lives of the Tunumiit have been extensively documented in over 10,000 images stored in the Netherlands today. These images depict them 'just as life looked' with little interference on the photographers' part. In that sense, the Nooter photographs can be labelled 'authentic', although the photographer's controlling hand is obvious:

> *The person behind the camera also intervenes... The photographer's selection and recording of a particular moment takes it out of its context in the flow of real-life experience and places it in another, possibly unrelated, context. The photographer can alter the elements of that moment by manipulating the setting, posing the subject of the image before recording it, and later, placing the image next to captions, text, other photographs, or in a particular form of presentation.* (Banta & Hinsley 1986:25)[30]

The term 'authenticity' in general, and more especially in relation to photography, is ambiguous. It is a selection process of aspects that outsiders label 'unique', 'original', 'real', 'traditional' and so forth, for instance in tourist literature. Looking at an isolated photograph omits the contextual information that makes it more relevant, and part of social life, although the mere sight of a picture is in itself a 'real' experience. To Nelson Goodman,

> *pictorial representation is always relative to the conceptual framework (that is, to the system of classification) within which a picture should be interpreted, in the same way in which vision is relative to the conceptual frameworks with which one approaches the visual world.* (Goodman 2010:10)

We have seen that in interpreting photographs one can scarcely avoid imposing one's own frame of reference and stereotypes. The mere presence of people taking pictures in the field influences the situation. 'Instead, a surrogate, covert "staged authenticity" emerges' (Cohen 1988:372).

Taking all this into account, we may conclude that authenticity is a constructed reality, bound up with selection and classification processes. Images, like representations and examples, are never absolute. As Goodman points out, 'they are relative, in particular relative to established use' (Goodman 2010:13). Museum publishing and exhibiting practices can thus be designated as 'established use'. 'Authenticity is a personally-constructed, contextual, and changing concept. Tourists are active creators of meaning in their tourism experiences

---

[30] For an extreme example of manipulating setting, see Edwards 2001:166, in which the death of Kwoiam was later posed and performed in a theatrical way, against the will and feelings of the people involved.

rather than passive receivers' (Littrell, Anderson and Brown 1993:199) – and so are anthropologists.

Whereas the very concept of authenticity is in itself 'unreal', we may conclude that photographs can be dealt with as evidence of a real situation and can be exchanged as objects (the 'real stuff'). That photographic experience creates new social contexts that are part of social life and possess value to relatives of those pictured. This experience reveals 'real' reactions, also from other viewers like museum visitors, in 'artificial contexts'. Or to put it differently: what we see is only partly what we get.

## Acknowledgements

I am most grateful to the people of East Greenland, the Tunumiit, who supported me for so many years in several ways while I did my research and lived amongst them. Their enthusiasm for the Roots2Share project has been very important for me. I would like to thank my colleagues Carl Erik Holm and Aviâja Rosing Jakobsen from Greenland for their kind cooperation and Diederik Veerman, my colleague at the Museon in The Hague, for sharing some information with me from his master's research on Nooter's photography in the widest sense of the word. Last but not least I am very grateful to Taco Hidde Bakker who commented on numerous details in this article on the basis of his expertise as a photographic scientist.

## References

Aird, Michael (2003), 'Growing up with Aborigines', in Christopher Pinney & Nicolas Peterson (eds.), *Photography's Other Histories*, 32-40. Durham, London: Duke University Press.

Banta, Melissa & Curtis M. Hinsley (1986), *From Site to Sight, Anthropology, Photography, and the Power of Imagery.* Cambridge, Massachusetts: Peabody Museum Press, Harvard University Press.

Bernardin, Susan, Melody Graulich, Lisa McFarlane & Nicole Tonkovich (eds.) n.d., *Trading Gazes, Euro-American Women Photographers and Native North Americans, 1880-1940.* New Brunswick, New Jersey. London: Rutgers University Press.

Berger, John & Jean Mohr (1982), *Another Way of Telling.* New York: Pantheon Books.

Broekhoven, Laura & Cunera Buijs (2010), 'Introduction', in Laura van Broekhoven, Cunera Buijs & Pieter Hovens (eds.), *Sharing Knowledge and Cultural Heritage Heritage: First Nations of the Americas. Studies in*

*Collaboration with Indigenous Peoples from Greenland, North and South America*, 13-22. Leiden: National Museum of Ethnology and Sidestone Press.

Brown, Alison K. & Laura Peers (2006), *Pictures Bring Us Messages, Photographs and Histories from the Kainai Nation*. Toronto, University of Toronto Press.

Buijs, Cunera (2006), *The East Greenland Collections of G.W. Nooter (1930-1998)*. Leiden: National Museum of Ethnology, http://www.volkenkunde.nl/collections/e-publications, accessed 30 April 2008.

Buijs, Cunera (2010), 'Related Collections, Sharing East Greenlandic Material Culture and Photographs', in Laura van Broekhoven, Cunera Buijs & Pieter Hovens (eds.), *Sharing Knowledge and Cultural Heritage: First Nations of the Americas. Studies in Collaboration with Indigenous Peoples from Greenland, North and South America*, 17-39. Leiden: National Museum of Ethnology and Sidestone Press.

Buijs, Cunera & Aviâja Rosing Jakobsen (2011), 'The Nooter photo collection and the Roots2Share project of museums in Greenland and the Netherlands', *Etudes/Inuit/Studies* 35 (1-2): 185-187.

Buijs, Cunera & Peter van Zuylen (2003), 'Jaap van Zuylen, En Hollænder i Østgrønland (1932-1934)', *Tidskriftet Grønland* 5: 203-214.

Cohen, Erik (1988), 'Authenticity and commoditization in tourism', *Annals of Tourism Research* 15: 371-386.

Collier Jr., John & Malcolm Collier (1986), *Visual Anthropology, Photography as a Research Method*. Albuquerque: University of New Mexico Press.

Edwards, Elisabeth (1997), 'Beyond the boundary: a consideration of the expressive in photography and anthropology', in Marcus Morphy & Howard Banks (eds.), *Rethinking Visual Anthropology*, 53-81. New Haven, London: Yale University Press.

Edwards, Elisabeth (2001), *Raw Histories, Photographs, Anthropology and Museums*. Oxford, New York: Berg.

Edwards, Elisabeth (2006), 'Photographs and the Sound of History', *Visual Anthropology Review* 21 (1-2): 27-46.

Edwards, Elisabeth & Janice Hart (2004), 'Introduction: Photographs as Objects', in Elisabeth Edwards & Janice Hart (eds.), *Photographs Objects Histories, On the Materiality of Images,* 1-16. London, New York: Routledge.

Evans-Pritchard, Deirdre (1989), 'How 'They" see "Us", Native American Images of Tourists', *Annals of Tourism Research* 16: 89-105.

Fienup-Riordan, Ann (2005), *Yup'ik Elders at the Ethnologisches Museum Berlin: Fieldwork Turned on Its Head.* Seattle: University of Washington Press.

Gerbrands, Adriaan A. (1990), 'Made by man. Cultural anthropological reflections on the theme of ethnocommunication', in Pieter ter Keurs & Dirk Smidt (eds.), *The Language of Things: Studies in Ethnocommunication in Honour of Professor Adrian A. Gerbrands*, 45-77. Leiden: National Museum of Ethnology, 25.

Graburn, Nelson (1984) 'The evolution of tourist art', *Annals of Tourism Research* 11: 393-419.

Johnson, Leise (2010), 'Speaking images. Digital repatriation of the Jette Bang photo collection to Greenland', in Laura van Broekhoven, Cunera Buijs & Pieter Hovens (eds.), *Sharing Knowledge and Cultural Heritage: First Nations of the Americas. Studies in Collaboration with Indigenous Peoples from Greenland, North and South America*, 53-60. Leiden: National Museum of Ethnology and Sidestone Press.

Goodman, Nelson (2010), 'Goodman's Aesthetics', *Stanford Encyclopedia of Philosophy*, http://plato.stanford.edu/entries/goodman-aesthetics/#Aut

King, J.C.H. & Henrietta Lidchi (eds.) (1998), *Imaging the Arctic.* London: British Museum Press.

Krupnik, Igor & Vera Oovi Kaneshiro (2011), *Neqamikegkaput, Faces We Remember, Leuman M. Waugh's Photography from St.Lawrence Island, Alaska, 1929-1930.* Washington: Smithsonian Institution Scholarly Press.

Krupnik, Igor & Elena Mikhailova (2006), 'Landscapes, Faces, and Memories: Eskimo Photography of Aleksandr Forshtein, 1927-1929', *Alaska Journal of Anthropology* 4 (1-2): 92-112.

Laxon, Joan D. (1991) 'How "we" see "them", Tourism and Native Americans', *Annals of Tourism Research* 18: 365-391.

Littrell, Mary Ann, Luella F. Anderson & Pamela J. Brown (1993), 'What makes a craft souvenir authentic?' *Annual of Tourism Research* 20: 197-215.

Marcus, Alan Adolph (1998) 'Reflecting on Contested Images', in J.C.H. King and Henrietta Lidchi (eds), *Imaging the Arctic*, 190-197. London: British Museum Press.

Morphy, Marcus & Howard Banks (1997) 'Introduction, rethinking visual anthropology', in Marcus Morphy & Howard Banks (eds.), *Rethinking Visual Anthropology*, 1-36. New Haven, London: Yale University Press.

Nooter, G.W. (1971), 'Old Kayaks in the Netherlands', *Mededelingen van het Rijksmuseum voor Volkenkunde* 17. Leiden: E.J. Brill.

Nooter, G.W. (1975) ' Ethics and Aquisition Policy of Anthropological Museums in the Netherlands', in P. Kloos & H.M Claessen (eds.), *Current Anthropology in the Netherlands*, 156-164. Rotterdam: Anthropological Branch of the Netherlands Sociological and Anthropological Society.

Nooter, G.W. (1976) *Leadership and Headship; Changing Authority Patterns in an East Greenland Hunting Community*, Mededelingen van het Rijksmuseum voor Volkenkunde 20. Leiden: E.J. Brill.

Nooter, G.W. (1980) 'Improvisation and Innovation; Social Consequences of Material Culture', in W.R. Van Gulik, H.SS. Van der Straaten and G. D. Van Wengen (eds.), *From Fieldcase to Showcase: Research, Aquisition and Presentation in the Rijksmuseum voor Volkenkunde*, 113-122. Amsterdam, Uithoorn: J.C. Gieben Publishers.

Nooter, G.W. (1984) '1884-1984: A Century of Change in East Greenland', in G.W. Nooter (ed.), *Life and Survival in the Arctic, Changes in the Polar Regions*, 121-144. The Hague: Staatsuitgeverij.

Peers, Laura (2010), 'Afterword', in Laura van Broekhoven, Cunera Buijs & Pieter Hovens (eds. ), *Sharing Knowledge and Cultural Heritage: First Nations of the Americas. Studies in Collaboration with Indigenous Peoples from Greenland, North and South America*, 187-193. Leiden: National Museum of Ethnology & Side Stone Press.

Peers, Laura & Alison K. Brown (eds.) (2003), *Museums and Source Communities*. London, New York: Routledge.

Peterson, Nicolas (2003), 'The Changing Photographic Contract: Aborigines and Image Ethics', in Christopher Pinney & Nicolas Peterson, *Photography's Other Histories*. 119-146. Durham, London: Duke University Press.

Pinney, Christopher & Nicolas Petersen (eds.) (2003), *Photography's Other Histories*. Durham & London: Duke University Press.

Price, Sally (1989), *Primitive Art in Civilized Places*. Chicago: University of Chicago Press.

Richter, Anne and Bruce W. Carpenter (2011), *Gold Jewellery of the Indonesian Archipelago*. Singapore: Editions Didier Millet.

Roots2Share (2011), Roots2Share website (online at: www.roots2share.gl; several updates).

Smith, David A. (2008) 'From Nunavut to Micronesia: Feedback and Description, Visual Repatriation and Online Photographs of Indigenous Peoples', *Partnership: The Canadian Journal of Library and Information Practice and Research* 3(1): 1-19.

Steenhoven, Geert van den (1959), *Legal Concepts among the Netsilik Eskimos of Pelly Bay, N.W.T.*. Ottawa: Northern Co-ordination and Research Centre, Department of Northern Affairs and National Resources, NCRC-59-3.

Thompson, Della (1993), *The Oxford Dictionary of Current English*. Oxford: Oxford University Press.

Veerman, Diederik & Cunera Buijs (2012), 'Roots 2 Share, From Archive photographs to Digital Heritage Forum', *Digital Journal of the European Museum Academy* (EMA). http://www.europeanmuseumacademy.eu

# Alternative Authenticities (and Inauthenticities)[1]

## Prof. Sally Price

Anthropology and Art History have traditionally been very different beasts, dealing with different kinds of materials, making different assumptions, asking different kinds of questions, and even – it could be argued – adopting different positions on political and ethical issues. But one point of intersection is the keen interest that both anthropologists and art historians have shown for dealing with the concept of authenticity. This paper addresses the issue of authenticity via a simultaneous interrogation of inauthenticity – both forgery and falsifications of other sorts.

I begin with a quote by Ernst Gombrich, arguably the most distinguished art historian of the twentieth century, in a discussion about art forgery from his book *Art and Illusion*:

> *Logicians tell us ... that the terms 'true' and 'false' can only be applied to statements, propositions. And whatever may be the usage of critical parlance, a picture is never a statement in that sense of the term. It can no more be true or false than a statement can be blue or green. Much confusion has been caused in aesthetics by disregarding this simple fact. It is an understandable confusion because in our culture pictures are usually labeled, and labels, or captions, can be understood as abbreviated statements. ... Without much reflection, we can all expand into statements the laconic captions we find in museums and books. When we read the name 'Ludwig Richter' under a landscape painting, we know we are thus informed that he painted it and can begin arguing whether this information is true or false.* (Gombrich, 1959: 67-68)

Eric Hebborn, a notorious forger, seconded Gombrich's position, declaring in his autobiography that

> *It is the labeling, and only the labeling, of a picture which can be false, and contrary to popular belief there is not and can never be a false painting or drawing, or for that matter any other work of art. A drawing is as surely a drawing as a rose is a rose is a rose, and the only thing that may possibly be false about it is its label – its attribution. What a relief this truth should be for the art world! No longer need the expert, the collector, or anybody else worry about fakes. The term can be expunged from the art lover's vocabulary.*

---

1   This paper is a published version of a talk given on 30 November 2012, at the Symposium 'What is authenticity? Questions of authenticity and authentication in ethnographic museums' (Rijksmuseum Volkenkunde/National Museum of Ethnology, Leiden).

*All we need worry about now is educating the experts to attach the right label.*
(Hebborn 1991: 357)

And Orson Welles, devoting his last major film ('F for Fake/Vérités et mensonges,' 1974) to what Wikipedia dubbed 'a meandering investigation of the natures of authorship and authenticity,' traced responsibility for the divide between truth and falsehood directly to the experts who authenticate attributions rather than to the forgers: 'The experts' he declared, 'are God's own gift to the faker'.

In other words, if art can't be true or false any more than statements can be blue or green, deception about 'authentic' versus 'inauthentic' artworks can only take place in attributions, labels, and stories about the objects, not in the objects themselves. It follows that fakes aren't created by artists, but rather by the experts who authorize attributions. Physical objects are never inauthentic; only the claims that are made about them can be inauthentic. This is a crucial distinction. And it's in that sense that forgery and plagiary are two sides of the same coin – plagiary being a person's fraudulent claim to be the creator of a particular text, and forgery being a person's fraudulent claim *not* to be the creator of a particular object.

Now, still by way of introduction to my concrete examples (and in order to create balance in my comments between art history and anthropology), let's listen to an anthropologist/historian who comes at the subject of authenticity in a very different mode. Greg Dening, writing about the Marquesas Islands in the Pacific, uses the metaphor of the beach to talk about the ways that objects can be stripped of their original meaning (and hence their cultural authenticity) as part of their physical (spatial) displacement to a Western museum. He underscores the conceptual transformations that occur when relics pass from 'one side of the beach to the other' and come to exist, as he puts it, 'only by virtue of the fact that [they] are preserved in museums, archives and libraries around the world'. He continues:

> *To discover them in their Diaspora demands a pilgrimage to cities on every continent .... Old men's white beards, ankle-bands of hair, gorgets of turtle shell, stone tiki clubs, spears and paddles, stilt-stirrups, bowls and tapa-covered skulls ... lie under glass or on shelves and walls, their colors faded to dull browns and grays. They seem disconnected and disembodied, trophies of adventurous moments, not expressions of the spirit ... who made them. They tell no stories. No one really knows them. Usually they are marked 'Marquesan this' or 'Marquesan that'. ... They are traded, exhibited, prized. They become part of aesthetic conversations about art or primitivity. ... They become evidence in debates about dispersal points and cultural relationships. Or they are classified, made into typologies. ... They become problems of preservation and committees will sit and wonder what is the effect of air-conditioning on old men's beards. They are thus transformed, made over into a currency of other cultural values.*
> (Dening, 1980: 271, 273).

The common ground in these two, very differently oriented, approaches is the fact that neither one is talking about the physical objects themselves, but rather about the discourses that are attached to them – either intentionally invented for them or created as a result of their transfer from one setting to another. In both cases it is the discourses and not the objects themselves that are used to claim authenticity... and that are also responsible for their inauthenticity. So, keeping that bi-disciplinary recognition in mind, let's move on to some concrete examples.

I'll begin with a case from close to home. Two years ago, during a visit to the Netherlands on other business, Richard Price and I went through an extraordinarily rich exhibition in the Great Hall of the Tropenmuseum called 'Kunst van Overleven: Marroncultuur uit Suriname'('Art of Survival: Maroon Culture from Suriname'). This ambitious attempt to present the six Maroon peoples of Suriname to the general public of their former colonizer, which filled the Great Hall of the Tropenmuseum (successor to the Colonial Museum), was aimed at bringing these little-known cultures to the attention of the Dutch and raising consciousness among the large Suriname population in the Netherlands (who tend to hold negative stereotypes of Maroons). Drawing on the museum's own rich collections as well as those of other (mainly European) museums, the exhibition made ample use of videos showing Maroons, usually speaking in Dutch, on a variety of topics. It was organized in seven modules: Religion, Memory/History, Wealth/Natural Resources, Gender, Music, Domestic Life, and Present-day Maroon Art.

For us, two of the cases in this exhibition raised questions about authenticity – both of which hinged on the *discourse* about objects rather than the objects themselves, and both of which involved objects that had been stripped of their original meaning by having, in Greg Dening's metaphor, 'crossed the beach'. One of the cases was devoted to musical instruments of the Maroons of Suriname. Among the seventeen instruments it contained were two from a museum in French Guiana that we were familiar with, since we had spent several years tracing their history (along with all the other carvings from the same source) at the request of the museum, in the 1990s. Following Gombrich's caution, we have to say that the authenticity of all these instruments, as physical objects, was not in doubt. Each was an authentically handcrafted object, and an interesting one at that. But a *double* level of inauthenticity had been introduced by the discourses that were attached to them at different points in time.

First, when they were sold to the Cayenne museum they were said to be instruments made in the late eighteenth or early nineteenth century by slaves on a plantation in Suriname. But investigation over a two-year period disclosed that they were in fact crafted during the 1980s by a French high school teacher – using special chemicals, resins, and even bits of bone – in a small workroom in his apartment in Cayenne. (For the full story, see R. & S. Price 1995.) When this was discovered, museum staff placed the instruments in a back area of their storage facility (together with others from the same tainted source), with the intent of protecting the acquisition from potentially embarrassing exposure to the public. So without even leaving Cayenne we're already dealing with a discourse of blatantly serious inauthenticity.

The second deviation from what we might call 'the authentic discourse' on these objects occurred when they arrived in Amsterdam and had labels attached to them at the Tropenmuseum. We know, from having spoken with museum staff in Cayenne, that when the Dutch curators came to Guyane to choose objects for the exhibit, they were told about the origin of the instruments as products of the schoolteacher's creative imagination. In fact, they were specifically warned not to exhibit them as 'authentic' slave-made instruments. But one of the two curators, a professional artist who seems to have privileged aesthetic considerations over ethnographic detail, felt that they would be a stunning addition to the exhibit and shouldn't be left out. So, there they were, described, authenticated, and dated: 'Wood. Suriname. c. 1800 (probably)' and 'Wood. Suriname. c. 1900.'

The Tropenmuseum exhibit also provides a link to my next example. The 'Kunst van Overleven' cases that displayed Maroon textiles included two pieces of clothing labeled 'Skirt and top with Aukan motifs. Cotton. Auka/Ndyuka Suriname. 2008'. For these items no detective work was required to understand the inauthenticity of the museum label's claim, since anyone who looked closely could see the small manufacturer's label. The two garments reflect the artistry of a talented British textile designer named Hatt Eaton who had spent several years in a Maroon village as the wife of the French doctor assigned to the local clinic (see http://www.hatteatondesign.com/EN/societe/default.asp). As an artist, she was taken by the Maroon designs she saw around her and approached Franky Amete, a gifted Maroon artist who had, among other things, produced a children's colouring book that nicely captured the colors and designs of Eastern Maroon art (2004). She convinced him to help her learn the style, creating her own designs, and being totally transparent about the fact that they were her own handiwork. Once she'd created a design, she would send it to Indonesia, where a commercial company would integrate it in beach towels, pareos, handbags, and tablecloths for sale. She never passed these items off as Maroon-made objects. .... but the 'Kunst van Overleven' curators did.

As a footnote to this story, which I learned only after I'd published an article on Franky Amete and Hatt Eaton (Price 2007a), there was another twist. It turns out that Maroons in the interior of French Guiana and in the border town of St-Laurent found Hatt Eaton's textiles very attractive, and began integrating them into their own life in the villages. One of her pareos, for example, was used as decorative banner for a dugout canoe. And more pareos with the same design were adopted as the costume for contestants in the 2007 Miss St-Laurent beauty contest in the Suriname/French Guiana border town of St. Laurent, whose population is dominated by Maroons.

This story raises some questions about *cultural* authenticity. Specifically, how should we classify Hatt Eaton's Maroon-style artistic output? Has she appropriated Maroon art by making things that were sufficiently good facsimiles so that they became ingredients in the Tropenmuseum exhibition of Maroon artifacts? Does the fact that Maroons admired and adopted them for their own uses change the equation? Also, does the fact that she always labeled them clearly with her own name (appending to them a discourse of perfect authenticity) mean that they're simply the product of intercultural inspiration of the sort that goes on all the time in the art world? After all, as one art critic once put it, 'all artists are essentially scavengers'.

Now on to some examples from the museum world of early twenty-first-century Paris concerning art objects whose cultural authenticity, I would argue, has been violated. These cases differ from those involving forgery/plagiary in that there has been no manipulation of the objects' authorship. Rather, it is their life histories and/or their intended meanings that have been distorted in motivated ways. I begin with the galleries of the Louvre Museum devoted to the arts of Africa, America, Asia, and Oceania – the pavillon des Sessions that was opened in 2000.

Following standard art museum conventions, the label for each object in these galleries specifies, in addition to the materials involved and the general geographical and cultural provenance, mention of its Western pedigree – that is, notation that prior to its arrival in the Louvre, an object had formerly been owned (for example) by Claude Lévi-Strauss, Helena Rubenstein, Paul Tishman, or some other well-known collector. All of the pieces on display are labeled according to this same template – all, that is, except the two terracotta statues from the Nok culture in what is now Nigeria, statues that were looted by tin miners, exported illegally to Brussels, and sold to France in 1998 by an art dealer well known for his active involvement in archeological trafficking.[2] When the Louvre galleries opened two years later, a telling exception to the general practice of listing former owners was made for these two remarkable pieces; their past was silenced, and their identity as looted treasures was cleansed for public consumption.[3]

While laundering the Nok statues consisted of sanitizing their collection history and provenance, other objects in the Louvre were cleansed of their cultural meaning. In these cases, neither the object nor its authorship nor its provenance is falsified, but I would argue that its 'authenticity' is nonetheless dealt a serious blow. Consider, for example, a wooden house post from the

---

2   Journalists in France were quick to jump on the tainted provenance of this sculpture and there was an extensive debate in the press as France and Nigeria held complex negotiations aimed at working out a mutually acceptable solution. The sculpture is now listed as being a 'deposit of the Federal Republic of Nigeria'. For a picture and further details about the story, see Price 2007b: 66-71.

3   The curators in Paris had no problem about identifying the same Belgian art dealer as the source for objects when they had not been the subject of an ethical outcry in the press. See, for example, Viatte 2006: 48 (fig. 18).

Solomon Islands that depicts a tightly embracing couple.⁴ Sandra Revolon, an anthropologist who conducted long-term fieldwork in the area and knew the great-grandchildren of the sculptor, explained that it

> represents a sexual encounter between a wealthy man and an aurao – a sacred prostitute who embodies a malevolent spirit called Matorua. At night this androgynous spirit wanders along isolated paths looking for a solitary person, takes a male or female form depending on the sex of its victim, and seduces him or her. As the couple make love, as portrayed on this post, the human victim contracts a fever which leads to certain death.⁵ (Brutti 2003: 25)

But this explanation was rejected by the art dealer who had been given carte blanche to design the exhibits – that is, Jacques Kerchache, the same close friend of Jacques Chirac who had collaborated with him on an earlier Taino exhibition. Kerchache made it abundantly clear that he had absolutely no interest in ethnography... that as far as he was concerned explanations like Sandra Revolon's interfered with aesthetic appreciation. Time and again he explained that he looked for only one thing in the objects that he collected and bought and sold, and that was their formal beauty. So he was certainly not about to label this house post in terms of malevolent spirits. Rather, what he read in it, with his connoisseur's impeccable eye, was erotic sensuality. So here's the description that he provided for the house post:

> *In spite of the simplicity and crudeness of the material, the subject is treated with extreme delicacy. The play of the arms and legs and the hands gently placed on the woman's lower back are full of sensuality, devoid of vulgarity... Through this primordial couple, the sculptor has been able to convey the sacred character of this essential act for the perpetuation of the clan... All is signified with such subtlety, with such dignity, that this tenderly clasped couple emerges from the material in total intimacy.*

And the catalogue to the Louvre galleries pleads ignorance regarding the house post's meaning: 'The two figures do seem to be coupling, but it is impossible to say with certainty what significance to lend to this representation' (Deborah Waite, in Kerchache 2000:287).

Next, an example from the musée du quai Branly, which opened next to the Eiffel Tower in 2006. Once again, we're dealing with objects that, in both Dening's metaphor and a very literal sense, had 'crossed the beach'.

First, a little background. The MQB (as it's known) was the brainchild of Jacques Chirac who, even before becoming president of France, had always been a passionate fan of non-European cultures, and especially non-Western art. His first move to promote French appreciation for what he called 'the forgotten arts' was, as we have seen, to introduce them into the sacred halls of the Louvre

---

4  For a picture, see Price 2007b: 77.
5  This reading of the house post is confirmed by Maurice Godelier (2002).

Museum, putting them on display in the Pavillon des Sessions. But as he expanded his ambitions, a plan was put together to group the entire collections of the former colonial museum (the musée des arts d'Afrique et d'Océanie) and all the ethnographic holdings of the anthropology museum (the musée de l'Homme) – some 300,000 objects, once the donations and new acquisitions were counted in. A prestigious site next to the Eiffel Tower was chosen and an architectural competition was launched.

The winner, internationally acclaimed architect Jean Nouvel, declared that his aim was 'to create ... a disjunction between the aesthetic presentation of objects ... as works of art, and their scholarly presentation.' As the head of the construction project put it, repeating an approach that had been used in the Louvre galleries, 'We wanted to privilege a sense of mystery, to allow people to discover the work in itself ... putting as much distance as possible between the object and the information relevant to the object.' Nouvel described his vision for the museum in distinctly poetic terms:

> *It's a space marked by the symbols of the forest, the river, and obsessions with death and oblivion... It's a haunted space, inhabited by the ancestral spirits of the men who, awakening to the human condition, invented gods and beliefs. The place is unique and strange. Poetic and disturbing... In a gentle shift, a Parisian garden becomes a sacred grove and the museum dissolves into its depths...* (Musée du quai Branly 2006: 1)

Nouvel quickly became a central decision maker in the project, and it was his vision of life and art beyond the European orbit that determined much about the museum, not only the external architecture, but also the interior spaces and the disposition of exhibited materials. (He even designed the dishware, glassware, and silverware for the museum restaurant.) This meant that he was in a position to convey his ideas of what life must have been like in the cultures represented in the museum – ideas that came directly from popular stereotypes of primitive people, and contradicted pretty much all the understandings that anthropologists have developed since at least the mid-twentieth century. This concentration of decision-making power in a man whose field of expertise lay far from the realm of ethnographic understandings led to short cuts and distortions of many kinds in the information provided on exhibited objects. I'll cite just one set.[6]

Nouvel devised an innovative proposal to integrate contemporary Aboriginal artworks in one of the four museum buildings. The idea was to reproduce them, blown up many times their original size, on walls and ceilings. Much was made of his plan to install mirrors and around-the-clock lighting that would make them visible to passers-by on the street even at night. Negotiations were launched by the French ambassador to Australia and involved exchanges of

---

6   For others, see Price 2007b.

letters between President Jacques Chirac and Australia's prime minister, John Howard. Four men and four women representing a variety of Aboriginal groups were selected and generous financial donations to the museum arrived from the Australian government and Australian foundations, since the official view from Down Under was that involvement in the MQB offered a unique opportunity to boost indigenous artists' international exposure and Australia's image in the world. Lavish attention to the project in the press made one of the Australian artists, John Mawurndjul, into a kind of exotic poster boy for the project, with ecstatic reports that, to my mind, were not unrelated to the French excitement over Josephine Baker in the 1920s and 30s.

Installation of the artworks was entrusted to the Australian architectural firm of Cracknell & Lonergan. The challenge was to reproduce delicately hand-painted originals at many times their original size using industrial-strength materials, a process requiring adjustments in both scale and texture. One Australian journalist described how 'An aged Tommy Watson was seen looking bemused as project manager Peter Lonergan held up a half-meter square metal panel containing the hugely magnified dots he'd taken from a few square centimeters of Watson's original painting ... Heaven only knows what the old man made of it' (Eccles 2006). And after one of Watson's wild red paintings was selected for inclusion in the museum, no one asked him whether it was all right for Cracknell & Lonergan to add in some green.

Or again, Lena Nyadbi's painting, designed in contrasting white and black, was converted to gray-on-gray, which harmonized better with the upscale Haussmannian residences across the street on the rue de l'Université. When she expressed reluctance to sign off on the result (objecting that it made her art look like sausages), she was threatened with severance from the project.

And a painting by Paddy Nyunkuny Bedford was originally supposed to be sandblasted onto a ground floor window, but because a steel beam across the window was in the way, this ceased to be an option, so a series of alternatives were proposed, and in the end a decision was taken to patch together pieces of two Paddy Bedford paintings and move the resulting amalgam to a different location where no steel beams would get in the way. As one journalist remarked, 'The scale is changed, the story is meaningless, the artist's moral rights are trampled' (Eccles 2006).

The objections of some of them to the way parts of their work were transformed for purposes of the architectural design were disregarded and the critical/political intent behind their work was largely whitewashed into a primitivizing stereotype. A text on the museum's website says that 'the themes of Aboriginal paintings are taken from mythical times. They may illustrate the creation of the world or of a particular places [sic.], inscribing their stories in the landscape' (Peltier 2002). How, then, could visitors to the MQB understand that a number of the paintings depict a twentieth-century massacre by poisoning of Aborigines by a white landowner? What would allow them to understand

*Fig. 1a. Paddy Nyunkuny Bedford, Thoowoonggoonarrin 2006*

*Fig. 1b. A photo labeled 'Thoowoonggoonarrin 2006' on the website of the musée du quai Branly*

urban artist Judy Watson's graphic references to toxic waste produced by French nuclear testing in the Pacific? And what hint are they given that Michael Riley's photographic images are condemning the Christianity that was imposed to replace traditional Aboriginal beliefs? The museum's vague mention of 'symbols of resistance and survival' or 'the opposing values of Aboriginality, Christianity and pastoralism' hardly suffice for capturing the very specific historical, political, and autobiographical allusions in their work.

Prior to a visit to the museum in May 2012, my understanding of the installation of Paddy Nyunkuny Bedford's painting, 'Thoowoonggoonarrin 2006', was based on a photo that I found on the MQB website (on a page that was expressing gratitude, not to the artists, but rather to the donors who had made the inclusion of the Australian artworks possible). I was struck that only one of the three elements in the painting had been reproduced, that it had been reversed left-to-right, and that a black expanse had been added above it.

But in May 2012 I was summoned to the museum by the curator of the Americanist collections who wanted my help with plans underway for an upgrade of the Maroon exhibit in the main gallery. After we finished working on the plans, I asked him to show me the installation of Bedford's painting. He said he'd never actually seen it, but he made some inquiries and got directions. Off we went, down some back stairs, through some hallways, and into a very tall narrow service corridor used for deliveries that was strictly off-limits to museum visitors, to passers-by on the street, and thus to the public in general. This delivery entrance lay at the extreme far corner of the museum complex, as far as possible from the visitors' entrance. No mirrors, and no all-night lighting to make this installation visible to the public. It is even invisible to the museum staff, except for workmen charged with accepting deliveries. But let's forget about its unfortunate placement for a moment and consider its physical authenticity – the way in which the lines and shapes and colors of Bedford's painting were replicated by the firm of Cracknell and Lonergan.

*Fig. 2: My sketch of the full installation, based on the museum's architectural diagram and the photos I took in May 2012.*

What I had seen in the photo turned out to be only part of the actual installation. To the right of the stairs, the painting loomed up nearly nine meters – solid black except for an oval shape in white, modeled on a piece of a different Bedford painting. I couldn't photograph it because of the tightness of the space, but later I found an architectural diagram for the installation that showed the difference between the *Thoowoonggoonarrin 2006* Bedford painted and the so-called '*Thoowoonggoonarrin 2006*' at the quai Branly. My rough sketch, based on that diagram, shows the scale compared to a person.

One final detail of the museum's treatment of the Australian Aboriginal artists whose work it used for the building might seem trivial, but it's still worth mentioning. It concerns the care that's taken (or not) with artists' names. The MQB website offers no entries on the eight artists, but there are wall plaques in French, English, and Spanish, placed on an outside wall next to the back entrance of the museum just outside the delivery door where Paddy Bedford is represented – thus visible to staff arriving for work, though not to museum visitors coming to see the collections. Bedford's close friend and executor Peter Seidel has pointed out that 'the sign outside the building has Old Man's Gija name spelled incorrectly. It should be Nyunkuny not Ngunkuny. We made it clear time and again ... to no avail'.[7] And this is not an isolated case. In the same insouciant spirit, a book on acquisition policies by the quai Branly's museological director Germain Viatte refers to Paddy Bedford as 'Patty'; the museum's inaugural portfolio opted for 'Pady'; and the museum's 2011 website also responded positively to searches for 'Pady' Bedford.[8] (In that same book Viatte also got tripped up on other Aboriginal names, misspelling both Ningura and Napurrula.)

---

7    Email of 27 May 2012.
8    See Viatte 2006: 61, 187.

Ultimately, the gaze adopted by the movers and shakers of the MQB – whether or not you want to call it 'primitivizing' or 'pan-exotic', as many critics have – leaves little room for according any kind of priority to the faithful rendering of details in the discourses attached to objects from non-Western sources. Details such as artists' names surely do matter to the people concerned, but once the products of their creativity 'cross the beach' and make their way to, for example, a museum in Paris, they may be treated as if they were unimportant. This contrasts with the careful attention paid to details concerning the individuals who have provided sustenance to the museum as colonial officers, military commanders, explorers, or collector-donors. We would be quite astonished if a typo in the name of a colonial officer or a museum donor were allowed to slip through the cracks.

Looking at the MQB's representation of Paddy Bedford's painting, what can we say about its authenticity? It is, regardless of its unfortunate placement, a physically imposing work and not uninteresting to look at (for those very few people who find themselves in the service corridor). The falsification is introduced in the text of the museum's plaque on the exterior wall of the building that declares it to be Bedford's 2006 painting, *Thoowoonggoonarrin 2006*. The painting has been appropriated by the museum in order to comply with the Parisian architect's vision for the museum and the structural constraints of the walls and beams that took precedence over the faithful reproduction of the artist's creativity. In my opinion, it is no longer *Thoowoonggoonarrin 2006*.

All of the examples I've invoked have, in Dening's metaphor, been 'transformed, made over into a currency of other cultural values', and all are in Gombrich's terms, objects whose inauthenticity resides strictly in the discourses that have been attached to them after they have crossed the beach. One final question that arises, then, is whether artworks that *don't* cross the beach are as frequently treated to the same kind of distorting discourse. That is, when museum curators are dealing with objects from closer to home, are they more conscientious in their treatment of them? Comparing the Quai Branly's wall and ceiling installations of Australian Aboriginal with the installation of a work by a *European* artist in another part of the museum suggests, to me at least, that a kind of double standard is in play. An artwork by Scottish artist Charles Sandison on the floor of the long ramp leading up to the permanent galleries, fully installed under the direct supervision of the artist, was accompanied by an extensive exegesis that he composed. And – not surprisingly – his name is free of misspellings each of the several times that Sandison is mentioned, with expressions of gratitude, on the MQB website.

Given all this, it might be useful to conceptualize 'authenticity' as a quality that resides in (and depends on) the truthfulness of *all* the discourses connected to a given object rather than simply those concerning (personal and cultural) authorship and provenance. Clearly, this makes the goal of producing authentic representations in the context of museums more difficult, given the sometimes competing political and aesthetic agendas that enter into curatorial decisions. But it could also contribute importantly to public awareness of the larger context in which objects cross beaches to reside in European and American museums, and the very rich meanings that are attached to them in their original cultural settings.

## References

Amete, Franky (2004), *Colorie Tes Tableaux Tembé!* Cayenne: Editions Plume Verte.

Brutti, Lorenzo (2003), 'L'ethnologie est-elle soluble dans l'art premier? Essai de lecture ethnographique du musée du quai Branly par le regard d'un observateur participant', in Yolaine Escande & Jean-Marie Schaeffer (eds.), *L'Esthétique: Europe, Chine et ailleurs*, 13-36, Paris: Éditions You-Feng.

Dening, Greg (1980), *Islands and Beaches: Discourse on a silent Land: Marquesas 1774-1880*. Honolulu: University Press of Hawaii.

Eccles, Jeremy (2006), 'Art World Away from Paris', *Canberra Times*, 3 June.

Godelier, Maurice (2002), 'For the Museum Public: Combining the Pleasures of Art and Knowledge', Barbour Lecture, University of Virginia.

Gombrich, E.H. (1959), *Art and Illusion*. Princeton NJ: Princeton University Press.

Hebborn, Eric (1991), *Drawn to Trouble: The Forging of an Artist. An Autobiography*. Edinburgh: Mainstream Publishing Projects.

Kerchache, Jacques (ed.) (2000), *Sculptures: Afrique Asie Océanie Amériques*. Paris: Réunion des Musées Nationaux & Musée du Quai Branly.

Musée du quai Branly (2006), 'Un musée composite: Une architecture conçue autour des collections'. 16-page document compiled for the museum's inauguration.

Peltier, Philippe (2002), 'Aboriginal Ceiling Paintings: Presentation'. December 2002 statement posted on the MQB website.

Price, Richard, and Sally Price (1995), *Enigma Variations*. Cambridge: Harvard University Press.

Price, Richard, and Sally Price (2010), 'Review of "Kunst van Overleven"', *American Anthropologist* 112: 655-656.

Price, Sally (2007a), 'Into the Mainstream: Shifting Authenticities in Art', *American Ethnologist* 34(4): 603-620.

Price, Sally (2007b), *Paris Primitive: Jacques Chirac's Museum on the Quai Branly*. Chicago: University of Chicago Press. (Expanded French edition: *Au musée des illusions: Le rendez-vous manqué du quai Branly*. Paris: Éd. Denoël, 2011)

Viatte, Germain (2006), *Tu fais peur tu émerveilles: Musée du quai Branly acquisitions 1998/2005*. Paris: Musée du quai Branly & Réunion des musées nationaux.

# AUTHENTICITY AND CURATORIAL PRACTICE

## Dr. Laura N.K. Van Broekhoven

In daily curatorial practice, questions of authenticity and authentication remain highly complex and confusing – and for this very reason immensely interesting and important. The focus in this book has shifted away from a more panoramic view of authenticity, as seen by the academic field, towards the more practical perspective as experienced by museum professionals and by visitors.

Some scholars have convincingly argued that 'authenticity', with its numerous conceptualisations, is an ontologically problematic term (Belhassen & Caton 2006; Reisinger & Steiner 2006; Steiner & Reisinger 2006). Others note that in everyday life the term is still very much alive throughout the public media and leisure industries such as tourism, films and museums (Belhassen & Caton 2006; Rickly-Boyd 2012). 'Authenticity' is to a large extent at the heart of museums' concerns in their displays, collections, and interaction with visitors. In relation to tourism, Mkono (2012) and Belhassen and Caton (2006) argue that scholars cannot simply abandon a concept that continues to figure so prominently in the minds of tourists and tourism brokers. Perhaps you will allow me to tell you a little story that exemplifies some of the many questions about authentication we confront, as curators, in our everyday working lives.

In our daily practice, the questions asked most frequently are about the authentication of objects that people have in their own collections. Every first Thursday of the month, we at the NME allow people to bring their objects to the museum to find out more about them. Virtually everyone wants to know if the object in question is 'real', authentic and therefore valuable. Another such category consists of queries as to whether objects exhibited in the museum are 'authentic' or 'real'. The authenticity of the object seems to influence the 'realness' of the personal relationship visitors experience with it. When we displayed an Inca mummy in 2003, virtually all the questions we received about the mummy related to its authenticity. Many visitors even assumed that it could surely not be a 'real' mummy. Visitors desire to experience what is known in Tourism Studies as 'existential authenticity', a state of being that, in the museum context, can be pursued only through visitor interaction with an object's 'objective authenticity'. On the one hand, people will gladly enter openly staged experiences in theme parks or travelling shows such as the Tutankhamen Experience staged in Amsterdam throughout 2013. In a 'real' museum setting, however, they seem to value not being lied to, and expect the museum to truly present what they claim: authenticated objects. In brief, no one wants to cry in front of a Van Gogh, to later find out that the Van Gogh was a forgery or fake.

## Real Replicas

Last year I travelled to Guatemala to give a lecture in a series of conferences organised in celebration of the Oxlahun Baktun date that was celebrated on 21 December 2012. I had been invited by the Ministry of Culture of Guatemala and by the Dutch Embassy, since the then Dutch ambassador, Jan Jaap van de Velde, had contacted the museum from Guatemala City to ask about a famous object we have in our collection called the Leiden Plate. This jade celt pendant is displayed in our permanent Mesoamerica Gallery, and features prominently on the one-quetzal note of Guatemala. Imagine the ambassador's surprise when one day, while inspecting the images on the banknotes, he stumbled on the name of 'Leyden' beneath an otherwise clearly Maya iconographic and hieroglyphic image. He was flabbergasted: he had studied at Leiden. Now, he asked himself, what was the name of the city of his university doing on a Guatemalan banknote? It did not take him long to trace the Leiden Plate to our museum, the National Museum of Ethnology (fig. 1a & figs. 1b & 1c & 1d). A Dutch engineer who had been hired by a lumber trade company to dredge a canal in Guatemala brought the Leiden Plate to the Netherlands in 1864 and gifted it to the museum.[1] The plate travelled the world, was published in numerous exhibition catalogues, and even though far more beautiful pieces are to be found in Guatemala's national collections, in 2006 the Leiden Plate ended up being chosen as one of the images to be depicted on Guatemala's national currency.

The Ministry of Culture asked if it would be possible to ship the Leiden Plate to Guatemala City for the 13th Baktun Ending Celebrations. We looked into the possibilities but in view of the current frequency of violence and robbery and the general lack of security in Zona 1 of Guatemala City, it seemed unwise to have the object travel there. The Guatemalan Ministry of Culture agreed with this decision. We considered having an exact replica made, which could be reproduced and gifted to several Guatemalan policy-makers and politicians. The museum explored various options and asked for quotes from makers of 3D-print replicas and of handmade replicas in the Netherlands. In some cases the quotes we received were extravagantly high, and in the case of the 3D-prints, companies were reluctant to accept the commission, since they predicted that the quality of the reproductions would be fairly low. Present-day techniques could not do justice to the surface colouring, shine and feel, or delicacy of the incisions. The Dutch ambassador then had the excellent idea of exploring local possibilities, and

---

[1] A critical period for Maya epigraphy is situated around the 1880s, when many aspects of the Maya writing and astronomical system were being deciphered by scientists around the world. Partly thanks to the images on the Leiden Plate, important advances were made in the deciphering process, and the celt soon became world famous, travelling from one conference to another as one of the most important pieces of the Maya. It records a very early historical date, and until a few decades ago, the hieroglyphs engraved on it represented the earliest written historical date known of the Maya. At present, the eldest Maya historical date is the Long Count date 8.12.14.8.15 (AD 292) recorded on Tikal Stelae 29 which is almost 30 years earlier than the 8.14.3.1.12 1 Eb 0 Yaxkin (AD 321) date recorded on the Leiden Plate.

Fig 1a The original Leiden Plate (glyphs) 1403-1193
Fig 1b The original Leiden plate (ruler) 1403-1193
Fig 1c The Leiden Plate (original) displayed at NME Leiden
Fig 1d The Leiden Plate (replica) displayed at the Museo Nacional de Etnología y Arqueología in Guatemala City.

contacted a large jade atelier in Antigua, Guatemala. Jade Maya, a jade jewellery seller and producer in the city of Antigua notified us that if we could send the exact measurements, accompanied by detailed pictures, they could make the replica for a reasonable price. Not only would it be made out of jade from the same sources as the original (which other replicas were not), but it would also be made by a team of five Maya artists, working in the atelier; and we would be able to have as many copies as we wanted on demand. This all came much closer to what would be classified in heritage studies as an object containing elements of 'existential authenticity'.

Naturally, I visited the atelier where the replicas were being made, and was able to buy a copy for our museum and meet the artists who had made it. While to me it seemed a miraculous achievement that this project had finally culminated in a replica of the plate, the artists did not see anything remarkable about it. Much to my dismay, the atelier told me that the plate had been replicated for decades. All that time, our museum had lived in blissful ignorance of the fact that copies of the Leiden Plate had been circulating since 1986.[2] Even so, the artists were very enthusiastic about the opportunity to work with the more detailed measurements provided by the museum, to make the replica more accurate. The replica they had made before was hardly worthy of the name, since it was too square, too thick, and a lighter shade of jade, besides which the images were placed somewhat incorrectly and important details were missing. Plans were made to have one of the artists travel to Leiden to come and study the original in 2013.

After my lecture in Guatemala on the Leiden Plate and its scientific enigmas, I visited the locations in the city where the latest replicas are now on display (or included in collections): the National Museum of Archaeology and Ethnography; the Dutch Embassy, the Palacio Nacional, the Miraflores Museum; the Popol Vuh Museum and the museum in Tikal (from where it is believed to have originated).

It gradually became obvious that with millions of one-quetzal notes in circulation since 2006, numerous pictures of the plate in scientific, virtual and tourist publications and now at least five replicas of the 3D plate simultaneously on display throughout Guatemala and the Netherlands, the Leiden Plate was, for a while, the most widely and diversely disseminated iconographic representation of an object in our museum's collection.

While two-dimensional images of the plate on banknotes, on the internet, in books and tourist folders did not raise questions of authenticity or authentication; the 3D replicas and the commemoration in which their display was staged, did. The replicas were exhibited in the festivities surrounding the Oxlahun Baktun, the 13th Baktun on 21 December 2012, a date that many

---

2   In 1986 the Leiden Plate was published in Linda Schele's famous catalogue *The blood of Kings*; Schele often visited Jade Maya to give workshops and work at the atelier.

believed to correspond to the end of the Maya Calendar, supposed Maya end-of-the-world predictions, and the coming of age of our universe, a completely fictitious New Age construction. So-called Doomsday Preppers, who believed this to be an authenticated fact, were indeed preparing for the end of the world, by building arks or safety shelters. And although in Guatemala, where the large majority of the population is Maya or of Maya descent, people fortunately knew that the Maya calendar was not coming to an end, the authenticity of any 13th Baktun Ending Celebrations was highly questionable from a scholarly vantage point, since the Maya Long Count system fell into disuse almost 1,000 years ago. In fact, what did the Leiden Plate have to do with the Celebrations of the 13th Baktun Ending at all? The plate was used to decipher parts of the Maya calendrical system, but aside from that, in all honesty it has nothing to do with the 13th Baktun, there is no reference to that date inscribed on it, nor is it easy to connect any of the images depicted on it to the 13th Baktun. So we were dealing with questionable replicas made to be presented at the questionable celebration of a questionable 13th Baktun Ending.

The ambassador had warned me that at every lecture he had given, he had been asked about the *real* plate and when it was going to be returned to Guatemalan soil. There was ample time for questions after the lecture. I came prepared for this key question: that of the plate's possible repatriation to Guatemala. It was still in Leiden; its replicas now possessed more precise measurements and had been distributed more widely throughout Guatemala thanks to the Dutch Embassy's project, but even so, the *real*, the *original*, the *authentic* Leiden Plate was still *not* in Guatemala. In the event, I – who represented the authority of the museum holding the plate in its collections – was never asked that question. I gave two lectures, one to a group of approximately 150 high school students and their teachers, and one to a smaller group of distinguished Guatemalan professionals from the museum sector, the deputy minister of culture, policy makers, a number of archaeologists, and ambassadors. Many questions were touched upon concerning the plate's object biography and use, but the issue of repatriation simply never came up. At the same time, everyone involved was fully aware of the absolute distinction between the real, authentic, pre-colonial Leiden Plate and its copies. And everyone involved would have liked it to have been possible for the plate to travel to Guatemala in the near future. In any case, we decided to keep improving the quality of the replica. To some extent, we feel that perfecting the reproduction process and the replicas' technical quality might somehow make up for an absence felt by all. Walter Benjamin's notion of auratic value may help us understand:

> *'Even the most perfect reproduction of a work of art is lacking in one element: its presence in time and space, its unique existence at the place where it happens to be. This unique existence of the work of art determined the history to which it was subject throughout the time of its existence… The whole sphere of authenticity is outside technical – and, of course, not only technical – reproducibility. … that which withers in the age of mechanical reproduction is the aura of the work of art'.*
> (Benjamin 1968: 220-222)

*Fig 2a: The Buddha's as exhibited between 1883 and 1937 in the then called 's Rijks Etnografisch Museum on the museums location at Rapenburg in Leiden. Copyright Rijksmuseum Volkenkunde*
*Fig 2b: The Buddha room in the NME at Steenstraat 1 (current location of the museum) 1937-1999*
*Fig 2c: The Buddha statues exhibited within the Japan gallery of NME 2001-2012*
*Fig 2d: The Buddha Room as inaugurated in 2012*

Benjamin writes of the loss of the aura as a loss of a singular authority within the work of art, which has itself been culturally and ritually shaped in time and space. So should we conclude that the Leiden Plate replicas will always be without auratic value? Or can a half manually and half mechanically produced replica, handmade by Maya artisans in Guatemala in the 21$^{st}$ century, with the same ancient Maya jade extracted from sources similar to those of the original, and proudly exhibited to a largely Guatemalan public, acquire a sense of aura all by itself?

## Staging Authenticity

Questions on how we use and mould authenticity are part of a museum's everyday practice in relation to techniques of representation and the displays we create for our visitors. 'The timber industry processes timber. The metal industry processes metal. If the tourist industry processes tourists' (Krippendorf 1987:19), does the museum industry process visitors and object experiences?

This year we reopened a Buddha Room in our museum. This fulfilled a long-standing wish on the part of our visitors. During the last major refurbishment, the Buddha statues had been incorporated into the Japan gallery instead of having their own separate space. Many of our visitors reacted in dismay, having cherished the sacredness and seclusion of the former Buddha Room. The museum received numerous complaints. It was therefore decided, after a decade of complaints, to reinstate the old Buddha room as part of the general refurbishment project carried out between 2010 and 2012. During the refurbishment of our Buddha gallery, our curator, Matthi Forrer, said that if our museum wanted to provide an impression of a present-day Japanese temple, we should certainly not display the Buddhas in such a serene, aesthetic manner, as the designers had suggested. In Japan, Matthi explained, you would never find Buddha statues standing alone; temples are jam-packed with objects used for the various rituals. Nonetheless, as any visitor to our museum will be able to observe, our exhibitions department decided against that approach (figs. 2a, 2b, 2c, 2d). Ultimately, the intention was not to give the visitor an experience of visiting a Japanese Buddhist temple, but to restore to our museum a room that would fulfil the public's need for an experience from the past, a room that our public would be able to relate to, hopefully reviving the fond memories they had had as children or younger adults when visiting the museum and coming into our Buddha room, filled with the smoke of people meditating while enjoying a joint.

Making representations involves creating the illusion of an authentic experience. In this light it is interesting to examine another aspect of the creation of authentic experiences through our exhibition spaces in terms of Erving Goffman's 'front versus back' distinction. Goffman concludes that tourists try to 'enter back regions of the places they visit because these regions are associated with intimacy of relations and authenticity of experiences. It is also found that tourist settings are arranged to produce the impression that a back region has been entered even when this is not the case'(MacCannel 1973: 589).

Museums create 'back region spaces' in much the same way. In our museum this involves the setting up of an 'open storage' space in the museum's attic – a space in which our visitors can experience more fully the look and feel of our museum storage. Our museum contains 240,000 objects, and another 500,000 items in our multi-media library including photographs, audio and film items, an extensive library, and archives. Only about four per cent of the object collections is on display. This means that the open storage offers a more 'authentic' sense of the representation of the museum's traditional backspace, and it was designed to show the public how we preserve our collections. Unlike our main storage facility, it is located on the museum's premises. The remainder of our collections is stored in an industrial complex over 20 miles from Leiden, in hangars that were built during the Cold War to stock emergency medical supplies in the event of a Russian invasion. When our museum applied for a government grant in 1996 to build more storage space in Leiden, the request was denied. By then, the possibility of a Russian invasion seemed remote, and the hangars could be put to better use.

In tourism studies it has been found that tourists try to enter the back regions of the places they visit because these regions are associated with intimate relations and authentic experience (see e.g. MacCannell 1973; Ivanovic 2008). Somehow, the accumulation of so much 'aura' in our storage hangars does indeed generate feelings of awe, amazement and wonder to almost all who visit them for research purposes or work. Since our collections lie at the core of our practice, we decided we wanted to share this experience with our visitors. In consequence, some of our exhibition space was arranged to produce the impression that visitors are entering a 'back region', even when the space is actually designed to serve as a front stage, albeit at irregular opening hours.

## Conclusion

Views on the societal role of museums have changed down the ages, partly in response to changes in society itself. Most ethnographic museums originally set out to preserve cultural historical knowledge, building on objects as containers of cultural information, and as a result, our museum collections have necessarily become the cumulative products of past collection policies. In recent decades, museums have come to realise that they are not merely heritage keepers, nor are they solely places of learning where the public comes to be educated and learn from a single authenticated voice of authority. Today, aside from serving as society's store-house of memories (Saldanha 2008), museums also want to be bridges between cultures, instruments of societal transformation, forgers of new futures and strong community anchors. New technologies are making it possible for a wide spectrum of stakeholders to express themselves and link up, and museums need to explore ways of connecting to them, if all these diverse goals are to be fulfilled. The current generation of visitors wants to play an active part and is less inclined to play a passive role than those of earlier decades. The percentage of 'prosumers' – or consumers who are co-producing – continues to rise. All this is happening on a global as well as a local scale, and these scales affect ethnographic museums in particular, since they hold collections relevant both to local and global stakeholders. Technologies such as the internet, personal computers and wireless telephony have turned the globe into an increasingly interconnected network of individuals, subcultures, groups and governments. Museums and government institutions are working toward making their cultural heritage widely available on the internet. Within the Netherlands, organisations such as the Foundations of Ethnographic Museum Collections (SVCN) and Digital Heritage Netherlands (DEN) have steadily improved accessibility by digitising their collections, and since the late 1990s, their entire collections have been accessible online. Projects such as *Europeana* have taken these efforts to a whole new level, and millions of objects are being made accessible for the world to enjoy.³ Nonetheless, merely placing collections online in their entirety does not necessarily build bridges with local or global stakeholders. The co-creative production of knowledge about cultural heritage offers the scope to develop new tools, new museological vocabularies, syntaxes and grammar to interconnect with present-day stakeholders, to enable us as museums to take on a role as catalysts of social change. We therefore find ourselves exploring more and more tools that will allow us to share curatorial authority with stakeholders. For museums to truly assume their role as instruments of social cohesion, which inspire global cultural competence, our praxis needs to revolve around facilitating co-creative knowledge production with stakeholders at the global and local levels, so that together with our diverse stakeholders we can develop a multitude of authenticated voices. For as Barbara Kirshenblatt-Gimblett and Edward Bruner argue, authenticity is 'less [a question] of authenticity and more one of authentication: who has the power to represent whom and to determine which representation is authentic' (Kirshenblatt-Gimblett and Bruner, 1992:304)

In theory I agree that authenticity is an ontologically problematic term, and must also agree with Regina Bendix, who argues on this topic, 'the crucial questions to be answered are not "what is authenticity?" but "who needs authenticity and why?" and "how has authenticity been used?"' (Bendix, 2009:21). Do we, as museums, need authenticity? Does our public? Do our partners abroad? How do we, as curators, use the concept of authenticity? How do we interact with questions of authenticity when we curate, collect, repatriate, and make (re)presentations?

In analogy to what has been argued for the tourism industry (Ivanovic, 2008: 325), could we argue that creating novel cultural museum experiences is the core business of the museum industry, whereas consuming 'authentic' object or exhibition experiences is the core business of being a museum visitor? While the tourist industry creates opportunities for individuals to encounter their authentic selves, ethnographic museums are in the business of creating opportunities for their visitors to encounter authentic (or authenticated) objects placed in a context of staged authenticity within a heterotopic space.⁴

---

3   See http://www.europeana.eu/.
4   Foucault introduces the concept of heterotopia in his essay on *Des Espace Autres* (Foucault 1986). He uses it to refer to places and spaces that function as spaces of otherness, semi-permeable spaces that are both parts of the space where they are located and spaces of difference. They are spaces in which the relations between elements of a culture are suspended, neutralised, or reversed. Unlike utopias, heterotopias are real places incorporated into the very institution of society in which all the other real emplacements of a culture are 'at the same time, represented, contested, and reversed, sorts of places that are outside all places, although they are actually localizable' (Foucault 1986: 24). Examples of heterotopias include ships, cemeteries, asylums, prisons, homes for the elderly, libraries and museums.

## References

Belhassen, Y. & Caton, K. (2006), Authenticity matters, *Annals of Tourism Research* 33(3): 853–856.

Bendix, R. (2009), *In Search of Authenticity: The Formation of Folklore Studies*. Madison: University of Wisconsin Press.

Benjamin, W. (1968), 'The work of art in the age of mechanical reproduction', in Hannah Arendt (ed.), translated by Harry Zohn, *Illuminations*, 217–252. New York: Schocken Books.

Chhabra, D. (2012), 'Authenticity of the objectively authentic', *Annals of Tourism Research*, 39(1): 480–502.

Chhabra, D., R. Healy & E. Sills (2003), 'Staged authenticity and heritage tourism', *Annals of tourism research: a social sciences journal* 30(3): 702-719.

Foucault, M. (1986), 'Of Other Spaces'. *Diacritics* 16 (Spring): 22-27.

Goffman, E. (1956), *The Presentation of Self in Everyday Life*. New York: Doubleday.

Ivanovic, M. (2008), *Cultural Tourism*. Cape Town: Juta & Company.

Kirschenblatt-Gimbell, B. (1988), 'Authenticity and Authority in the Representation of Culture', in Ina-Maria Greverus et al. (eds), *Kulturkontakt — Kulturkonflikt* 28, 59-70. Frankfurt: Institut fiir Kulturanthropologie und Europäische Ethnologie.

Kirshenblatt-Gimblett, B. & Edward M. Bruner. 1992. 'Tourism' In *Folklore, cultural performances, and popular entertainments. A communications-centered handbook*, ed. by Richard Bauman. New York: Oxford University Press, 300-307.

Krippendorf, J. (1987), *The Holiday Makers: Understanding the Impact of Leisure and Tourism*. Oxford: Routledge.

MacCannel, D. (1973), 'Staged authenticity: arrangements of Social Space in Tourist Settings', *The American Journal of Sociology* 79(3): 589-603.

Mkono, M. (2012), 'Authenticity does matter', *Annals of Tourism Research* 39(1): 480–483.

Reisinger, Y. & Steiner, C. J. (2006), 'Reconceptualizing object authenticity', *Annals of Tourism Research*, 33(1): 65–86.

Rickly-Boyd, J. M. (2012), 'Authenticity & aura: A Benjaminian approach to tourism', *Annals of Tourism Research* 39(1): 269–289.

Saldanha, A. (2008), Heterotopia and structuralism. In *Environment and Planning A,* 40 (9): 2080-2096.

Schele, L. & M. E. Miller (1986), *The Blood of Kings: Dynasty and Ritual in Maya Art.* New York: George Braziller, Inc., in association with the Kimbell Art Museum, Fort Worth.

Steiner, C. J. & Reisinger, Y. (2006), 'Understanding existential authenticity', *Annals of Tourism Research* 33(2): 299–318.

## List of contributors and addresses

1. Alexander Geurds [a.geurds@arch.leidenuniv.nl]

    Assistant Professor Adjunct University of Colorado, Boulder
    Associate Professor Leiden University
    Faculty of Archaeology
    Leiden University
    PO Box 9515
    2300 RA Leiden
    The Netherlands

2. Martin Berger [martin.berger@volkenkunde.nl]

    Junior Curator Middle and South America Department
    Rijksmuseum Volkenkunde/National Museum of Ethnology
    PO Box 212
    2300 AE Leiden
    The Netherlands

3. Rosemary Joyce [rajoyce@berkeley.edu]

    Richard and Rhoda Goldman Distinguished Professor of Social Sciences
    Professor of Anthropology
    University of California, Berkeley United States

4. Oliver Watson [oliver.watson@orinst.ox.ac.uk]

    I.M. Pei Professor of Islamic Art and Architecture
    Khalili Research Centre for the Art and Material Culture of the Middle East
    University of Oxford 3, St John Street,
    Oxford, OX1 2LG United Kingdom

5. Fransje Brinkgreve [fransje.brinkgreve@volkenkunde.nl]

    Curator Insular Southeast Asia Department
    Rijksmuseum Volkenkunde/National Museum of Ethnology
    PO Box 212
    2300 AE Leiden
    The Netherlands

6. Cunera Buijs [cunera.buijs@volkenkunde.nl]

   Curator Arctic Department
   Rijksmuseum Volkenkunde/National Museum of Ethnology
   PO Box 212
   2300 AE Leiden
   The Netherlands


7. Sally Price [sallyprice123@gmail.com]

   Duane A. & Virginia S. Dittman Professor of American Studies and Anthropology College of William & Mary
   http://www.richandsally.net/


8. Laura Van Broekhoven [Laura.vanbroekhoven@volkenkunde.nl]

   Head Research Department, Curator Middle- and South America Department and Assistant Professor Leiden University
   Rijksmuseum Volkenkunde/National Museum of Ethnology
   PO Box 212
   2300 AE Leiden
   The Netherlands

# Mededelingen van het Rijksmuseum voor Volkenkunde

No. 1   J.P.B. de Josselin de Jong, *Archeological Materials from Saba and St. Eustatius, Lesser Antilles*, 1947. 54 pp. + 19 figs. + 16 p. plates.

No. 2   J.L. Swellengrebel, *Een vorstenwijding op Bali. Naar materiaal verzameld door H.J.E.F. Schwartz*, 1947. 27 pp. + 18 p. plates.

No. 3   C. Nooteboom, *Quelques techniques de tissage des Petites Iles de la Sonde*. With Discussion et données complémentaires à propos de l'ouvrage de M. James Hornell, Watertransport, Origin and Early Evolution, par Pierre Paris 1948. 46 pp.+ 8 p. plates + 10 figs.

No. 4   P.J.L. Vandenhoute, *Classification stylistique de masque Dan et Guéré de la Côte d'Ivoire occidentale (A.O.F.)*, 1948. 48 pp.+ 7 p. plates, map.

No. 5   T. Volker, *Ukiyoe Quartet: Publisher, Designer, Engraver and Printer*, 1949 vi + 29 pp. ill.

No. 6/7   T. Volker, *The animal in Far Eastern Art and especially in the Art of the Japanese Netsuke, with references to Chinese origins, traditions, legends and art, 1950*. 190 pp. + 19 p. plates.

No. 8/9   P.H. Pott, *Introduction to the Tibetan Collection of the National Museum of Ethnology, Leiden*, 1951. 184 pp.+ 32 p. plates.

No. 10   J.P.B. de Josselin de Jong, *Lévi-Strauss's Theory on Kinship and Marriage*, 1952. iv + 59 pp. + figs. Reprinted 1970.

No. 11   Tijs Volker, *Porcelain and the Dutch East India Company, as recorded in the Dagh-registers of Batavia Castle, those of Hirando and Deshima and other contemporary papers, 1602-1682*, 1954. 243 pp. + 32 p. plates, maps.

No. 12   Adriaan A. Gerbrands, *Art as an Element of Culture, especially in Negro-African*, 1957. x + 158 pp. + 16 p. plates. Translated from the Dutch by G.E. van Baaren-Paape.

No. 13   Tijs Volker, *The Japanse Porcelain Trade of the Dutch East India Company after 1683*, 1959. 92 pp. + 26 p. plates.

No. 14   Herman H. Frese, *Anthropology and the Public: The Role of Museums*, 1960. viii + 253 pp. +16 p. plates.

No. 15   *The Wonder of Man's Ingenuity. Being a Series of Studies in Archaeology, Material Culture, and Social Anthropology by Members of the Academic Staff of the National Museum of Ethnology, Published on the Occasion of the Museum's 125th Anniversary*, 1962. 165 pp. + 24 p. plates, map.

No. 16   Simon Kooijman, *Ornamented Bark-Cloth in Indonesia*, 1963. viii + 145 pp. + 32 p. plates and 235 drawings.

No. 17   Gert W. Nooter, *Old Kayaks in the Netherlands*, 1971. 76 pp. ill.

No. 18   Freerk C. Kamma and Simon Kooijman, Rowawa Forja, *Child of the Fire. Iron Working and the Role of Iron in West New Guinea (West Iran)*, 1973. viii + 45 pp. ill. map.

No. 19   Ger D. van Wengen, *The Cultural Inheritance of the Javanese in Surinam*, 1975. iv + 55 pp.

No. 20   Gert Nooter, *Leadership and Headship: Changing Authority of the Patterns in an East Greenland Hunting Community*, 1976. viii + 117 pp. ill.

No. 21   Simon Kooijman, *Tapa on Moce Island, Fiji: A Traditional Handicraft in a Changing Society*, 1977. x + 176 pp. ill.

No. 22   W.R. van Gullik, *Irezumi: The Pattern of Dermatography in Japan*, 1982. xviii + 308 pp. + 72 p. plates.

No. 23   Ted J.J. Leyenaar, Ulama*: The Perpetuation in Mexico of the Pre-Spanish Ball Game Ullamalitzli*, 1978. viii + 120 pp. ill.

No. 24   Simon Kooijman, *Art, Art Objects, and Ritual in the Mimika Culture*, 1984. xix + 173 pp. Translated from The Dutch by Inez Seeger.

No. 25   Pieter ter Keurs and Dirk Smidt (eds.), *The language of Things. Studies in Ethnocommunication, in Honour of Professor Adrian A. Gerbrands*, 1990. 208 pp. ill.

No. 26   Gerard W. van Bussel, Paul L. T. van Dongen and Ted J.J. Leyenaar (eds), *The Mesoamerican Ballgame. Papers presented at the International Colloquium 'The Mesoamerican Ballgame 2000 BC-AD 2000', Leiden, June 30th-July 3rd, 1988*, 1991. 300 pp.ill.

No. 27   Rita Bolland, with Rogier M.A. Bedaux and Renée Boser- Sarivaxevanis, *Tellem Textiles, Archaeological Finds from Burial Caves in Mali's Bandiagara Cliff*. Published in Cooperation with the Tropenmuseum, Royal Tropical Institute Amsterdam, 1991. 321 pp. ill.

No. 28   Dirk A.M. Smidt, Pieter ter Keurs and Albert Trouwborst (eds.), *Pacific Material Culture. Essays in Honour of Dr. Simon Kooijman, on the Occasion of his 80th birthday*, 1995. 336 pp. ill.

No. 29   Michael Prager and Pieter ter Keurs (eds.), *W.H. Rassers and the Batak Magic Staff*, 1998. 152 pp. ill.

No. 30   Reimar Schefold and Han F. Vermeulen (eds.), *Treasure Hunting? Collectors and Collections of Indonesian Artefacts*, Mededelingen van het Rijksmuseum voor Volkenkunde Leiden, no. 30 / CNWS Publications, Vol. 116, Leiden 2002, ISBN 978-90-5789-078-9, 324 pp. incl. Index out of print.

No. 31   Laura van Broekhoven, *Conquistando Io Invencible. Fuentes históricas sobre las culturas indígenas de la region Central de Nicaragua*, 2002 ISBN 978-90-5789-083-3, 352 pp. Incl., bibl., app., index, € 36,00.

No. 32   Cunera Buijs, *Furs and Fabrics. Transformations, Clothing and Identity in East Greenland*, Mededelingen van het Rijksmuseum voor Volkenkunde Leiden, no. 36 / CNWS Publications Vol. 129, Leiden 2004, ISBN 978-90-5789-094-9, 300 pp. Incl. photogr.,figs., app., index, out of print.

No. 33   R. Bedaux, J. Polet, K. Sanogo & A. Schmidt (éds), *Recherches archéologiques à Dia dans le Delta intérieur du Niger (Mali): bilan des saisons de fouilles 1998-2003*, Mededelingen van het Rijksmuseum voor Volkenkunde Leiden, no. 33/ CNWS Publications Vol. 144, Leiden 2005, ISBN 978-90-5789-107-6, 560 pp., richly ill,. Incl. figs., bibl., annexes, € 48,00.

No. 34   Pieter ter Keurs, *Condensed Reality. A study of material culture. Case studies from Siassi (Papua New Guinea) and Enggano (Indonesia)*, Mededelingen van het Rijksmuseum voor Volkenkunde Leiden, no. 34 / CNWS Publication Vol. 148, ISBN 978-90-5789-112-0, 240 pp. Ill., incl.,append., bibl., index, € 36,00

No. 35   Joost Willink, *Stages in Civilisation, Dutch museums in quest of West Central African collections (1856-1889)*, Mededelingen van het Rijksmuseum voor Volkenkunde Leiden, no. 35 / CNWS Publicaties, € 49,95.

No. 36   Pieter ter Keurs (ed.), *Colonial Collections Revisited*, Mededelingen van het Rijksmuseum voor Volkenkunde Leiden, no. 36 / CNWS Publications Vol. 152, Leiden 2007, ISBN 978-90-5789-152-6, 270 pp. Ill. € 36,00.

No. 37   Rudolf Effert, *Royal Cabinets and Auxiliary Branches. Origins of the National Museum of Ethnology 1816-1883*, Mededelingen van het Rijksmuseum voor Volkenkunde Leiden, no. 37 / CNWS Publications No. 159, Leiden 2008, ISBN 978-90-5789-159-5 340 pp. € 45,00.

No. 38   Véronique Degroot, *Candi, Space and Landscape. A study on the distribution, orientation and spatial organization of Central Javanese temple remains*. Mededelingen van het Rijksmuseum voor Volkenkunde Leiden, no. 38, Leiden 2009, ISBN 978-90-8890-039-6, 497 pp. Ill., Incl. bibl., index, € 49,95.

No. 39   Laura Van Broekhoven, Cunera Buijs & Pieter Hovens (eds), *Sharing Knowledge & Cultural Heritage: First Nations of the Americas. Studies in Collaboration with Indigenous Peoples from Greenland, North and South America*. Mededelingen van het Rijksmuseum voor Volkenkunde Leiden, no. 39, 2010, ISBN 978-90-8890-066-2, 250 pp. Ill., Incl. bibl., € 29,95.

No. 40   Karen Jacobs, *Collecting Kamoro. Objects, encounters and representation on the southwest coast of Papua*. Mededelingen van het Rijksmuseum voor Volkenkunde Leiden, no. 40, Leiden 2011, ISBN 978-90-8890-088-4, 288 pp. Ill., Incl. bibl., index, € 29,95.

No. 41   Jimmy Mans, *Amotopoan Trails, A recent archaeology of Trio movements*. Mededelingen van het Rijksmuseum voor Volkenkunde Leiden, no. 41, Leiden 2012, ISBN 978-90-8890-098-3, 332 pp. Ill., Incl. bibl., € 34,95.

To order volumes 30-37, please visit www.cnwspublications.com.

Mededelingen van het Rijksmuseum voor Volkenkunde is currently published by Sidestone Press: www.sidestone.com